Aesthetics

Colin Lyas

McGill-Queen's University Press
Montreal & Kingston. London. Buffalo

ISBN 0-7735-1646-8 (bound)
ISBN 0-7735-1647-6 (pbk.)

First published in 1997 by UCL Press
The name of University College London (UCL) is a registered
trade mark used by UCL Press with the consent of the owner.

Published simultaneously in Canada by
McGill-Queen's University Press

Legal deposit first quarter
Bibliothèque nationale du Québec

Canadian Cataloguing in Publication Data
Lyas, Colin
Aesthetics

(Fundamentals of philosophy)
Included bibliographical references.
ISBN 0-7735-1646-8 (bound)
ISBN 0-7735-1647-6 (pbk.)

1. Art-Philosophy. 2. Aesthetics. I. Title
II. Series

BH39.L93 1997   701'.17   C97-900027-0

Typeset in Century Schoolbook and Futura
Printed and bound by
T.J. International Ltd., Padstow, Cornwall.

For Hild Leslie

But often, in the world's most crowded streets,
But often, in the din of strife,
There rises an unspeakable desire
After the knowledge of our buried life;
A thirst to spend our fire and restless force
In tracking out our true, original course;
A longing to inquire
Into the mystery of this heart which beats
So wild, so deep in us – to know
Whence our lives come and where they go.
And we have been on many thousand lines,
And we have shown, on each, spirit and power;
But hardly have we, for one little hour,
Been on our own line, have we been ourselves –
Hardly had skill to utter one of all
The nameless feelings that course through our breast,
But they course on forever unexpressed.
And long we try in vain to speak and act
Our hidden self, and what we say and do
Is eloquent, is well – but 'tis not true.

Only – but this is rare –
When a belovèd hand is laid in ours,
When jaded with the rush and glare
Of the interminable hours,
Our eyes can in another's eyes read clear,
When our world deafen'd ear
Is by the tones of a loved voice caresss'd –
A bolt is shot back somewhere in our breast,
And a lost pulse of feeling stirs again,
The eye sinks inward and the heart lies plain,
And what we mean we say, and what we would, we know.

Matthew Arnold, The buried life

Contents

Preface

This is not a book for those who know but for those who want to know. In writing it I had in mind three possible audiences. The first is the general reader who hears from afar of exciting controversies about art and who would like to know what is going on. The second is the student who might be thinking of embarking on a course in philosophical aesthetics and wants a survey of that field. Thirdly, the publishers of this work wish to offer it as a text for undergraduate aesthetics courses. With that in mind this book is offered as a springboard into the subject. It tries to orientate the reader by outlining a central problem in aesthetics and some solutions which have been offered to it.

I have no great confidence that anything that I say is right in any absolute sense. Nor is that important as long as the book provokes thinking. I will be happy if readers take away an impression of a vigorously boiling pot, and even happier if they are moved to add fuel to the fire under it.

This book owes much to the thinking provoked in me by various philosophers, some of whom I have, alas, never met, and who I envy for their achievements in combining a love of, and often high skills in, the arts with the ability to think with power and imagination about them: Cyril Barrett, Stanley Cavell, Ted Cohen, Ray Elliot, Lydia Goehr, Gary Iseminger, Peter Kivy, Roger Scruton, Bob Sharpe, Michael Tanner, Ben Tilghman and Richard Wollheim. Over everything I have written hovers the influence of the late Frank Sibley, whose friendship and example over 30 years influenced my thought and enhanced my life.

Parts of this book were written at Carleton College in Minnesota and owe a very great debt to the influence of the life of that admirable institution.

Edinburgh 25 May 1996

A note on references

Two kinds of references are included in the text. At the end of each chapter there are guides to further reading. The full reference is given only on the first occurrence. In addition there are references in the text of each of the chapters. These consist of the name of the person cited and a date. At the end of the work a bibliography gives the full source for each such reference.

Introduction

The disconsolations of philosophy

The bedrock

Everything we are to study rests on the bedrock of the spontaneous reactions that we make, from earliest infancy, to nature and to created things. A child hears a piece of music and reacts by marching up and down, swinging its arms: it listens enraptured to storytellings: it may begin by simply throwing paint, but soon takes an intense interest in the precise choice and positioning of colours: it delights in the movement of trees and clouds and the textures and fragrances of the world. These responses are a form our life takes, as natural to us as eating and sleeping. They are the beginning of what would issue, were education systems designed to reinforce rather than to frustrate our aesthetic development, in being moved by Janáček, entranced by Kundera and fascinated by Kitaj.

These bedrock responses are initially spontaneous. They may, by education, individual psychology and social pressure be deflected into this or that set of preferences, but if, initially, we did not spontaneously respond as we do, we could not develop as aesthetic beings.

1

Such responses are, moreover, ubiquitous. We know of no culture in which people do not dance, listen to stories, ornament themselves and construct representations. That these forms of activity have been suppressed (as a religion might suppress art as infringing on God's monopoly position as a supplier of created objects) merely testifies to their ubiquitous existence. What *may* differ is the reasons people give for engaging in such activities. A dance in one culture may be danced to bring the rain down, a motivation, even in the dry seasons, far from the minds of the Ballet Rambert and its clients.

The bedrock responses are ubiquitous in another way. The ways we fulfil ourselves aesthetically are extraordinarily wide and various. Our fictions include novels, films and plays that embrace Tarantino, Bergman, Tolstoy, Barbara Cartland, Kundera, *East-Enders*, *Bay Watch* and *Twin Peaks*. Music ranges across Dire Straits, Wagner, Michael Nyman, Take That, Joni Mitchell, raga, Elgar, reggae, yard, garage, Mozart and jungle. The visually aesthetic ranges across Amerindian body decoration, Pollock, Warhol, Vermeer, Hopi sand-painting, Hindu temple decoration, subway wall-painting and Gothic sartorial embellishments.

But to that we can add another fact, from which in the end our study gets whatever importance it has. For all that aesthetics can be marginalized by those who think of it as an optional extra, to be enjoyed when the serious business of vocational training is done, we know that our encounters with art and nature go not merely wide but also deep, and, moreover, go as deep as anything in our lives can go.

Thus, Wordsworth, recalling an earlier visit to the Wye above Tintern Abbey, felt that he had in the interim possessed, by virtue of that earlier visit, something deeper than merely pleasing memories of an enchantment of his eye by certain scenic beauties. He owed to it:

That blessed mood
In which the burden of the mystery,
In which the heavy and the weary weight
Of all this unintelligible world
Is lightened: – That serene and blessed mood
In which the affections gently lead us on, –

Until, the breath of this corporeal frame,
And even the motion of our human blood
Almost suspended, we are laid asleep
In body, and become a living soul:
While with an eye made quiet by the power
Of harmony and the deep power of joy,
We see into the life of things.

(Lines composed about Tintern Abbey)

A striking expression of the feeling that art, too, reaches deeply into us is to be found in the remarkable Chapter 5 of E. M. Forster's *Howards End*, in which the central characters attend a performance of Beethoven's Fifth Symphony. Helen Schlegel feels her life to have been changed by the music that she hears:

Helen pushed her way out during the applause. She desired to be alone. The music had summed up to her all that had happened or could happen in her career. She read it as a tangible statement, which could never be superseded. The notes meant this and that to her, and they could have no other meaning, and life could have no other meaning. She pushed right out of the building, and walked slowly down the outside staircase, breathing the autumnal air, and then she strolled home.

That such experiences are not confined to "high art" is testified to by one of my students who wrote:

I was walking to a friend's house listening to U2 . . . on my Walkman . . . . The song "One" started to play . . . . Looking at the lyrics by themselves fails to stir much emotion in me at all. However, when this was mixed with the musical arrangement it turned me into a mess. Even now, when I listen to the track a shiver judders me to a standstill.

In the introduction to *Endymion* Keats asserted, somewhat dubiously, as those who tire of last year's fashions might suspect, that a thing of beauty is a joy forever. More pertinently, after a list of the things that entrance us, including such natural objects as "daffodils and the green world that they live in", and such works of art as "all lovely tales that we have heard and read", he remarked on something that has always struck me, namely, the *sheer volume* of the stream of aesthetic stimulation in which we are immersed. He speaks of it as "an endless fountain of immortal drink". So it is.

A sense of deprivation

And yet many feel aesthetically deprived. At Open University summer schools in aesthetics one encounters people who feel that they have missed out on art, who are anxious to participate in a form of life that, they are constantly told, offers more solid joys and more lasting treasures than the world of getting and spending, on the receiving end of which many of them have been. Newly arrived university students, too, scent a world in which people talk of Michelangelo and can pronounce Tannhäuser. Since that is held up as the acme of civilization, they want to be in that world.

Of course, they are not deprived of a rich aesthetic life. They choose their clothes with an attention to aesthetic detail scarcely second to that with which Cosimo Medici would have chosen an etching; the bodies of those who frequent the rave clubs of the world's urban jungles are adorned with a richness not less than those of the bodies of the Amazonians; their ears are constantly stimulated by music; they dance with astonishing rhythm and dynamism; they are saturated with the narrative drama of the screen; they walk the hills, climb the rocks, ride the waters and are uplifted by those experiences; their poetry is the sometimes great poetry of the contemporary song lyric. So what is the worry about aesthetic deprivation?

Some worry for a simple reason. They see certain things held up as aesthetic *icons*, worthy of veneration: things produced by such people as Rembrandt, Monteverdi, Mahler, Joyce and Henry Moore. But my friends, in all humility, concede that although these things may be great, they get nothing from them.

Then, too, they worry because what they do get from art is often derided, as when their genuine delight in the scenes painted by Constable is written off as irrelevant compared with something mysteriously characterized as "the formal features" of a painting. Someone, too, deeply moved by Auden's beautiful *Lullaby*, is told instead to attend to some hocus-pocus involving such barbarisms as "signifier" and "metonymy". Many music students, too, will know of the way in which the deep stirrings engendered by *The dream of Gerontius* can vanish into the orifice of Schenkerian musical analysis (see Sharpe 1993 and *The New Grove dictionary of music*).

Then, again, they worry that, although they are more moved by Queen's "Bohemian rhapsody" than by Schubert's *An die Musik*, they are told that the Schubert is vastly better. Then they feel *put down* and can't see why.

The situation of these would-be appreciators is summed up by someone who asked me what she should look at on her visit to the Walker Gallery in Liverpool. I suggested a recently acquired Poussin. "No," she said, "I don't want to know what *picture* to look at. I want to know what I should look at when I look at a picture".

It is a sobering fact, in a country in which even the most barbaric politician pays lip service to art as a prime manifestation of civilization, which spends extraordinary sums of money, and at least 11 years, on educating each of its children, that so many people in Britain can reach the age of 22 (or even 92) and have no idea what to do when standing before a picture. For many, art galleries are places where stains, largely rectangular, hang on walls. Standing before these stains, other people, often with a certain kind of accent, proclaim, often in voices meant to be overheard, that looking at these stains has given them experiences so profound that a failure to have them would have left their lives impoverished. And others look and just can't see any of this, just as others can make no sense of the noises in the sonic museum of the concert hall, or resolve the words of *The waste land* into sense.

The collision between those who see a value in such art and those who cannot generates a variety of responses. One is to claim that the works of art that are standardly held up as icons are only so to those who have had a certain kind of education. Further, that kind of education is the class-based prerogative of an economic elite, a conclusion reinforced by the fact that the accents in which the appreciation of art is expressed are more often those of the corridors of power than the corridors of an inner-city hospital.

If this approach is meant to deal with those who can't see why people have been so drawn to Botticelli, Rembrandt, Monteverdi, Eliot and other icons of art, and who worry that they are missing something, it can only do so by drawing the conclusion that there *is* nothing being missed by those unable to participate in the art preferred by a more privileged cultural group.

But, aside from the fact that preferences for this or that sort of art do not correspond neatly to the tastes of this or that culturally determined group, that conclusion simply does not follow. The true claim that one group is culturally disposed to like Verdi and another culturally disposed to like graffiti art does not entail that there is nothing we can miss in the art preferred by a different group. Indeed the contrary is true. People come lovingly to value things for which no previous education prepared them. The boundaries between such group preferences as do exist are not impermeable membranes. Someone brought up on Barry Manilow can come to see what is to be found in Handel, no less than someone brought up on Monteverdi might come to see what is to be found in King Oliver.

Suppose, however, one does have a reason for believing one is missing out on something to be seen in galleries and heard in concert halls. How is one to get access to it?

The disconsolations of philosophical aesthetics

A tempting inclination is to believe that one can get access to art by the study of philosophical aesthetics, and it is because a decision to study that subject is sometimes thus motivated that it can be such a disappointment. This is because a subject bearing such a title creates the not unreasonable expectation that its study will impart a greater capacity to reap those rewards of the art that are so loudly trumpeted by those whose hands are already on the ropes. People hope to come to see what is great about certain works of art and why some so confidently claim these works to be better than some of the icons of popular culture. And, as generations of students of aesthetics have complained, this simply does not happen.

One explanation for this disappointment is that beginners confuse *aesthetics* with *philosophical aesthetics*, and wrongly expect to get from the latter what only the former could give them. To explain this I need to touch on a problem about philosophy.

One of the recurrent embarrassments for a philosopher is having to explain to nonphilosophers what being a philosopher involves.

For although everyone understands the notion of someone being a physicist or a mortician, even professional academics can be vague about what being a philosopher involves.

It is not difficult to tell a story about how this uncertainty about the nature of philosophy arises. At one time, so the story goes, philosophy was *philo sophia*, the love of wisdom. In the innocent dawn that is alleged to have preceded the division of labour that now characterizes intellectual life, *philo sophia* was an undifferentiated curiosity about anything whatsoever. Gradually, the story continues, the specialist disciplines carved out, from the huge undifferentiated carcass of aboriginal human enquiry, their own subject matters, to be studied by their distinctive methodologies. Mathematics was first, perhaps, then, in the Renaissance, physics, then, in the late nineteenth century, psychology, and so on to linguistics in this century. The furniture of the universe is thus divided, each part to its own discipline, each discipline with its own distinctive methodology.

Now a crisis for philosophy arises. For what will be left for philosophy after the special disciplines have annexed their areas of study? What category of the furniture of the universe will be left for philosophy, and what distinctive methodology has philosophy for studying it? This is what puzzles many about philosophy. They wish to know what stands to that subject as atoms stand to physics, numbers to mathematics, neuroses to psycholoanalysis and mumbo-jumbo to research selectivity exercises. And the problem appears to be that nothing is left over that is not already the subject matter of some other special discipline.

Faced with that, *one* tactic is to retreat to higher ground. Instead of practising a discipline, we step back and think about what is done when it is practised. To take some simple instances: a mathematician *uses* the word "number" ("a proof that there is no highest prime number is . . . "). Likewise a religious person uses the word "God" ("In the beginning God created the heavens and the earth"). An aesthetic appreciator might use the word "better", as in "the wider lapels look better on you". Most of us use the word "ought" ("You ought to have passed it to Cantona"), and the word "mind" ("I know exactly what you have in mind"). In these practices we also use arguments: "the proof that there is no highest prime number is . . ."; "a reason for believing God exists is . . ."; "those lapels look

7

better because of your broad shoulders"; "you ought to have passed to Cantona because Giggs's run drew the defender"; "I knew what he had in mind because . . .". In these practices we *use* words. But, so the argument goes, we can step back and think about these uses. Then, so the claim is, we are philosophizing.

In that activity our questions can take two forms. First, we can ask what is *meant* by a term: "what did the Pope mean when he used the term 'God'?"; "what are numbers?"; "what is the force of the word 'ought'?"; "what is mind?". And secondly we can ask about *arguments*. We can ask about particular arguments, as when we ask "is the ontological argument a good reason for believing in God?"; "is that a sound mathematical proof?". Or we can ask about types of arguments, as when we ask: "can we support our judgements about what ought to be done by any arguments at all?". Of course, we then *use* the terms "meaning" and "argument", and we can think about these in their turn: "what is meaning?", "what is argument?", questions that generate what is called philosophical logic. And since questions about meaning and argument are so central to philosophizing, philosophical logic, which seeks to understand these terms, becomes a fundamental area of philosophy.

Now we can understand one notion of *philosophical* aesthetics. There is, we saw, a bedrock of response to art and nature articulated in infinitely rich and varied words and behaviour. Being struck dumb by the Taj Mahal is one case; being reduced to silence by Juliet Stevenson's performance in *The doll's house* or by Hurt and Keitel in *Smoke* is another; George I's spontaneously standing up during the "Hallelujah Chorus" is yet another. There are different forms of verbal responses, too: "I love it", "It's stupid", "You ought to hear *The hissing of summer lawns*", "Pavarotti's is the better voice, but Domingo is the better actor", "It's the use of the clarinet that makes Glenn Miller's sound distinctive", "Sullivan wrote the music for *Iolanthe* just after his mother died", "It's been badly restored", "I don't like Mahler", "Like a pot of paint thrown into the faces of the public", "Auden wrote *Lullaby* for a male lover", "How am I to take Hardy's late poems, in which he purports to grieve for the wife he treated so badly?", "Ugh!", "Bis!", "Boo!", "Too sentimental", "Not blue enough", "She avoided the temptations of the minor key", "Why is Lear's wife never mentioned?", "Men conspired to conceal the work of great women painters", "That air again: it has a dying fall", "How *blue* the Mediterreanean is!", "How can a sawn-up cow be art?" In these, and in countless other ways, we articulate encounters we have with art and nature.

To be initiated into and to grow in those ways of expression, to be able to react thus with understanding, is to be an enfranchised member of the aesthetic community. When people express a sense of missing something about "great art", what they are saying comes to this: they cannot use the kinds of aesthetic vocabulary that I have just instanced in the presence of those works of art, because those works do not occasion in them any response that needs articulation in those ways.

On the one hand, then, there is the bedrock of aesthetic response. And, given the recently sketched model of philosophizing, above this hovers philosophical aesthetics. Its questions will include, "what did you mean when you said 'better'?", "are the reasons given for those judgements good ones?", and, more generally, "does the notion of a good reason make sense in these contexts anyway?", or "isn't it all subjective?".

Now we can see why aesthetics, as taught in philosophy departments, might disappoint. I shall argue in this work that the problem for those who feel left out by art is that they simply can't see or hear something. I shall also argue that the corrective to this, the acquisition of an ability to perceive the features of art and nature, is a matter of practice. We begin by marching up and down in response to what we perceive in simple rhythms. Given we can do that, the rest is practice. If we are constantly exposed to music of developing complexity, we end up able to respond to more complex musical forms and to articulate that response, just as our eyes can be trained to discriminate finer shades of colour. So, what is needed is guided exposure to the art one wishes to understand.

That, on the account I have given, will not come from philosophical aesthetics. For that explicitly stands back from the practices of the competent in order to reflect on what the competent do. The not untypical student wishes to acquire the competence to respond to art. The philosophical aesthetician wishes to reflect on the utterances of those who have acquired the competence. Put bluntly, the student wanted aesthetics, but is offered philosophy.

This explains the bleakness that surrounds some essays in courses on philosophical aesthetics. Many who come to the subject have little experience of "high" art. They may even have enrolled in order to remedy a sense of inadequacy in this respect. But philosophical aesthetics, as it is often practised, reflects upon the words used by those who can talk about high art and assumes that those who wish to study philosophical aesthetics are also competent enough to call up examples from "high" art to illustrate their contentions about those uses of words. In this task, because of the inadequacy of the average aesthetic education, the student is often predetermined to fail. (The same happens in philosophy of science, alas, too often, taught to and by people who have no culture of active science.)

Remedies

Four remedies suggest themselves.

The first is simply, in the spirit of a Trades Descriptions Act, to warn off those possessed of no knowledge of the high arts from those courses in philosophical aesthetics that take those arts as grist for the mills for their philosophizing.

The second alternative would be to take one's examples from wider aesthetic situations, for example, from recent fashion and music. That tactic will be undermined by the fact that academic teachers can have an ignorance of new wave music and fashion that is symmetrical with the ignorance of high art in many of those being taught.

The third alternative is to devise ways both of giving the grounding in aesthetics that the student seeks and showing how philosophy arises from that. Though I do some of this in my courses, this would go beyond what a book of this length can do.

The fourth alternative is to demonstrate that, whether or not philosophical aesthetics satisfies those who wish to learn about high art, the questions with which it deals have a compelling interest for anyone who wishes to be alive to what is happening in our culture, globally conceived. The philosophical problems of aesthetics are not simply problems about high art (although high art is one of its problems). They are, simply, problems about aesthetics, and since everyone is part of a ubiquitous aesthetic community, they are everyone's problems.

Here are some examples of the kinds of questions I have in mind.

First, why do we need art at all? We can be immersed in the aesthetic in ways that don't need the term "art". Stand in Marks and Spencer and listen to the aesthetic discourse about clothes: "it's too long", "just right for your cheekbones". The participants don't think of this as art. Watch the dancers at any rave: they have no consciousness of being part of the art world. Overwhelmed by the sunset seen from Great Gable, I don't call it "art".

Yet alongside all of this we have art. There are places where things are *marked off* as art and solemnized, even sacralized, as such: there are galleries where these things are stored, locked up at night, protected by patrolling guards; there are halls where people pay art-music the tribute of formal dress, high prices and hushed attention; there are buildings that store literary art in silent rows. Why is this? Why are those things marked off? What additional importance are they thought to have over the lesser and possibly more popular manifestations of the aesthetic? And how do I get my work into that club? Does a pickled shark deserve to be there? Or videos taken through various bodily orifices? Or the *Four minutes and thirty-three seconds* of silence that John Cage offered to a concert audience?

These questions take on a special form when we realize that art has a cost. Part of this is simply financial. The temples in which art is practised, the priests who practise in those temples and the acolytes who attend them, claim public money that quite simply could be (though it never would be) spent on other desirable things, for example, soup for the starving. What is the basis of *that* claim on our finite resources, a claim that will become more pressing as the resources increasingly diminish?

A second question: it is claimed that certain objects, usually those associated with what I have called "high art", are *superior* to other aesthetic products. Beethoven is ranked above Paul Simon, Vermeer over Superman comics, *Les enfants du paradis* over *Batman forever*, and *Middlemarch* over *Gone with the wind*. Some will simply shrug and go on liking what they like. But few can do this, and for two reasons. Firstly, the effect of making one thing better than another is seldom charitable to the thing of lesser worth. To say Beethoven is superior to Paul Simon is to put the latter down. And if my taste is for the latter, I feel put down, too. Then I'd like to know what right someone has to do this to me. Secondly, what is raised up is not simply raised up. It is raised very high, so that high art is said to be *supremely* worthwhile. That can make us suspect we are missing something. Again we would like to know whether we are, and if so what.

A third set of questions arises when we note that we do not merely find people articulating their responses to art and nature. We also find massive volumes of talk about how *others* should respond. So one person says that, when looking at paintings, we should ignore representational features; another says that, when reading books, we should ignore information about their authors; yet another will say that, when listening to music, we should not imagine pictures. These people purport to tell others, including those who would like to get access to what are treasured as the great icons of our culture, what the best way is to attend to art and nature. We have to ask whether they get it right. For if they don't, then they impoverish response; I shall argue later that those who say that we should ignore representation, authors and emotions have maimed rather than enhanced the responses of those that they influenced. A small example: purporting to teach the appreciation of poetry, I take a poem, say Owen's "Anthem for doomed youth", and I point out an alliteration in line three. The strong-minded student will ask "So what?". For lots of useless poems have alliterations in them. The typical learner, anxious to please, will assume that alliteration is a relevant thing to cite without knowing why. Hence the standard essay, when asked to assess a poem, simply lists its alliterations, its litotes, and other such fruits of oxymoronic teaching.

Finally, there is the deep question that underlies all this. When we look, from that supposed vantage point of philosophy, at the practices of those who deal with art and the aesthetic we come across responses such as those articulated on behalf of Helen Schlegel by Forster. We are reminded that art and nature seem to have profound importance.

We might just note this fact. But I am not in the end quite content to do so.

Here perhaps I may confess that I love the practice and enjoyment of the arts. If I had three hours to live and a choice between attending a magnificent performance and philosophizing about why magnificent performances matter so much to me (other possible ways of spending the time, alas, being excluded), I would go to the performance. That may show I am not at heart really a philosopher. But here and now I don't have to make a choice. As it stands with me, I love the magnificent in art and nature (and many lesser splendours, too). But I also have a wonder that I am so moved and a wish to understand why I am. And if, as Socrates is reported as saying, philosophy begins in wonder, and if its goal is "know thyself", then my philosophical aesthetics begins with that self-wonder. This, it seems to me, is the right reason for asking what art is. If I knew that, I might know why so many thought great art supremely worth pursuing, and why any culture worthy of that name should foster and support it. That in turn might generate a truly radical criticism of the culture, hinted at in the envoi of this work, in which I and you now live.

In the first part of this book, then, I shall be looking at the stories that have been told about the source of the power of art and in the next chapter I shall begin with a plausible and influential account of the power of art.

Guide to reading

Reference

First of all, a good dictionary of philosophy is not a bad thing to have. At one end of the scale there is a very useful short dictionary, A. Flew (ed.), *The dictionary of philosophy* (London: Pan, 1979). At the other end I commend T. Honderich (ed.), *The Oxford companion to philosophy* (Oxford: Oxford University Press, 1995), which has much on aesthetics and aestheticians in it. Academic libraries at least should have the multi-volumed P. Edwards (ed.), *The encyclopedia of philosophy* (New York: Macmillan, 1967) that has articles on everything and everybody in aesthetics. It will shortly be updated by Edward Craig's *Encyclopedia* to be published by Routledge, London, with a comprehensive coverage of aesthetics. Keep an eye out, too, for the appearance in libraries of the magisterial *Macmillan dictionary of art*, which will do for the visual arts and their theory what the equally magnificent Grove dictionary does for music. D. Cooper (ed.), *The Blackwell companion to aesthetics* (Oxford:Blackwell, 1992), now in paperback, is admirable for browsing about in and a good place to start on any of the topics I mention.

Philosophy

Philosophical aesthetics is a part of philosophy and is affected by what happens in philosophy. For that reason it is not a bad idea to have some grasp of the history of philosophy. Here try, first, J. Shand, *Philosophy and philosophers* (London: Penguin, 1994) for the overall picture. I also commend the eminently readable R. Scruton, *A short history of modern philosophy* (London: Routledge, 1995). A. C. Grayling, *Philosophy: a guide through the subject* (Oxford: Oxford University Press, 1995) is just what it says it is, and will authoritatively take you further.

Those interested in pursuing the question of what philosophy and philosophical aesthetics might be, can be referred to R. Shusterman, *Analytical aesthetics* (Oxford: Blackwell, 1989). This book promotes alternative art forms such as rap. A very informative and intelligible essay on the issues about what philosophy ought to be is Essay XIII in G. P. Baker & P. M. S. Hacker, *Essays on the philosophical investigations volume 1: Wittgenstein; meaning and understanding* (Oxford: Blackwell, 1980). An alternative tradition to the one I sketch, emanating from Husserl and running through Heidegger, Sartre and Merleau-Ponty, is the phenomenological tradition. That is explored, for those interested in more advanced and difficult things, in M. Hammond, J. Howarth & R. Keat, *Understanding phenomenology* (Oxford: Blackwell, 1991). Excellent and authoritative discussion of recent continental European aesthetics is to be found in P. Crowther, *Critical aesthetics and post-modernism* (Oxford: Clarendon, 1993). An interesting offshoot of that is Merleau-Ponty's remarks on Cezanne, to be found in his *Essential writings*, ed. A. L. Fisher (New York: Harcourt Brace & World, 1969). On this matter see P. Crowther, "Merleau-Ponty: perception into art", *British Journal of Aesthetics* **22**, 1982, pp. 138–40.

Histories of aesthetics

A good overall history is M. Beardsley, *Aesthetics from classical Greece to the present day* (New York: Macmillan, 1966).

Aesthetics

A. Shepherd, *Aesthetics* (Oxford: Oxford University Press, 1987) is a useful short introduction as is M. Eaton, *Basic issues in aesthetics* (Belmont, California: Wadsworth, 1988). The most up-to-date intermediate book is O. Hanfling (ed.), *Philosophical aesthetics* (Oxford: Blackwell, 1992) (the basis for the Open University degree course in philosophical aesthetics). When you know your way around aesthetics you should be ready for some influential and more advanced (sometimes much more advanced) recent works including R. Wollheim, *Art and its objects*, 2nd edn (Cambridge: Cambridge University Press, 1980), N. Goodman, *Languages of art* (Indianapolis: Indiana University Press, 1976), R. Scruton, *Art and imagination* (London: Methuen, 1974), A. Savile, *The test of time* (Oxford: Oxford University Press, 1982) and M. Mothersill, *Beauty restored* (Oxford: Oxford University Press, 1984). Grayling's *Philosophy: a guide* (1995) has a very well-informed section on aesthetics by Sebastian Gardner that will help you build a map of the whole field of aesthetics, including what is happening now.

Collections

Most libraries should have F. Tillman & S. Cahn (eds), *Philosophy of art and aesthetics* (New York: Harper and Row, 1969), which is a valuable collection of much of the material cited in this book. A modern, good and very affordable collection has been put together by the admirable A. Neill & A. Ridley (eds), *Philosophy of art: readings ancient and modern* (New York: McGraw Hill, 1995).

Journals

The British Journal of Aesthetics publishes a wide range of articles, often accessible to the less advanced reader. It, and its American equivalent, *The Journal of Aesthetics and Art Criticism*, are the way to keep up with what is happening near the cutting edge. *Philosophy and Literature* also publishes articles of interest to aestheticians that are readily accessible to the nonspecialist.

The arts

Since philosophical aesthetics as I have described it is parasitic on aesthetics it is as well to supplement your native grasp of matters aesthetic with some more detailed knowledge. Some fun can be had by reading R. Hughes, *The shock of the new*, rev. edn (London: Thames and Hudson, 1991). (Even more fun can be had from a cruel little squib by T. Wolfe, *The painted word*, Toronto: Bantam, 1976.) The great compendium of twentieth century writing about the arts (often by artists themselves), with some glorious nonsense in it, is C. Harrison & P. Wood (eds), *Art in theory: 1900–1990* (Oxford: Blackwell, 1992). This is a book to browse in.

As to whether art is an elitist imposition see R. Taylor, *Art an enemy of the people* (Brighton: Harvester, 1978), elegantly dissected by Tom Sorrell in Hanfling, *Philosophical aesthetics*, pp. 328–35.

Finally, there are now lavish Internet resources in aesthetics. These are best accessed via the American Society for Aesthetics-hosted *Aesthetics On-Line* (http://www.indiana.edu/~asanl). From this site there are links in all directions in philosophy and the arts. I also recommend joining the aesthetics e-mail list that is both a notice board and often a very amusing forum for discussion. Aesthetics On-Line will tell you how to join, or you can email majordomo@indiana.edu with the message "subscribe aesthetics" (no quotation marks). Thereafter you join in by sending an e-mail to aesthetics@indiana.edu.

Chapter 1

Anglo-Kantian attitudes

Natural and man-made things, as we have seen, excite our attention. But then questions arise. Firstly, since not everything that attracts attention does so aesthetically (as when one's attention is caught by a rustle in the grass when nervous about snakes), which attractions are aesthetic? A second question is why these attractions can be, and in what ways they can be, so powerful.

Which attractions are aesthetic?

Although this is a common question in introductions to aesthetics, I am uncertain about what is being asked when it arises.

Let us note first that our words reflect the various forms our evolution has taken. We did not first have certain experiences and then invent words with which to express them. Our words emerged as our lives developed, and emerged to express capacities acquired during that development. It was, for example, in the course of our development as colour-sighted beings that our colour language emerged. It is because we evolved as creatures who make mistakes that such words as "doubt", "belief", and "knowledge" gained their functions.

So it is with aesthetic terms. It is because we are struck by rainbows, entranced by fictions, moved by rhythms, unsettled by certain colour combinations, that we developed the words and behaviour that articulate aesthetic responses. As small children we simply marched up and down to music or turned from discordant colours. To develop aesthetically is, in part, to augment those responses with words and gestures that allow infinitely more complex and subtle ways of articulating our aesthetic reactions: words like "too", "trite", "garish", "beautiful", and countless others.

In knowing how to use that vocabulary, we show a knowledge of the attractions that are aesthetic. But what, then, in addition to that, does the *philosopher* want to know when asking what the characteristic features are of aesthetic responses? It cannot be how and why we evolved our capacities for aesthetic response. That is a question for evolutionary biology. It cannot be how to use aesthetic terms, for that is already mastered. It cannot be how to extend one's capacities so that one can use these terms of paintings by Giotto as well as, or instead of, paintings by Holman Hunt. That is a matter for experience and for art historians and critics and not for philosophers to teach us. It cannot be whether we should respond to something aesthetically, as if we had any choice in the matter. And if the question is whether it is more worthwhile to enjoy a film than to play korfball or work in a hospice (granted that these are exclusive alternatives), that is not a question about the nature of aesthetic experience but about its ranking.

So what drives these *philosophical* questions about the defining characteristics of aesthetic experience?

Firstly, some philosophers have an impulse to classify things, apparently just for the sake of doing so, so as to report, for example, that aesthetic experiences, say, are the class of experiences marked off by these or those sorts of characteristics. Whether or not that motivation appeals will depend on whether one has that classificatory impulse. I don't, but let that not stop anyone who does.

Secondly, some seem struck by the fact that we cannot always say whether a response is aesthetic. Being startled by a rustling in the grass seems clearly not to be aesthetic, whereas being stirred by the colours of a picture clearly is. But then I find myself stirred by the tilt of a retroussé nose. Is that aesthetic, too? My heart moves when I see eagles soar. Is that an aesthetic response? I am elated by the try scored by the Barbarians in 1973. Is that aesthetic? I look into the eyes of a bat and am stirred by its otherness. How aesthetic is that reaction? And then the hope might emerge that if we could distil the characteristic features of aesthetic response, we would be able to determine whether these cases are or are not aesthetic. But again I need to know why that question is a pressing one. Why is it important that I be able thus to classify my experiences?

A better reason is suggested by Kant, whose philosophical aesthetics will be more fully examined later in this chapter. Kant certainly sought the defining characteristics of the aesthetic, one being that aesthetic experience be "disinterested". However, he did not leave the matter there. He also asked why disinterested experiences are so important to us. This suggests that a reason for enquiring into the defining qualities of aesthetic experience is that an answer might also solve the fundamental question of why art and nature can have such power over us.

We can find another good reason for seeking defining features of the aesthetic by following up the striking fact that we can use a word perfectly well and yet fall into confusion and error when asked to say what we are doing in using it. I can ask if you have the time, admire your mind, know where I left a book, believe that you are lying and yet, when asked what time, mind, knowledge and belief are, I can fall into confusion. So it is in aesthetics. We can delight at a sunset, gasp at the denouement of *Seven*, laugh at *Bullets over Broadway* and be moved to tears by the conclusion of *Vanya on 42nd Street*. But when asked what aesthetic response *is*, people say the daftest things. That would not concern me (I simply carry on laughing at *Bullets over Broadway*), save that those same people don't leave it there. They have the temerity, on the basis of their mischaracterizations of aesthetic experience, to say how others *should* respond aesthetically. Others, taking this advice seriously, miss out on sources of enjoyment. For example, they are told (Bell 1920) that aesthetic responses should ignore representation. And so they miss the significance of the expressions in Rembrandt self-portraits. That impoverishes their response. So, one reason for involvement in discussions about the defining features of the aesthetic is to detect misleading characterizations.

I begin there, with a way of going wrong (and one with pernicious consequences) in characterizing the aesthetic and I take as my example the influential attempt to define the aesthetic in terms of something called the "aesthetic attitude".

The aesthetic attitude

Consider the dangerous situation in which fog descends while I am sailing. The manuals indicate practical things to do when this happens, such as sounding audible warnings. But the captain finds me admiring how creamy the sea looks, how vaporously delicate the fog. He might justly say that I am taking an unduly *aesthetic* attitude. Consider, next, a man looking forward to an evening out with his wife at a performance of *Othello*. He comes home and finds a note reading "Have gone off with Gordon". In a turmoil of rage and jealousy he still goes to the play and, at the moment when Desdemona is killed by the jealous Othello, applauds. Here one might say that his particular situation has prevented him from taking the proper aesthetic attitude.

These cases fuel the influential notion that the aesthetic involves putting "psychical distance" between oneself and the object to which one responds. In the fog, I responded aesthetically by distancing myself from practical action. At the play, the jealous man could not distance himself enough to respond aesthetically, no more than did those, possibly mythical, early cinema audiences who fired at the screen. So we have the claim that a certain stance defines the aesthetic. This is the so-called "aesthetic attitude", which establishes "psychical distance" between viewer and work.

I object to this still popular account that it is feeble, that it gives no answer to the fundamental questions about the source of the power of art and the aesthetic, and that it results in damaging advice to would-be appreciators.

That the account is feeble is easily shown. It is true to say that we can switch our attention to the aesthetic aspects of our surroundings. Moreover, if I am in danger, it may, indeed, take a special effort to focus on the aesthetic aspects of my environment. This is because danger diverts me from paying attention to them. But when I do attend to them, I do not take up a special sort of attitude, as a sycophant might on meeting a princess. I simply attend, often with no sense of effort, to the aesthetic features of the situation. And the way I attend to *them* is no different from the way I attend to anything else. What makes my attention aesthetic, then, is *what* I attend to, not *how* I attend to it.

The account is equally feeble when applied to art rather than nature. My uncomfortable seat may interfere with my attention to music, my stiff neck may interfere with my efforts to view the architectural features of the Lloyd's building, and my toothache with my attention to *Trainspotting*. But this is not because something called "distance" is lost. It is simply that my attention is distracted from the aesthetic aspects of those things and events to which I wish to give my undivided attention.

Drama and other fictions may seem to offer more scope to notions of distance. There is something not quite right about shooting at Dirty Harry, serving a vagrancy order on Estragon and Vladimir, applying for a job at the Rover's Return, or writing to Dr Watson for some methadone. But if, as the case of the fog at sea was meant to show, distancing requires an effort of some sort, then fiction involves no distance. The notion that I spend my time at a play holding myself back from intervening is plain daft. I learn the notion of fiction as involving the logical impossibility of intervention and that is all there is to it.

The notion of distance is radically useless. The theory does not even say that to distance oneself is to have an aesthetic experience. It says no more than that certain things can interfere with enjoyment of the aesthetic properties of things. This explains nothing about the aesthetic. For until we know to what experience of the aesthetic distancing gives us access, we know nothing about the aesthetic. We are, to be sure, told that some experiences are aesthetic, for example, the delight we take in the visual qualities of fogs. But now we really are making noises in a vacuum. We already knew about the possibility of delight in the visual qualities of fogs. What we were expecting was some account of the central features of such experiences. Instead we get a recipe for obtaining them.

The other class of experiences that is mentioned as aesthetic is the experiences to be had by attending to fictions. The claim is that we need to put ourselves into a certain condition in order to have these experiences. But again we are not told what these experiences are nor why it is worthwhile putting oneself in the condition to have them. So we have been told nothing about what makes experiences aesthetic.

Edward Bullough, to whom talk about psychical distance is due, spoke of "the antinomy of distance". He clearly saw that a play must engage and involve our sympathies. To that extent we can't be totally distanced. Yet at the same time he noted that if we become too involved, as a jealous man might, we can lose the proper experience of the play. So he concluded that there were degrees of distance, the best approach being to get as involved as possible without finally losing the last bit of distance.

However, it is wrong to suppose that distance in the cinema or theatre, say, exists on a sliding scale, so that the loss of distance of the jealous man at a performance of *Othello* is further along the scale than the child who shouts "he's behind you" or the cinemagoer who yelps with fear as the Blob approaches. This can be seen by considering our earlier example of the jealous man at the performance of *Othello*. If when he applauds the killing of Desdemona he believes that a real murder is taking place, he is simply unbalanced. Or if he is participating empathetically in the make-believe he is joining in the fiction. There are no degrees between these two alternatives. Note, too, that although in the second case, the jealous man has maintained distance, since he knows he is joining in a fiction, yet he still gets the play wrong, since to ally oneself with Othello is entirely to miss the valuation the play puts on that character. We cannot express that aesthetic error in terms of loss of distance, for the man has preserved that.

Accounts of fictional distance, moreover, entirely ignore problems to which I return in the next chapter. One is that it seems possible to become emotionally involved with fiction. But nothing in talk about the distance necessary to fiction tells us *how* we can become emotionally involved with things that don't exist. If, having distanced myself, I simply know that no-one is really leaving anyone at the end of *Casablanca*, how can I be moved to real tears, any more than I can stay angry with you if I find that you didn't, contrary to my belief, really insult me behind my back.

My final objection to the notion of distance is to the noxious effects on our dealings with art and the aesthetic, of the connotations that the term ingloriously trails. "Distance" suggests a non-involvement and cool detachment and is likely to encourage the notion that some sort of icy contemplation is *de rigueur*, so that (and the case of the fog at sea suggests this) one's posture in front of art ought to be like that of a stiff upper lip at the funeral of a lover. This might appeal to someone suffering from emotional constipation but is no recipe for enjoying art.

As we have seen, Bullough did not rule out the possibility of emotional involvement with a work, though he gave no sensible account of what this involves. Would that some of his disciples had read him more carefully, especially the crazy individual who suggested that the necessity of distance for proper aesthetic response entailed that children shouldn't clap their hands when asked to by Peter Pan, a recommendation that entirely overlooks the ways in which one is, from earliest childhood, actively involved with one's fictional imaginings.

Talk of aesthetic distance from a work is of a piece with that whole tradition that makes aesthetic experience a matter of detachment and disinterestedness. The notion of detachment, I suspect, collapses to the notion of distance and is prey to its ills. But the notion of disinterestedness, which is also there in Bullough's writing, inherits the thought of a formidably difficult philosopher, who for good or ill has towered over philosophical aesthetics, Immanuel Kant. To his vastly more demanding, and instructive, characterization of the aesthetic I now turn.

Kant's project

It is not difficult to give enough of an idea of Kant's general project to make sense of the place allotted to the investigation of the aesthetic in that project. Traditionally, Kant supposed, it was believed that an ordered world impinges upon our senses and that those senses convey a knowledge of that world into the mind. The world imposes its order on us. And now, just as Copernicus reversed the claim that the sun goes round the earth, so Kant reversed the claim that the world gives its order to the mind. The mind, rather, gives order to a world, which has no structure save what the mind gives it.

It is, I think, important, as we shall see when we come to talk of Kant's aesthetics, to understand that one who thinks that the mind structures reality must start by accepting the world as it actually shows itself in our dealings with it. The world, as it is for us, cannot but have the structure that our mind has in fact imposed on it. (The fun starts when we imagine the possibility, as Kant did not, that different cultures might impose different structurings on the world, including some we find repugnant. Granted Kant's view that there is no world independent of human structurings against which the correctness of this or that structuring can be checked, how are we going to object to the ways in which others structure their worlds?)

Given this account there are a number of questions that constitute the Kantian philosophical programme. One is: "What is the character of the structuring the mind has imposed?" Well, for example, we have so structured the world that we think of it as containing physical objects with spatio-temporal locations and which causally affect each other in law-like ways. Again, as we have structured the world, we think of it as containing moral agents, free to act in certain ways and having a duty to act in some of these ways. We think, too, that these agents have feelings, desires and inclinations. Finally, we have so structured things that we think of these agents as moved by the beautiful and the sublime in art and nature.

To appreciate the full flavour of Kantian philosophy, and its bearing on aesthetics, however, consider this: if we are to talk of the mind as structuring, then there must be two distinct things: something to which structure is to be given, and something that gives the structure. The latter is provisionally indicated in saying that the mind is what gives the structure. What receives the structure is less clear, but we can get by with the notion of our being bombarded by an inchoate welter of sensory stimuli to which the mind gives structure. William James spoke of the mind of the new-born as bombarded by what must seem to the infant a blooming, buzzing confusion. That is a way of grasping Kant's initial notion.

Now we can ask some Kantian questions. Granted we know that the mind has given order to the world, we know what order it has given by seeing what order *the world* has. But we can also ask what structure *the mind* must have in order to make it possible for the stimuli that bombard it to have been structured in the way in which they have been. To give a simple example: the stimuli we receive have been organized so that we do not merely receive a random set of disconnected sensory imports, but perceive discrete things. So there must be some power of the mind that makes that possible. Next, we talk of the same sorts of things as encountered at different times and places. So there must be some power of the mind that makes it possible for us to have the notion not merely of, say, a particular cat here and now, but of the *general* notion of a cat. For Kant the organization of random stimuli into perceived objects is the work of the *imagination* and the production of conceptual categorizations of those objects is the work of the *understanding*.

Kantian aesthetics

Vastly more than that is going to be needed, of course, before we have the full story of why things are structured the way that they are. (What, for example, makes possible a world structured in space and time?) We have enough now, however, to grasp the main features of Kant's account of the aesthetic. His investigation must be rooted in what he took to be the structure of our practices in responding to art and nature. For these amount to the way in which the mind has structured its world aesthetically. Then he asked how the mind itself must be structured if that kind of aesthetic structuring of the world is to be possible. The outcome of that enquiry will be nothing less than a full understanding of the place of the aesthetic in the whole life of the mind and, with that, answers to questions about the power of art over us.

What apparent facts about our practices struck Kant? One is that the aesthetic is a source of a certain sort of delight to the individual. The questions then become what the mind must be like to make that sort of delight possible and why that pleasure and delight is so important to us.

To appreciate Kant's answer to the first of these questions, think again about his account of what is involved in seeing an object: a flower, say. In through the avenues of the senses pours a welter of chaotic stimuli. The imagination synthesizes them into the discrete objects. To that synthesis the understanding applies concepts and classifications, which make the synthesis knowable and communicable. Here the understanding confines the imagination by binding its synthesis to a general concept. However, in the aesthetic case, the imagination is not thus confined. For, Kant says, somewhat obscurely, that in aesthetic judgement imagination and understanding enter into a "free play". It is from this free play that aesthetic delight arises.

The hard part here is understanding the notion that in aesthetics there is a "free play" between imagination, which organizes the randomly bombarding stimuli, and understanding, which imposes conceptual understanding on that organization.

To help make sense of this consider, first, the case in which I say "Turn at the tree by the pub". Here, on Kant's view, the imagination is only active minimally in organizing the stimuli that will be conceptualized as trees and pubs. Now consider the way in which a child, in play, does not merely thus *label* trees but *imagines* some tree as a spectral figure and, moreover, richly embroiders that imagining, so that the tree is personified, given a life, history and a role, the details of which might proliferate for ever. Here the imagination *plays*.

Second, consider next that I might say "True love isn't fickle". Here I formulate a somewhat dry piece of thinking. But then I read this Shakespeare sonnet:

> Let me not to the marriage of true minds
> Admit impediments. Love is not love
> Which alters as it alteration finds,
> Or bends with the remover to remove.
> O, no! it is an ever fixèd mark,
> That looks on tempests and is never shaken;
> It is a star to every wandering bark,
> Whose worth's unknown, although his height be taken.
> Love's not Time's fool, though rosy lips and cheeks
> Within his bended sickle's compass come;
> Love alters not with his brief hours and weeks,
> But bears it out even to the edge of doom.
> If this be error, and upon me proved,
> I never writ, nor no man ever loved.

Again my imagination is released to play. These words trigger in me a complex of images that in turn trigger thoughts and associations of my own which I might weave about them: imaginings of stars, and ships, legal proceedings and of sickles. Here there is delight in that play.

Consider, too, this lovely piece of writing:

When our attention is absorbed in a symphony sometimes a melody will appear as a single being floating or gliding or making a tender gesture; the music of the symphony itself may appear as a single being making some sort of journey, turning this way and that in search of something, and we may identify with it, as we identify with a character in a play or picture; a horn-call may be heard as if it were a voice, which some other instrument seems to answer; the sounds of the various instruments of the orchestra as a multitude of voices restlessly discussing or expressing something, or as a crowd of beings moving restlessly about; or the sounds may suddenly seem to fly up, like a flock of birds; or they become again one thing and assume the momentum of an immensely powerful force or machine. (Elliott 1973, p. 94)

There, too the imagination plays.

But Kant says that the origin of aesthetic delight is a free play between the imagination *and* the understanding. How is the understanding involved?

Consider the random free play of the mind in daydreaming, where the stream of consciousness has no constraints. Contrast that with my cases. The child's mind is active in weaving imaginings around the tree, but the tree constrains those imaginings. If it lends itself to spectral and skeletal imaginings, it will not lend itself to imaginings of Friar Tuck. Again, the words of the poem and the sounds of the music *constrain* and shape our imaginings. The "play" to which Kant refers occurs because in imagination we push the limits of those constraints. But the understanding lodged in those words and sounds pushes back.

Granted this picture we can understand the powerful delight in what Kant calls the "purposeless purposiveness" of the beauty of natural things, as when we marvel at the way a snowflake seems to be wrought like a jewel. For there the imagination plays with finding a purposefulness where the understanding knows there is none.

That now leaves the question why the delight occasioned by this free play is so important to us. This brings us to another Kantian theme, the notion of disinterestedness.

Disinterestedness

Kant asserts that aesthetic judgement is disinterested. There are three parts to this. Firstly there is the claim that an examination of our practices reveals that we have so structured the world that aesthetic judgement is disinterested. Secondly there is an investigation of what in the structure of the mind makes that structuring possible. The third part is the role that the notion of disinterestedness is to play in questions about the objectivity of aesthetic judgement.

Aesthetic judgement as disinterested

What might lead Kant, on inspecting our practices, to the conclusion that aesthetic judgement is disinterested?

Firstly imagine that we are outside a theatre on the night that a new play takes the audience by storm. One person comes out smiling because he invested in the play, another because her daughter wrote it, another because the boss – who likes his employees to enjoy culture – saw him there, and another because she simply enjoyed the play. If asked which is the aesthetic response, the temptation is to say the last, and to go from that to saying that this aesthetic response is *dis*interested. This does not mean that it is *un*interested or that those who respond disinterestedly sat there passively (or distanced). Rather, they had no personal stake in the fate of the play.

Secondly, many of our personal interests presuppose a concern with the real existence. If I am avidly interested in owning a Ferrari, I'd better believe that Ferraris exist. But now, if I look at Picasso's *Woman weeping*, I can react in two ways. I can ask whether this is a picture of some real woman. But I can also be intensely moved by that picture-face without worrying about whether it had any real counterpart. And that is one of the things that may suggest to Kant that an interest in the aesthetic is "disinterested", meaning not interested in the real existence of the object contemplated (which is entirely compatible with being deeply moved by that pictured face).

Thirdly, an example of a *personal* judgement is "I like it". Here one expresses one's purely private personal interest. But for Kant the example of an *aesthetic* judgement would be "this is beautiful". Here we have different claims. The claim to like a thing, say jam on one's kippers, does not assert that others should do so too. But the claim that a thing is beautiful does appear to assert that others should like it too. Since the judgement of liking expresses a personal interest and the judgement of beauty is not like that, so, Kant could conclude, the latter is disinterested.

Fourthly, I think Kant was also tempted to suppose that our interest in art differed from our interest in, say hammers. In the latter case, part of our interest lies in what we could use the hammer for. The interest would be practical or utilitarian. But, we might suppose, an aesthetic interest in a picture-face would not involve asking what one could use the image for (though one could use it as a prop for one's fantasies), but would content itself with solely contemplative attention.

The possibility of aesthetics: reality

Granted we treat aesthetic judgements as disinterested, we turn to the question of what makes this possible. Here we meet for the first time the notion of representation.

Kant uses the term "representation" more widely than the way we usually now do. On Kant's account, whenever imagination fuses the bombardments received by the senses into the perceived object it does so by forming a *representation*. It helps to think of representing something in this way as like creating a representational picture. Consider Turner painting a sunset. The sensory input he receives from the sunset is fused by him into his picture.

Now we can see what makes it *possible* to be disinterested, in at least one of the senses in which Kant thought aesthetic responses to be disinterested. Granted we have a representation, say of a sunset, we have the power to delight in the picture-sunset without ever taking an interest in whether some real sunset was its model.

What goes for the contemplation of paintings goes for the contemplation of natural objects.

To see a flower, on Kant's view, is to impose an order on our sensory input in just the way that a painter imposes order on the impinging stimuli of a sunset. The imagination creates the representation of a flower. Then either we can take an interest in whether there is some such flower, or alternatively we can just enjoy the representation as we may enjoy any representational picture, that is, without asking whether what it represents really exists. We simply attend to the look of the flower.

So what makes a disinterested response possible is the power to form representations and the possibility of ignoring questions about the real existence of what is represented.

How does this connect with the examples we gave of being disinterested?

Why might we be interested in the real existence of something, say a Ferrari? One reason is that we want it. That binds an interest in real existence to something that is not disinterested but partial. We *could not* wish to possess the picture-face in this way (although we could wish to possess the original picture in which that face first made its appearance). Another reason is that we have hopes and fears that would be affected by real existence. These too are partial. Alternatively we can ask why one might think ignoring real existence to be aesthetically relevant. One answer is, having abdicated interest in real existences, we can only attend to the picture-object. All we can do is contemplate it. That will mean entering imaginatively into the world of the picture, the mind being freed to weave its controlled imaginings about it. Disinterest in this case engenders the very delight that was earlier said to arise from the free play of imagination and understanding.

The possibility of aesthetics: objectivity and subjectivity

Kant is quite certain my aesthetic judgements appear to be rooted in my feelings of delight. Yet on the basis of these purely personal, subjective feelings, I appear to claim the right to say how others, too, should respond. The aesthetic judgement is, thus, entirely rooted in my subjective likings, and, yet, at the same time makes claims on others. Kant's great problem is what makes *this* possible.

I deal with this matter more fully later. Here I note that the notion of disinterestedness has a role to play. The argument goes thus: if my interest is personal and partial, I have no right to claim that simply because *I* have such an interest, *you* should share it.

But if purely personal interests don't come into the matter, there is more hope of agreement because no partiality gets in the way. So if we could show that our attention to the aesthetic was disinterested, in some way impersonal, then we would have some right to expect more agreement. For what personal interest *could* divide us? I return to that important argument in Chapter 6.

Importance: rapture

Whatever one thinks of Kant's account it attempts an answer to the question why the aesthetic has such power. On that account an intense delight arises as the mind roams in controlled acts of imagination through the world of art and natural things. This delight is rapture. Think of the utter delight of music heard so deeply that, as T. S. Eliot put it, it is not heard at all but you *are* the music. Nor is rapture merely mental. Many of my readers will have been lost in the kind of dancing in which the body spontaneously acts out what we imagine the music is intimating that we should do.

In a striking analysis Ray Elliott (1973) deepens this. Rapturous imagination, he says, is valued because in it our *freedom* is celebrated. We are not passive receivers of the world but, as the child's imaginings remind us, active in shaping, glorifying and consummating it. In these moments it is as if we rise transfigured from the deadness of our habitual lives. And we have, too, the promise of the continual possibility of such spiritual renewal. That, indeed, is an experience of rapture offered by the greatest art.

Importance: community

It is possible to feel that great though rapture is, it does not give us all we want from an account of the importance of art. We are told how certain experiences are valuable to individuals. But some have thought that art ought not merely to celebrate the powers of humans considered in isolation, but some more social vision. Kant appears to me not unmindful of this and offers two thoughts, one clear enough, one deeply obscure.

Firstly he stresses the role of the aesthetic imagination in helping us all to comprehend what he calls "rational ideas", abstract notions such as justice, peace, honour, which do not appear among the physical objects of the world and which are not as fully comprehended as physical objects are. These notions, he claims, can take on an appearance of reality through being represented in images that the senses can take in. He says:

> The poet attempts the task of interpreting to the sense the rational ideas of invisible beings, the kingdom of the blessed, hell, eternity, creation, . . . death, envy and all vices . . . love, fame and the like . . . to present them to sense with a completeness of which nature affords no parallel. (Kant 1951, pp. 157–8)

Consider as an example here the following lines from *The merchant of Venice*:

> The quality of mercy is not strain'd,
> It droppeth as the gentle rain from heaven
> Upon the place beneath: it is twice blessed,
> It blesseth him that gives, and him that takes,
> 'Tis mightiest in the mightiest: it becomes
> The throned monarch better than his crown.

Here the poetic imagination weaves about the notion of mercy a wealth of images that enrich our conception of the nature of that quality in a way in which merely saying, however eloquently, that mercy is a good thing cannot do. Only the active imagination can thus sensuously embody the idea of such abstract ideas. Since these are integral to us as social beings, art serves those communal purposes.

Secondly, Kant posits a connection between the aesthetic and the morally good that takes the aesthetic out of the realm of private indulgence. Kant does not mean that we have pictures, like those Victorian masterpieces *The awakening conscience* and *The self-abuser's doom*, the contemplation of which might be morally uplifting. Rather he suggests that an intense attention to the aesthetically valuable leads to reflection on the morally good.

This is deeply obscure. There *are* similarities between the aesthetic and the morally good as Kant perceives them. Attention to the aesthetic is disinterested, as we expect moral action to be. The aesthetic celebrates freedom, a prerequisite for moral action. But these parallels do not necessarily bring communal moral concerns into the realm of art.

About Kant

I think that Kant's aesthetic ought to be attempted by anyone who seriously wishes to be a philosophical aesthetician, and his philosophy by anyone who wants to be a serious philosopher. This is because of the intrinsic interest of the view he has of philosophy and the seriousness of the questions he raises. Moreover he set the agenda for much that has happened in aesthetics. Indeed he sets an agenda to which I turn next. For central to Kant's analysis is the belief that the proper objects of aesthetic interest are representations and the attempt to say why we should be so interested in them.

That analysis of representation is linked to Kant's belief that our construction of the world involves creating representations of it. That has advantages. Kant's theory enables him to give a unified account of our interest in nature and our interest in art. Looking at a wild flower is as much looking at a representation as is looking at a painting of Macbeth. Of course, if we drop Kant's notion that to look at anything is to create a representation, and attach the notion of representation simply to the notion of things like representational paintings, then a rift opens between what we are doing when we enjoy nature and what we are doing when we enjoy art. For myself I welcome this conclusion, if only because, as I argue in Chapter 10, our enjoyment of art differs from our enjoyment of nature, particularly if, as I shall argue, representation is part of the essence of the former and not of the latter. A painting or a play can be a representation in the way in which a tree cannot (though a tree may figure in a representation, as in those parks in which trees are planted in the formations of the regiments at the battle of Waterloo).

However, even granted that representation lies at the root of our dealings with art and the world we still need an account of what goes on when we *see* a representation. How, for example, *do* we manage to see smears of paint on a two-dimensional surface as a three-dimensional object? We might wonder, further, whether Kant has given an entirely satisfying account of why the imaginative interest in representations should be so compelling. True, he gives an account that explains why individuals should find such rapture in imaginative enjoyment of representations. But then we might wonder, as he did, if a reference to individual satisfaction is all there is to it. We might think here of the way in which Tolstoy, in a way to be examined, thought that the great feature of representational art was its power to bind humans together. Or we might think of Croce, who wished to stress that representations are important because they are bound up with expression. We need, then, to take a longer look at representation and the long-standing claim that representation lies at the root of the aesthetic, if only, as we shall now see, because the claim, in one form or another, that art is essentially a matter of representation is as old a claim as there is in aesthetics.

Guide to reading

The notions of aesthetic attitudes and distance are associated with Edward Bullough and can best be approached by his deceptively straightforward article "'Psychical distance' as a factor in art and as an aesthetic principle", *British Journal of Psychology* 5, 1912 and reprinted in Tillman & Cahn, *Philosophy of art and aesthetics*, pp. 397–414. This is a splendid article for a seminar discussion, determined to winkle out and scrutinize its various theses. Some further twentieth century examples of aesthetic attitude theories are given in J. Stolnitz, *Aesthetics and the philosophy of art criticism* (New York: Houghton Mifflin, 1960), pp. 29–64. The now classic piece of scepticism about aesthetic attitudes is G. Dickie, "The myth of the aesthetic attitude", *American Philosophical Quarterly* 1(1), 1964, pp. 56–65. See also his "Psychical distance: in a fog at sea", *British Journal of Aesthetics*, 13(1), 1973, pp.17–29. A more sympathetic view is that taken by Diane Collinson's "Aesthetic experience" in Hanfling's *Philosophical aesthetics*.

Any first reading of anything by Kant is a formidable undertaking. The relevant primary text is *The critique of judgement*, trans. J. H. Bernard (New York: Hafner, 1951). I'd be inclined to try to get the hang of what is going on before (or simultaneously with) getting stuck into the original. On the general philosophy R. Scruton, *Modern philosophy* is instructive as is John Shand's *Philosophy and philosophers*. There are helpful remarks on Kant's aesthetics in Diane Collinson's contribution to Hanfling's *Philosophical aesthetics*. Also to be commended as you get deeper into the matter is D. Crawford, *Kant's aesthetic theory* (Madison: University of Wisconsin Press, 1974). A more advanced, but helpful article by a noted Kant scholar and aesthetician is E. Schaper, "Taste, sublimity and genius: the aesthetics of art and nature", in *The Cambridge companion to Kant*, P. Guyer (ed.) (Cambridge:Cambridge University Press, 1992), pp. 367–93. And anything by Guyer on Kant is worth reading. The scope of the present introduction prevents me from going into theories that are related to Kant's, of which one of the most rousing is Schopenhauer's *The world as will and idea*, Vol.1, Book 3. There is a fair introduction to this in the Collinson piece referred to above. See also C. Janaway, *Schopenhauer* (Oxford: Oxford University Press,1994). Kant's influence is manifested in an entirely different way in Hegel's philosophy, on which see Scruton and Shand.

In the text, by way of getting a purchase on the notion of disinterestedness, I refer to the various ways in which an audience might be interested in a play. This is derived from an influential article by J. O. Urmson, "What makes a situation aesthetic?" *Proceedings of the Aristotelian Society*, supp. vol. 31 (1957), pp. 75–92. The Ray Elliott article to which I refer is the remarkable "Imagination in the experience of art", in *Philosophy and the arts*, G. Vesey (ed.) (London: Macmillan, 1973), pp. 244–82. There is a discussion of the shortcomings of disinterestedness (especially in our dealings with nature) in A. Berleant, *Art and engagement* (Philadelphia: Temple University Press, 1991).

I have not dealt with John Dewey's important *Art as experience* (New York: Putnam, 1934). This is touched on in the Collinson contribution to Hanfling's *Philosophical aesthetics* (pp. 150–6). See also T. Alexander, *John Dewey's theory of art, experience and nature* (Albany: State University of New York Press, 1987). Dewey much influenced M. Beardsley who sketches an account of aesthetic experience in Beardsley (1958), pp. 527–43. Croce, incidentally, thought that much of Dewey's work in aesthetics was derivative from Crocean aesthetics, in which case what I shall say about Croce in Chapters 3 and 5 will apply also to Dewey. The matter is fully discussed by Alexander.

Chapter 2

Nature's mirror: imitation, representation and imagination

If we wish to understand the power of art, a way to start is by looking at situations in which people claim to feel this power. Here legend, art and history all supply examples of cases in which viewers are moved to awe by *pictorial representations*. In this originated an ancient and still popular account that links art with imitation, representation or, using a Greek term, *mimesis*.

From remote antiquity people were powerfully struck by representations and the power to produce them. Hence the legend, to which I shall return, of Pygmalion, whose sculptures excited awed marvel and one of which was good enough to be granted life by the goddess Venus. Browning's "My last duchess" begins:

> That's my last Duchess painted on the wall,
> Looking as if she were alive. I call
> That piece a wonder, now: Frà Pandolf's hands
> Worked busily a day, and there she stands.

Note the strength of the language used. The thing is called "a *wonder*". People, indeed, stand in amazement before representations. Something *powerful* is going on here.

Interest in representation is as ubiquitous as our involvement with the aesthetic. Pictures are bought in Woolworth's because representation appeals. The waterfront portraitist at Key West trades on a fascination with representation. People seem *driven* to festoon walls, trains and bridges with representational graffiti. There is an insatiable drive to represent the world, an insatiable wish to view those representations, and a propensity fervently to cherish those gifted as representers. That suggests a central role for representation in any account of the power of art.

If representation is to be made central to that account, two things have to be done. Firstly, we need to know what representation is. If the term is left vague then any account of art based on it is vague. Secondly, we must show that the power of art can be adequately accounted for in terms of representation. By way of a glimpse of some difficulties here, we might note that although music, as Helen Schlegel found, has enormous power, it seems not to be representational at all. How then, is the power of art generally to be accounted for in terms of representation?

Representation as imitation

It is said that some, Plato for example, have thought of representation as imitation. This is so implausible as to raise doubts that it has ever been seriously entertained. Imitation is quite useless as a general account of art, because so little in art has to do with imitation. Think of obvious cases of imitation: you have an odd gait and I follow you, imitating your walk; Percy Edwards could imitate to perfection the flutings of the nightingale. Little of art has to do with imitation in this sense.

There may be cases in which a composer puts into music a sound such that if one were to hear that sound in isolation, one might think "Ah! a corncrake!". But the composer is not imitating a bird, and, even if he or she were, music does not generally do that. Again, Annie Lennox doesn't imitate lost love in "No more I love yous", even if she feels the sentiment of that song. There are works of literature, Browning's *Dramatic monologues* for example, where the writer tries to catch the tone of voice of, say, an irritable monk. But, again, to suggest that literature generally does this, or that when it does it is imitative, is simply to understate and mischaracterize the variety of literary phenomena.

Even in performance, actors do not generally imitate the characters they play. One might note the walk of a real person and build that into one's acting, but that does not make one's acting an imitation. The notion that Charles Laughton was imitating Captain Bligh or Quasimodo is simply far-fetched. Actors do not imitate characters: they inhabit them. Hence Warren Mitchell's riposte to someone who queried his rendering of a character: "You've only seen him: I've been him".

What of pictorial representation? For, just as ducks are taken in by imitations of ducks issued from the reed beds by the lurking hunters, so there are reports of people and even animals being taken in by pictures. But again there is nothing to be said for the view that paintings generally take people in or are generally meant to do so. Even *trompe l'oeil* takes one in only momentarily. What would its point be, if never detected with a smile of admiration?

Representation as copying

Accounts of art as imitation sometimes suggest that imitation is a kind of copying. Copying can happen in the course of imitation. I can imitate your walk or your signature by copying it. But the notion of copying is neither general enough, nor good enough, nor creative enough to capture our dealings with art.

Firstly, it is not general enough. There are cases of art that involve copying, notably some mime. It is unclear, however, what is copied in *Edward Scissorhands*, "Nessun dorma", or the Judge Dredd comic strip. Secondly, the account misses the goodness of art. Copies are not always greeted with the approbation with which we tend to greet art, our reaction to finding a well-forged fiver in our change being, at best, a mixture of approbation for the skill and disapprobation for the deceit. Thirdly, the account leaves out creativity. A copy, for all the skill it commands, needs exhibit none of the creative or imaginative originality characteristic of art.

Much sport has been had with Plato's views on this matter. For Plato a representation is a copy, and as such always suspect, being a misleading and deceitful derivation from a true original, this being something existing in some transcendent world. Many of those who ridicule Plato's views confuse a rejection of his claims about the existence of a transcendent reality, copied third-hand by artists, with rejection of his claim that a copy is a second-best, a claim that they would, had Plato's metaphysical views not clouded the issue, probably accept.

Apart from this there are more recent, powerful objections to the view that representational art involves copying.

The copying model suggests that a painter stands before something and then copies what is seen, looking from the one to the other to check the match. That view presupposes that there is some way of identifying the world being copied or represented independently of the act of copying or representing it. How else could we compare the one with the other?

Against resemblance

There are two approaches to this copying model. One is simply to deny that one can thus produce resemblances of the world. The other is to concede that one can do so, but then to deny that representational art does that.

I associate the first approach with Kantian inclinations. To those with such inclinations, as we have seen, the notion that we passively receive a pre-existently structured world is denied. We do not copy the world. We make it. More recently, similar views have been expressed by Ernst Gombrich and, in an extreme form, by Nelson Goodman. We do not passively perceive a world, which we copy down in order to produce a representational resemblance. What is received is interpreted according to expectation, memory, cultural background and individual psychology. There is no reality to be resembled independently of these conditioned seeings. Hence Goodman's claim that artists make rather than take reality. Let us look a little more closely at this, taking Gombrich and Goodman in turn.

Gombrich

Gombrich suggests that talk of copying a pre-existent reality requires us to think of an innocent eye confronting and copying a pre-existently structured world. He denies that there are innocent eyes. Our seeings are always conditioned and that conditioning affects what we see.

I am suspicious of talk of eyes as innocent or not. Eyes are neither. It is the people who have the eyes who are innocent or naive or conditioned. The claim is better put as asserting that the way a person draws the world is conditioned by that person's personal and cultural baggage. Then there are two ways of continuing. One is to say that there are no right or wrong ways of drawing how things look, only the different ways that different people, with different baggages, in fact draw them. That is certainly Goodman's view. The other is to say that although the ways in which we represent the world are conditioned by our personal or cultural baggage, some ways of representing it capture it better than others. This is, I think, what Gombrich says. Thus whereas Goodman feels that perspective drawing is only one representational *convention*, Gombrich thinks of it as allowing us more closely to capture how things look. And for Gombrich, unlike Goodman, there really does seem to be some point in saying that a picture of a green apple on a red tablecloth might better capture a scene than a picture of a blue apple on a yellow tablecloth. But then the view that in representation we try to capture how a thing really looks is not wholly undermined.

Goodman

Goodman, however, does want to undermine it. We really do, he says, make rather than copy the world, arguing, indeed, in one place, that we make the stars themselves.

The arguments Goodman gives in the first chapter of his *Languages of art* do not engender confidence. A first argument is that there are very many things an object might be. A man may be a violinist, a buffoon, a billiard player and so on and so on. How is this plenitude to be captured by one picture? This is a verbal trick. It may be difficult to portray someone simultaneously as a violinist and as a billiard player. One can't do it because in the world as it exists independently of the portrayal, one cannot simultaneously play snooker and the violin. But there is absolutely no problem in depicting someone, say Rodney, who is at one and the same time a violinist, a buffoon and a billiard player. I simply depict Rodney, since if Rodney is a violinist, billiard player and buffoon, any picture of him is a picture of someone who is all those things.

Secondly, Goodman points to the fact that under the influence of prejudice, indoctrination, acculturation or whatever, we may see things wrongly. We do indeed. But that is no help whatsoever to Goodman. The very talk of prejudice entails that there is something against which our views can be checked.

Thirdly, Goodman argues that conventional perspectival drawing does not show how things look because an undoctored photograph doesn't look like that. In photographs, the poles beside the receding railway track aren't, as conventional drawing has them, receding parallel uprights. But far from that being a proof that there is no way things really look, it is an argument to the contrary. The camera shows us that things don't really look as the conventional drawing shows them.

I do not deny that our preconceptions, however formed, can influence our ways of seeing and depicting things. Convinced antecedently that young black males are dangerous, someone will exaggerate certain features in depicting them. But how do we get from that to the conclusion that there is no reality against which those depictions can be checked? Nor could I deny that there are conventions in representing, for example, the convention of representing the Virgin Mary in a blue robe or St Lawrence by a man carrying a gridiron. But that does not show that all representation is thus conventional.

I do not wish to claim that representational paintings can simply be checked against reality. For we know that Turner, Constable, Monet and Cezanne, confronted by the same sunset, will produce different looking paintings. Suppose we ask which produced the most accurate picture of a sunset? What stands in the way of a choice is that we see sunsets through paintings. We say things like "how Turneresque". Each artist gave a way of representing sunsets. Collectively they give us a repertoire of such ways. But we can believe this without denying that there is, independently of the depiction, a sunset to be represented.

So I am not sure there is enough in Goodman's radical arguments to undermine a feeling that, even if a work cannot simply be checked against reality, it may certainly be assessed for its resemblance to how things look.

But, and this is the second approach I mentioned, to say that a resemblance may exist between a picture and reality is not to say that the artist copies reality, even when the artist captures that resemblance. For, one thing, as Croce trenchantly argued, artists may be unclear when starting what the outcome will be. That they can say, after finishing, that that is how the world indeed looks to them, does not entail that this could be known and simply copied before the picture was painted. In Virginia Woolf's *To the lighthouse*, Lily Briscoe finds the one line that will unite her painting so that it represents her vision of the world. But she did not find it by copying. Until she found her vision she had nothing to copy.

The notion of art as a kind of copying fares badly in the literature. In those attacks on art as imitation or as copying, however, something is overlooked. We *do* delight in imitations, and imitation (think here of mime) can be an art form. Moreover, as we shall see, imitation throws light on a nest of problems. I shall return to these after a look at some other problems about representation.

The very possibility of representation

Whether or not a representation does or does not resemble reality, there remains a basic question of how we can see a representation at all. How is it that pigment on a two dimensional surface can be seen as a horse or a dog? Goodman is right in one thing: there is no sense in which a two-dimensional surface resembles, in the sense of sharing all the properties of, a three-dimensional object. So how can we see that three-dimensional object represented on that two dimensional-surface?

At first sight this seems more a question for philosophical psychology than aesthetics, which asks, granted we can see representations, how they figure in any story of the power of art. But one answer does suggest something about the power of art, so here are a few words on a possibility suggested by Richard Wollheim.

On Wollheim's account when I see the girl portrayed in Manet's *The bar at the Folies-Bergère* I see that girl *in* those pigments. Here the mind generates visual experiences out of itself. When I see an inkblot as a bat, or a cloud in the shape of a camel, an image generated by the mind is fused with an external object, an inkblot or an oil painting. So the painting represents an object if it is configured in such a way that that object is *seen in* it. This account becomes important when it is linked, as I shall link it in Chapters 5 and 7, to the notion of art as a means of expressing and so making clear our inner lives.

An alternative account is offered by Kendal Walton. Consider a doll that in the imaginative world of a child becomes a baby. This lifeless object is tucked up, consoled and, in some more ostentatious models, is fed by and even waters upon its surrogate parent. The child *makes believe*, and the doll becomes a prop for its imaginative musings. That, Walton suggests, is what happens in representation. To see a painting that represents Batman I, no less than the child, engage in the make-believe that that set of configured pigments is Batman.

These two views are kindred. In both cases the imagination is exercised and something is seen in something. Walton's account may, however, make the perception of pictures too voluntary. One makes believe that the pigments are Batman. I am aware of no such process. I simply see Batman. Wollheim's account seems to me to stress that fact. I shall return to Wollheim's account when I come to talk about expression in art.

Nonrepresentational art

I have discussed whether representation is imitation and how we see representations. These are hotly disputed matters. I suspect, though, that there are deeper questions than these. For even if we know how we can see representations, and even if we have something better than imitation as our account of representation, we are still no nearer to explaining the power of art by reference to representation. For, since not all art is representational (music for example), how can representation be a general characteristic of art? Indeed, not even all visual art is representational. Consider any so-called "abstract" design with which you are familiar. Nothing seems to be represented there in the way in which God is represented on the ceiling of the Sistine Chapel.

This is too hasty. Firstly, even the most abstract of works can have spatial depth. Certain lines or colour patches can be seen as lying behind others, even though the picture is two-dimensional. To see this is to see three-dimensional configurings in the two-dimensional surface, and that is representational seeing.

Secondly, whether or not abstract paintings are representational they share a feature with representations. We may say of them that they are angry, brooding, joyful, calm and jolly. If it is a reason for saying that a picture represents Christ that Christ is seen in the configuration of its pigments, then it seems there is some reason to say that an "abstract" picture does something like that in that anger is *seen in* the configurations of its pigmentation.

This goes for music, too. I may not merely hear a beating of drums. I hear an angry beating of drums. I hear it *in* those sounds. Similarly, when I read a literary work, I do not merely see ink marks, I see meaningful words *in* those marks, and *in* those meaningful words, in turn, I see described people, places and events. Something happens in these cases that seems related to seeing a face in a painting. I am required to go beyond a substratum to what is signified in it.

Before I come to the question as to why this kind of representation is important, I mention for completeness two other much debated issues about representation.

Photography

A woman sits in Picasso's fearsome picture, *Nude dressing her hair*. About her one might ask, "Is this a picture of an actual woman, and, if so, was she like the picture painted of her?". Alternatively we can put aside questions of whether the picture-woman has a correlate and simply study the picture-woman. We can take an interest in the fact that she is in a state of great tension and finds her body loathsome and also take an interest in the way in which the painter has organized the details of the painting to produce just that impression. Indeed, Wollheim has argued that this two-foldedness of our interest, a simultaneous interest both in what is represented and in the manner of its representation, is essential to our dealings with painting as an *art* form. To do this we must detach ourselves from questions of real existence and, by an act of imagination, engage with a picture-figure. That

Picasso, *Woman dressing her hair,* 1940. Oil on canvas, 51¼" × 38¼". The Museum of Modern Art, New York.

engagement, in which the imagination focuses on and is controlled by the image, is rewarding to us, this being part of the value of the aesthetic.

Now Scruton argues that there is a clear difference between paintings and photographs. When I see the harrowing image of the napalmed child in a famous photograph from the Vietnam war, I cannot put aside the questions of real existence in order to contemplate the picture-child as a representation. There is something more than faintly disgusting in saying such things as "see how the disposition of the limbs is used to reinforce the effect of terror". Nor, since the photographer cannot control the detail of the photograph in the way in which the painter controls the detail of the painting, would it make sense to do so.

Scruton is right that there is a clear difference between image in a representational painting and a photograph. Does it follow that photography isn't an art form? One can see why this might be alleged. What makes aesthetic contemplation possible for representational pictures is the fact that one can separate the question: "Was there a real correlate to the picture-thing?" from the question, "What is the character of this picture-thing?". Moreover, the way in which painters can control every last detail to achieve a particular effect, is part of the contemplative pleasure. Photographers do not have this control. The fly that happens, to humorous effect, to land on a nose as a photograph is taken is a grace of fate rather than art. As Croce put it, the element of nature is not subdued in photography as it is in the greatest of art.

To this conclusion, generations of students, for whom the epitome of the pictorial is the photograph and the film, have objected strenuously. One approach is to impute to the photographer painterly elements of control. That may be possible. Some photographers may be better than others because they have greater control over their effects. But nature is never totally to be subdued. Another approach is to think of portrait painting, where we do concern ourselves with real existence, and to ask whether portraiture is an art form. If it is, it may be because a portrait can, in some way, catch the nature of the sitter, a realization so distressing to Churchill and his family that they destroyed a remarkable portrait. But Karsh's photographs – and Churchill is again a case in point – show that photography, through the way that the photographer, no less than the painter, has controlled the way in which the figure is to be seen, can do that.

But a worry remains. The representational painting gives us the option of detaching it from its source in an act of imaginative free-dom. The photograph does not. We always know that the object photographed actually existed.

However all is not lost to those who wish to argue that photog-raphy is an art form. Firstly, not all representational paintings are to be treated in the same way. It seems important that a pic-ture like Picasso's *Guernica*, or Goya's *So it goes*, both of which portray actual horrors, be not detached from those events. Since this does not undermine them as art, it need not do so in the case of photography either.

Secondly, the image in a photograph *can* be contemplatively detached from its subject. With time any possible concern with the historical identity of the pictured figure withers, leaving us with only the image to contemplate. There may well come a time when the appearance of the historical Churchill is of no more concern to anyone than that of St Hild of Whitby. Someone could then simply look at the Karsh image for its overall effect and the cunningness with which the photographer achieved that effect. As to the claim that there is something disgusting in contemplating a photograph of a napalmed child as one might contemplate a representational painting, there is this reply. Not every photograph is disgustingly viewed when contemplated as one might contemplate a picture, and not every representational painting can be simply contem-plated without that contemplation being disgusting. Anyone who contemplated a Goya etching of a wartime rape purely aestheti-cally ("How interesting the arrangement is of the limbs!"), would commit a crime against that picture. Painters have felt the same repugnance in creating representational art of suffering as photog-raphers have felt in simply photographing it. Sylvia Pankhurst, a gifted painter of the scenes of horror in east London, one day looked at the faces of the poor and felt a great wrongness in creating from them an art to be contemplated with aesthetic satisfaction.

Thirdly, we might admit that photography differs from represen-tational painting by virtue of the fact that the image in the photo-graph cannot be detached from its connection with something real. But then one might claim that this opens a possibility not open to representational painting. For there is a distinctive pleasurable experience that surrounds the contemplation of a photograph that is connected with the ill-understood phenomenon of nostalgia. In nostalgia the past returns and excites a special kind of experience in which the past lives in the present. A Victorian boy in the sepia print, staring at the camera, frozen by its Medusa's eye, was a real person who stood *just there*, who turned and walked away, grew up and died and is returned to this present bearing the actual past in a way that occasions the special feeling of the past restored of which Proust so wondrously wrote. Representational paintings cannot give us that experience, save in the sense that they may give us a present image of a past time when people painted like that. But that is to root them in past reality.

Fiction

The second, much debated, issue I mention is fiction. For in a novel, too, to ask whether Mr Pickwick, say, had a real life model, is to deflect attention away from the aesthetic act, which is the imaginative contemplation of the fiction.

Some questions about fiction transcend philosophical aesthetics and reach into philosophical logic. Thus "Ace Ventura was kind to animals" is a perfectly meaningful statement about Ace Ventura. But how can it be about him if he doesn't exist? Further if we (wrongly) suppose that the meaning of a term is what it refers to, then how can that statement, which refers to nothing, be meaningful at all? That problem, which gets an early airing in Plato's dialogue *The sophist*, and a rigorous work out in, *inter alia*, the work of Peter Strawson and Bertrand Russell, is, however, more a problem for philosophical logic than aesthetics.

More directly related to aesthetics is the question: why are we so interested in fictions? People will queue to get into fictional films and I'd guess more fiction is read than fact.

All sorts of reasons suggest themselves. One is escapism. When the four walls begin to close in perhaps even escape to the glamour of Jilly Cooper's polo players can have its allure. Another is that a fictional world demands imaginative involvement, that being a source of enjoyment.

Next, why do we enjoy certain fictions? I go to see a play in which an old senile man divides his kingdom and is driven mad, his loving daughter is hanged and a man is brutally blinded. Yet I might be tempted to answer "Yes" if asked whether I enjoyed the play. How is that possible?

Here one has to be careful in saying what was enjoyed. Had I been asked what I enjoyed and replied that it was the putting out of the eyes, and did not mean the clever way it was done, then something would be seriously wrong. What I enjoyed was the *play*, the acting, the contrivance of plot, the majesty of the writing, the thoughts articulated for me, the scenery, the lighting and the cumulative effect. When I enjoy *King Lear*, I need not enjoy what happens *in* it and I need take no pleasure in blinding and dementia. And I suspect that some events are too horrible to be encompassed in a play. Dr Johnson certainly thought this of *King Lear*.

But the problem that most exercises many of my contemporaries is the apparent irrationality of fiction. By way of introduction to this intriguing matter, let us note that when I have an emotion such as fear, rage or sorrow, I *must* believe something *actually* obtains towards which my emotion is targeted. If I am afraid because I think my employer wants to dismiss me, I must really believe he wishes so to do. If I find that my employer does not wish to do so, then there is something irrational in continuing to fear that. An emotion seems to involve the belief that the situation that is its object actually obtains.

Now consider that great film classic *The Blob*. As I sit munching my popcorn, the Blob comes towards me. My hands sweat, my bowels turn to water; if someone tapped me on the shoulder I should jump galvanically. In short, I'm afraid. But how can this be? For me actually to be afraid, I must believe that I am actually threatened. But I don't believe this, else I wouldn't have come. And now, again, I watch the end of *Brief encounter*, and he's gone, and the tears flow because Laura, with her ridiculous hats and emaciated voice, is desolate. I am sad for her. Yet I do not believe that there is any such person.

Some try to save the rationality of fictional grief and fear by finding real objects for it. I cry because Laura's condition reminds me of real cases of suffering, or some general truth about it, and these thoughts make me weep. That seems unhelpful. Is it not Laura I cry for? Secondly how does this work for fear of the Blob. What general truths does that bring home? Is it that jellies can get out of hand? Thirdly, the account seems simply too depressing. The outcome would be that I leave the cinema moping or anxious, whereas I come out of *Brief encounter* exhilarated.

Colin Radford takes the opposite tack of saying that emotional responses to fiction are irrational. I know there is nothing to cry over, yet I cry over it. That account does not explain how we can knowingly act in irrational ways and so doesn't explain fictional responses. Confronted with the fact of my lover's infidelity, I can shut my eyes to it and this might be a rational way to behave. What I can't do is simultaneously act out the belief that she is faithful and faithless. How then can I cry for someone while *knowing* she does not exist.

In the case of my lover's infidelity I simply shut the fact out. Do I perhaps deliberately shut my eyes to the fact that the Blob does not exist in order that I can enjoy my emotions? But if it is possible to shut my eyes in this way, and if I have a reason for doing so, the action is not, as Radford claims, necessarily irrational.

If the question is, how can I cry for Laura when I know she does not exist, one answer is, by shutting my eyes to that fact and acting as if she does. I engage, *pro tem*, in innocent self-deception. The matter then ceases to be one for aesthetics and becomes a more general one of how that kind of action is possible in a wide range of cases, aesthetic and nonaesthetic. The question is not, "Is self-deception possible?". Nor is it "Can self-deception be rational?" (it can). The question is what account of the mind explains its possibility?

Sometimes shutting one's eyes to something, self-deception, is perfectly reasonable behaviour, as in the case of the cancer sufferer who is told hope of amelioration lies in not thinking about the desperate aspects of the matter. Can it be reasonable in fictional cases? Yes, if something we get out of fictional encounters makes this reasonable.

One thing is the enjoyment of imaginative activity. But that can't be all. I actually enjoy being terrified in films in the way in which I would not enjoy this in life and I am willing to shut my eyes to the fictionality in order to be terrified. The explanation of why this is so must go very deep and the full explanation will be related to answers to such questions as why pain can please and the forbidden attract. Those can only come from explorations of the mind's psychology. As far as aesthetics goes, the fact that terror excites us and that fictional terror offers the excitements without the inconveniences makes its pursuit seem a reasonable and not an irrational one.

Representation and art

Let us return to the question of whether the fact that art is representational helps us to understand its power.

I have tried to deal with the difficulty posed by the fact that not all art is representational. A more fundamental objection is that representation is not relevant at all, even when it is present. Clive Bell (1920) writes that representation is always irrelevant, for the power of art lies in the attractions of form. This is dubious.

Firstly it is unclear that Bell does dismiss representation, at least in the larger sense that I have given to that notion. He says that we should attend to "form, colour and three dimensional space". But to see a three-dimensional space on a two-dimensional plane simply is to see something in something, and thus to see a representation.

Secondly, we cannot exclude an interest in representation from considerations of form. In Stubbs' picture *The Duke of Richmond's racehorses at exercise*, we can only see the formal composition of the picture if we see in it the representation of a man pointing a whip. That directs our eyes to the organization of the picture as a mere line would not.

But for all that, Bell has had an unfair press, as least as far as his worries about representation go. For he is raising again an objection first envisaged by Plato and reiterated more recently by Ortega y Gasset: Why paint replicas of beds, to be looked at as beds are looked at, when we already have perfectly good beds to hand.

Part of what worries Bell stems from inclinations to believe that an interest in a representation can only be an interest in the object represented, the surface of a picture being a clear window through which one looks at these things. And countless people do buy pictures of ponds and fields and Benidorm as surrogates for viewing the real thing. This is why Bell thinks that photography has made representational painting otiose. A photograph can now do better what representation tried to, so representation can be dropped.

That confronts us with a challenge: what would we lose if we lost representation from art?

Imitation again

I approach that challenge by looking at one form that representation takes, a form in which the answer to the challenge shows itself in its clearest form, and that is imitation. I do not say that representation is always imitation (what does a representation of Bart Simpson imitate?). But there are grounds for thinking that imitation is a form of representation. If I walk down the street with a funny gait, I may present a ridiculous spectacle. If you imitate me exactly you re-present that spectacle.

The first thing I want to point out is that not every imitation is a subject of delight. The discovery that a splendid show of daffodils on your lawn consists of plastic flowers is hardly likely to please, and toupees are more a matter for jest than aesthetic delight. Imitations, then, need to be divided between cases where one wants the imitation to be enjoyed as such and cases in which we hope the imitation will not be detected. (When one signs someone else's name on a cheque one is hardly likely to point out to the cashier how perfectly one has caught the very curlicues of the Getty hand.) Artistic acts of imitation, those intended for our delight, are, unlike fake mink coats, in the class of things that are meant to draw attention to themselves. Secondly, when an imitation is appreciated, there is no necessity that one likes *what* is imitated in order to enjoy the imitation. The object of my imitation when I imitate a toothless man with a walrus moustache eating spaghetti without a fork does not have to be a spectacle of delight for you to delight in my imitation of it. What you delight in is not what is imitated (although you might independently delight in this, as when I do a perfect imitation of the speaking voice of John Gielguld). What you delight in is the act of imitating it. And we can generalize this. When we represent something it is not the object that is represented that is of interest when we are interested in the representation (although, as in the Gielguld case, we might independently be interested in this). It is the act of imitating it.

That allows us to deal with two conundrums. The first is why we bother to copy what we already have. Here we see the point of a famous piece of representational art. Magritte exhibited a representational drawing of a pipe that looks very like a pipe. Included in the drawing are the words "This is not a pipe?". Of course it isn't. It is a drawing of a pipe, and as such has quite different properties from a pipe.

Pictures of things offer us rewards other than those offered to us by the things pictured. Consider, again, Pygmalion and Galatea. Pygmalion created a marvellous statue of a woman, but if what he wanted was a companion, a stone statue probably offers less than the vicarious satisfactions of an inflatable doll. Hence Pygmalion beseeched Venus to give his statue life. But of course, once it had that, he had to forfeit the contemplative joys that statues offer. Similarly, a character in Tom Stoppard's *Rosencrantz and Guildenstern are dead* expresses surprise that a real execution on stage seemed unappreciated by audiences. Whatever delights are offered by the spectacle of an execution they are not co-extensive with the delights offered by representations of an execution.

What are these delights? One is the delight we take in acts of imitation – in the wit, perception and skill shown in such acts. We delight, too, in the way in which an artist bends all the (sometimes recalcitrant) elements of a picture and the media used in its production, to produce its effect: as when we are ravished by the placing of the colours, the eyes, the knotted tendons, the bright light, the deformed figure that produces the haunting image of Picasso's nude as she dresses her hair.

The other conundrum, to which we may now have the beginnings of an answer, may be approached by asking why we might think that certain subjects are, so to speak, off limits to art, a point hinted at by whoever said that in the face of the Nazi death camps art is silent. I enjoyed Martin Amis's *Time's arrow* as a remarkable feat of the novelist's skill. But I had a worry about using the Holocaust as subject matter for that exercise. Similarly, I have stressed the way in which in the presence of a representation we might point admiringly to the way in which the effect is achieved, as when we say, note how the open mouth of the smallest child in Kathe Kollwitz's blisteringly ironic and compassionate picture *Municipal lodging* clinches the overwhelming piteousness of the scene. But I feel uneasy in saying "Note how cleverly the almost luminous and putrescent green of Grunwald's *Crucifixion* helps capture the desolation".

Could it be said that if I am interested in the Grunwald or the Amis as art, then the way it is done is all I can take an interest in? It is merely that in these cases my ability to respond aesthetically is interfered with by what I know of the horror of the Holocaust and the Crucifixion. Some things are so horrible as to rule out the activities of creating and enjoying representations of them. In the face of the death camps art is silent because it not merely should not but cannot create enjoyable things out of them.

I worry about this answer. It seems, firstly, at odds with the fact that some of the greatest art has made art out of the truly awful. Grunwald's *Crucifixion* is great art.

Secondly, it marginalizes art. On this account it is fine for us to make representations of a great range of things, but when we come to things that most challenge comprehension, representation is forbidden and art has nothing to say. I shall accept that only as a last resort.

That there are other possibilities here might be indicated by considering the unlikely people who have suspected that however meaningless and bleak life might become, art intervenes to help us. At the end of Sartre's *Nausea* the sound of music, eternally transcendent to the scratched record that reproduces it, offers its protagonist a glimpse of a certain kind of salvation from time. With deeply moving poignancy it is music, at the end of Kafka's *Metamorphosis*, that brings the giant insect temporarily back to a better world. Consider too the most moving thing of all. Art was not silent in the Nazi death camps. Those in them produced operas, painting and literature. Why was that?

The way to an answer lies again in the simpler case of imitation. Not everything that is imitated is pleasing. But neither is every act of imitating, however well-wrought. If someone, for a cheap laugh, hobbles after a cripple, any brilliance of the impersonation does not erase the nasty taste. We feel that such acts *express* states of moral unawareness discreditable to their perpetrators.

That suggests this: representations are expressive. That fact begins to explain why those in the camps thought it important to produce representations. They wished to express something by them. That in turn suggests that we should ask if the importance of representation lies not *merely* in representing, for all that representations can ravish us in capturing the looks of things. Representations might have a deeper expressive significance, the exploration of which might take us deeper into an understanding of the power of art. So it is to expression I must now turn.

Guide to reading

Imitation, copying and resemblance

An overview can be had from Rosalind Hursthouse's "Truth and representation", Essay VI in Hanfling's *Philosophical aesthetics* and pp. 53–65 of Marcia Eaton's *Basic issues in aesthetics*. Also to be commended as you become more advanced is the chapter on representation in W. Charlton's rather neglected *Aesthetics* (London: Hutchinson, 1970). I very much enjoyed D. Peetz, "Some current philosophical theories of pictorial representation", *British Journal of Aesthetics* **27**, 1987, pp. 227–37, a rousing piece by a rousing philosopher.

Plato's eminently readable and challenging views on representation as second-hand imitation can be found in *Republic*, Book 10. Aristotle's *Poetics* 1–5 is often said to be an attempt to answer Plato's objections by finding a role for representation. More on these writers can be found in Beardsley's *Aesthetics from classical Greek to the present*, pp. 30–68. Tom Sorrell makes remarks about Plato and imitation in the Hanfling volume, pp. 297–311. See also Anne Sheppard, *Aesthetics*, pp. 4–17 and R. Woodfield, "Resemblance", in *The Blackwell companion to aesthetics*.

Ortega y Gasset's problems with representation are explored in *The dehumanisation of art*, trans. H. Weyl (Princeton: Princeton University Press, 1948).

Ernst Gombrich's views are to be found in his fascinating and instructive *Art and illusion* (London: Phaidon, 1977). A start can be made with pp. 3–25, but the whole book merits attention. For a criticism of Gombrich see Richard Wollheim, "Reflections on art and illusion" in his *On art and the mind* (London: Allen Lane, 1973). See also the very useful R. Woodfield (ed.), *The essential Gombrich* (Manchester: Manchester University Press, 1996) and R. Woodfield (ed.), *Gombrich, art and psychology* (Manchester: Manchester University Press, 1996). Goodman's views are best approached by way of Chapter 1 of his enormously controversial *Languages of art*. Criticism can be found in D. Pole, "Goodman and the naive view of representation", *British Journal of Aesthetics* **14**, 1974, pp. 68–80 and in Richard Wollheim, *On art and the mind*, pp. 290–314. Wollheim's own view is to be found in "Seeing-as, seeing-in and pictorial representation" in his *Art and its objects*, Essay V. Kendal Walton's views are to be found in his fascinating and important *Mimesis as make-believe* (Cambridge, Massachussetts: Harvard University Press, 1990). Since I said that Wollheim and Walton have a kinship in their views, take in also Walton's attempt to reduce seeing-in to make-believe in his "Seeing-in and seeing fictionally" in *Psychoanalysis, mind and art: perspectives on Richard Wollheim*, J. Hopkins & A. Savile (eds) (Oxford: Blackwell, 1992). I was impressed by Alex Neill's criticism of Walton to be found in his "Fear, fiction and make-believe", *Journal of Aesthetics and Art Criticism*, **49**(1), 1991, pp. 47–56. Recently there is also M. Budd, "How pictures look", in *Virtue and taste*, J. Skorupski & D. Knowles (eds) (Oxford: Blackwell, 1993), pp. 154–75. Those advancing in the subject should take in the remarks on seeing-as in Roger Scruton's *Art and imagination* and the rightly praised though more difficult F. Schier, *Deeper into pictures* (Cambridge: Cambridge University Press, 1986).

Photography

The startling essay by R. Scruton, "Photography and representation" in his *The aesthetic understanding* (Manchester: New Carcanet Press, 1973, pp. 102–26) started the hares running on this one, though it elaborates a point made in Chapter II of Croce's *Estetica* (translated 1992). Read also what Scruton says about film in *The aesthetic understanding*. S Sontag, *Photography* (London: Penguin, 1979, pp. 128–36) is also worth pondering.

Fiction

Much of the recent discussion in this area was prompted by C. Radford, "How can we be moved by the fate of Anna Karenina", *Proceedings of the Aristotelian Society*, supp. vol. **49**, 1975, pp. 67–80.

A full review of all the material is to be found in the monumental P. Lamarque & S. Olsen, *Truth, fiction and literature* (Oxford:

Clarendon, 1994). Different views on why we enjoy tragedies are fully discussed by Lamarque and Olsen.

A difficult but important discussion of various issues surrounding the rationality of self-deception is to be found in S. Gardner, *Irrationality and the philosophy of pyschoanalysis* (Cambridge: Cambridge University Press, 1993).

Chapter 3

Ne'er so well expressed (I)

We have arrived at a great story of the power of art, the story of art as expression. Many of my readers, indeed, will already intuitively feel that art is importantly to do with self-expression, for we are brought up in the aftermath of Romanticism with its image of the artist possessed of powerful feelings of joy or suffering and pouring them into art. Keats's nightingale, which, from the heavens, pours its full heart in the profuse strains of unpremeditated art, stands as the image of the romantic artist giving vent, in Wordsworth's phrase, to a spontaneous overflow of powerful feelings.

I shall discuss expression through two exemplary figures: Tolstoy and Croce.

Tolstoy's *What is art?*

What is art? is worth reading in its entirety. That Tolstoy was a great writer is well evidenced in the work, particularly in the passionate account, which begins the book, of his visit to a rehearsal at a great theatre. (Note, too, the later sardonically funny and deeply unfair description of his night at the opera.) Tolstoy is not engaged in an academic exercise, but cares about art and its effects on those who produce and consume it. He seems to me to ask the right questions about the huge cost, financial and emotional, of art and about its absurd hierarchies. The controversies that rage about such prestige organizations as London's Royal Opera House show these questions have not lost their relevance.

Part of *What is art?* is negative, the dismissal of various claims about art. In the catalogue of these rightly forgotten claims, boredom easily sets in. Howbeit, two claims get short shrift. One is that the importance of art lies in the pleasure it gives. Here there is an echo from Kant. For in Kant we noticed the suspicion that although art can give very great pleasure, it ought to do more than simply provide satisfactions to individuals. Tolstoy, too, attempts to show that art transcends its indubitable power to provide individual satisfactions. Since aesthetic pleasure can be rapturous, that begins to explain its power. But anyone who wishes to show that art should have a central place in *human* life may have to do more, for that life is social. So one might ask how art fits into the fact that we are not simply individuals seeking individual pleasures.

Tolstoy further denies that an interest in art is simply an interest in beauty. Firstly, we are not just interested in the beautiful. As every eighteenth century aesthetician knew, we are as interested in the sublime and the pretty. Secondly, if we ask why we are interested in the beautiful, we arrive back at the claim that beauty delights us, and so to the claim that pleasure is the chief end of art.

The shortcomings of such theories suggest (and as a primitive communitarian Christian, Tolstoy would have found the suggestion congenial) that any account of the importance of art must embed art in the social. Moreover, the society of art cannot be confined to a subset of rich aesthetes who patronize high art. Tolstoy is emphatic that such high art must be continuous with the forms of aesthetic life permeating a whole culture.

> We are accustomed to understand art to be only what we hear and see in theatres, concerts, and exhibitions; together with buildings, statues, poems, and novels . . . But all this is but the smallest part of the art by which we communicate with one

another in life. All human life is filled with works of art of every kind – from cradle-song, jest, mimicry, the ornamentation of houses, dress, and utensils, to church services, buildings, monuments, and triumphal processions. It is all artistic activity. (Tolstoy 1994, pp. 60–61)

Granted a wish to add a social dimension to art, it seemed natural to Tolstoy to give the following account. I may have an experience, say a feeling of revulsion at the treatment of serfs. If I can get you to share my feeling, a bond is established between us. Given this, doesn't the power of art lie in its capacity to establish that sharing? This leads directly to the so-called "infection" account of art.

Tolstoy puts it thus: "Art is a human activity consisting in this, that one man consciously by means of certain external signs, hands onto others feelings he has lived through, and that others are infected by those feelings and also experience them" (*ibid.*, pp. 59).

This picture relates three components. There are the artist's feelings, emotions or attitudes. There is the work in which the artist embeds these and which is passed to the audience. There is the audience that comes to share the artist's feelings, emotions or attitudes. Thus a bond is established between human beings, and that directly establishes the important social dimension of art.

It is essential to understand that Tolstoy's account involves two claims. One is that art is a matter of people coming to share feelings, emotions and attitudes. The other is a specification of the kinds of feelings that ought to be shared. For Tolstoy, as a communitarian Christian, these are feelings of love of God and one's fellow humans. Some have focused on the second component and written off the whole account as the absurd ravings of a born-again Christian. But Tolstoy is emphatic that the claim that art involves a sharing of feeling can be separated from any claim about what feelings should be shared. He thinks that these should be religious feelings, but he is tolerant enough to note that different lands have different religions. And since for him, anyway, religion is not a matter of doctrinal subscription but a matter of whatever is fundamental to a life, this allows alternatives to his own preferences. When, therefore, we discuss Tolstoy's account as an account of art, it is the claim that art is infective that should occupy us, not questions as to what the infection should be with.

To that account we find three main objections. The first is that it is wrong to assume, as Tolstoy does, that artists must actually have the feelings with which they seek to infect the audience. The second is that the theory places too little importance on the work of art as an object. If one simply wants to get a state of mind from one person to another, then anything that will do that will serve. Indeed, if a pill could be found to bring another to feel what I feel, then we could dispense with works of art altogether. The third is that the account is simply mistaken in believing audiences should come to have the feelings of the creator of the work. I can, thankfully, appreciate the works of D. H. Lawrence without coming to share all his views.

These criticisms are trotted out in most introductory books and are dutifully regurgitated by their readers. They deserve, however, a closer look than they usually receive.

The artist

Does Tolstoy wrongly assume that artists must actually feel what a work expresses?

A first observation is simply that Tolstoy does not assume this. Tolstoy's example is a child who goes into a forest, meets a wolf, is filled with terror and escapes. When he tells others the tale, he relives the terror and those hearing him tell of it come to share that terror and all the other emotions of relief and the like that the narrator lives through. This is precisely what happens in good story telling, as witness the effect of the great John Laurie's eye-rolling sagas told to the Walmington-on-Sea platoon in *Dad's army*.

Now even as Tolstoy tells it, it is obvious that the teller of the story is not, when telling it, in fear of the wolf. He imaginatively recreates that fear. Moreover, Tolstoy clearly says that it is not even necessary that the fear conjured up by the narrator be based on a real fear occasioned by a real event. He writes that "even if the boy had not seen a wolf but had frequently been afraid of one, and . . . invented an encounter with a wolf and recounted it so as to make his hearers share the feelings he experienced . . . that would also be art" (Tolstoy 1994, p. 58).

So much for the claim that the artistic creator must actually have the emotions expressed in the work. All Tolstoy needs is the pretty obvious claim that the creator must have had a sufficient actual acquaintance with emotions in order to have the materials out of which to build imaginative expressions of them. There is more to be said, however.

Let us begin by noting that it would not necessarily be an objection to Tolstoy that there can be emotions in a work that are not, and could not be, emotions had by its creator. Munch's *Puberty* portrays a girl whose face clearly expresses a confusion about the onset of that condition. Munch could not have had those feelings. Browning's "Soliloquy of a Spanish cloister" expresses the irritation of a monk. But Browning was not that monk.

Here it is essential to make a distinction between what may be expressed by the characters *in* a work and what may be expressed *by* a work in its portrayal of those characters. Camus's *The plague* contains a number of characters who express certain views, but, in addition, the novel itself articulates an attitude. Rembrandt's astonishing *Girl sleeping* shows us a girl asleep, but the picture itself expresses a tenderness towards the sleeper. It has recently been argued (and see here the guide to reading) that there are examples of this kind of articulation of attitudes in music.

If we make this distinction, then it is less implausible to say that in and through the work the creator articulates feelings, emotions and attitudes to the things depicted therein. The objection to this will be that we cannot assume that the attitudes of the work itself are those expressed there by its actual creator. That view is held by those who have talked about the death of the author and asserted the irrelevance of references to the authors of works. I shall answer that when I deal with those views in Chapters 7 and 8. Here I note only that we speak, with no sense of strain, about the attitudes that artists articulate in their works. Dickens does not merely depict Smike expressing himself but in that depiction expresses his own reaction to the sufferings of those like Smike.

The work itself

Does Tolstoy's account allow too little autonomy to the work itself, so that it is merely a means, in principle dispensable, for getting what is in one person into another person?

That claim would be true if Tolstoy were saying that before ever starting to create their works artists know exactly what they wish to express in them. It would then be just a matter of finding the means to get this across to someone else. I suppose Tolstoy's summary formulation might suggest that, but I cannot see that it entails it. When Tolstoy talks of having a feeling that one seeks to embody in a work, he might indeed mean that the feeling is there before the work begins. But he might equally mean that the feeling is inchoately there before the work begins and is carefully worked out in producing the work. Consider here some passages that appear later in the book than most critics reach. For, in remarks astonishingly like those later made in Wittgenstein's lectures and conversations on aesthetics, Tolstoy stresses how complex the work of embodying one's vision in a work is:

> Musical execution is only then art, only then infects, when the sound is neither higher nor lower than it should be, when exactly the small centre of the required note is taken . . . The slightest deviation . . . destroys the perfection and consequently the infectiousness of the work . . . It is the same in all arts . . . Infection is only obtained when an artist finds those infinitely minute degrees of which a work of art consists. (*ibid.*, p. 137)

The effect of this passage is to suggest that for Tolstoy there was nothing to be expressed that could be expressed equally well in another way.

Tolstoy certainly believes that the work of art is the way in which an emotion is conveyed. That leads to this argument: on Tolstoy's view if *An ideal husband* and *Wall Street*, say, both successfully convey the dangers of love of money-making, then one will serve as well as the other, so one can be dispensed with without loss. But there would be a loss if one were dispensed with. So Tolstoy's view is wrong.

That argument invites the simple reply that if we do feel we need them both, this is simply evidence that they do not convey exactly the same thing. Two works can "convey the same thing" in the sense of the same general sort of thing, love of money, say, while not conveying the same thing in the sense of a particular form that love of money can take. Why should we saddle Tolstoy with the former and implausible view?

The audience
Is it true that there is no requirement that the audience come to share what is in the work?

It is certainly true that there can be no requirement that the audience come to share the feelings expressed by a character in a work. Appreciation is harmed if we identify with a character and see the world of the work only from that point of view. That indeed is how a person in an earlier example misperceived *Othello* through seeing it Othello's way. But if the claim is that the audience need share what is articulated through the work, that is less clear.

Wittgenstein writes: "Only an artist can so represent an individual thing as to make it appear to us like a work of art. . . .. A work of art forces us – as one might say – to see it in the right perspective but, in the absence of art, the object is just a fragment of nature like any other" (1980, p. 4).

Tilghman glosses this thus:

> To see an object in the right perspective is surely to see it as having a certain spirit or expression, but the world certainly does not force us to see it in the right perspective; in fact it is doubtful whether there is a right way of seeing the world. There are, of course, ethically preferable ways of seeing it – as happy rather than unhappy, for example – but how we see is left up to us. A work of art, by contrast, shows us things as seen by someone else and thus does not leave its vision up to us, but forces us, as we might say, to see those things as the artist did. (Tilghman 1991, p. 52)

If a work embodies a certain perspective, then to engage fully with it, I have to make the effort to see it from that perspective, too. If it is objected that some perspectives are ones I don't and can't adopt, from squeamishness or on the grounds of their moral odiousness, say, then that is to say that I can't engage with those works at all, not that engagement does not involve grasping the perspective from which a work is constructed.

It will, however, be argued that it is one thing to enter, *pro tem*, the attitudes, feelings and emotions that constitute the perspective of a work, and another to come to share these in the fuller sense that Tolstoy clearly has in mind.

Here I have one suggestion, the full elaboration of which will have to await the discussion in Chapter 9, of the way in which considerations of truth or falsity bear on our assessment of art. It does simply seem that we find a fuller satisfaction in works whose perspective we can share or, as Ronald Hepburn (1990) puts it, that we can "inhabit" (as opposed to visit *pro tem*). This is not to say that we simply look for works we can agree with – though some do, and not just those who seek out the muscular ethics of Bulldog Drummond. Nor is it to say that our tastes are fixed for ever. I may come to wonder at the kinds of things I once inhabited. Nor must we forget that a work of art might bring us to its point of view. Indeed, as we shall see, the significance of imaginative representations rests in part on the epiphanic experiences they may give us.

There is no requirement, moreover, that we make the test of whether we can inhabit a work the sole test of whether it is or is not a great work of art. Leavis could think Swift a great writer although he felt, rightly or wrongly, that in Swift's world view the channels of life are blocked and perverted. All I suggest is that if I cannot fully inhabit a work then I will withhold some of my unqualified assent.

If I cannot share the perspective of a work, I am reminded that there are divisions in humanity. What else is Tolstoy saying when he says that shared artistic experience brings us together? That suggests that Tolstoy's introduction of religion into his discussion of art is not, given his notion of religion, out of place. For Tolstoy, religion is a matter of what one holds to be fundamental, what would express the view of life that one ultimately inhabits. But that would affect both the sorts of work one could create, that is, the kind of attitudes, beliefs and emotions that one could express, and the works of art one could engage with. That engagement would be related to what one could inhabit, given one's life set, or what Tolstoy would call one's religion.

Tolstoy's views do not have the knock-down stupidity often predicated of them. But although we are told that works of art embody the feelings and emotions of their creators and awaken those feelings and emotions in those who encounter them I still feel, after the best defence that I can muster, that Tolstoy has not made clear what happens when a vision is embodied in a work. Moreover, we are given no clear idea why we feel so moved by sharing the expressed visions of artists. In order to progress, we need to go beyond Tolstoy to Benedetto Croce, the greatest pioneer of the theory of art as expression.

Benedetto Croce

Croce's view

Italy has been a united and independent country for not much over 100 years, the history of those years being complex and compelling. Into that history, as a statesman, philosopher, cultural critic and as a political economist is woven Benedetto Croce, as if, for us, Churchill, Russell, Leavis and Keynes had been rolled into one. Croce published over 60 volumes, but he asserted that his first major work, *The aesthetic as the science of expression and of the linguistic in general* (1902; trans. 1992) was the rock upon which his whole theoretical and practical life rested. The work is truly seminal. It is not an easy read, in part because it was written in the joy of discovery, with ideas tumbling out, daring leaps of thought, and references continually made to unidentified opponents. Moreover, it is not a work about aesthetics, in the sense of being a book about the beauties and value of art and nature. They are certainly dealt with, but the book goes further than that to give a complete picture of what in Italian would be called *lo spirito*. This term would be feebly translated by "mind", since Croce wishes to deal with all our faculties and not merely, as the term "the mind" suggests, the intellectual. Some of the book is of little relevance to those specially interested in aesthetics, though it is never irrelevant to those interested in philosophy.

Croce begins, like Kant, with the notion of stimuli bombarding us. But now consider the difference between the rays of the sun bombarding and warming a stone and the rays of the sun bombarding our senses. The stone is passive. It simply warms up. We, however, have the power to respond actively to stimuli. In particular we have a power, which Croce calls "intuition", to organize them. Intuition does this work by ordering the stimuli into representations of particular things.

Mysterious though the word "intuition" sounds, it amounts to no more than a power to form representations. An exact analogy is the way in which painters have the power visually to organize sunsets in creating representations of them. Those representations are not copies of reality. Until intuition has imposed order on the world by producing representations, there is no reality to copy.

Croce *identifies* the aesthetic with intuition, that is, with a power to produce representations, and the representations produced by aesthetic intuition are of particular things, this stretch of water or this pen.

When the activity of forming the *representations of particular things* has operated, we can generalize from these representations to produce *general concepts*, so that we can talk not only of a particular stretch of water, but of water in general. This is the province of logic. But the aesthetic is the foundational activity. Until the formative act of producing representations of particular things has been performed, there is nothing from which to abstract general concepts.

The aesthetic and the logical give us *knowledge* of particulars and concepts and are thus theoretical. But we also want and will things to happen. This Croce calls "the economic". This is dependent on "the logical" that has given us concepts. How, he asks, could we want something if we had no concept of it? But then the economic will ultimately depend on the aesthetic, since the logical, on which it depends, depends in its turn on the aesthetic.

Finally we do not merely will. We will the right and wrong. This is the realm of the ethical. There would be no ethical willing if there were no willing, although there can be willing that is not ethical. The ethical, therefore, depends on the practical, the practical on the logical, the logical on the aesthetic. The aesthetic, then, is the foundation of the whole economy of the mind. The aesthetic is not, as often now happens, tagged onto philosophy, the serious business being done elsewhere. It is central. Croce, like Kant, and like Scruton and Wollheim in recent years, tries to show the proper place of the aesthetic in some full story of the mind's structure. That, as my final chapter makes clear, gives their accounts great depth.

The aesthetic, the logical, the economic, and the ethical make up the activities of the human spirit. Croce was to write a separate book on each of the last three and together these books make up what is known as the "Philosophy of the Spirit". Since the spirit makes its world, that philosophy is a form of idealism (the world created out of the ideas of the spirit) of which the work of Kant and Hegel are other forms.

Croce's work, together with that of Gentile, who certainly thought Croce's idealism lacking in rigour, led to a resurgence of idealism in Italy in the twentieth century. This neo-idealism fell under a cloud, in part because Gentile became for a while the official philosopher of fascism. It is quite unclear, however, that idealism is, as some have believed, especially congenial to the fascist temperament. Croce, for his part, was a heroic figure in the intellectual resistance to Mussolini and a deeply influential figure in the restoration of some kind of democratic rule to Italy.

So far Croce's view is cognate to Kant's. Assailed with a sensory bombardment, we have the power to impose an order on it by forming representations, organizing pictures of reality. But Croce goes beyond Kant in a way that is to have far-reaching consequences for his views on art. For, he claims, the representations produced by the aesthetic power of intuition are at the same time *expressions*. So we arrive at an account that places art as expression at the very root of the way in which we make sense of the world.

Why does Croce say that aesthetic representation is expression? I have said that at the core of Kant's theory lies a picture of ourselves at birth as suddenly bombarded by a blooming buzzing confusion of stimuli that are to be organized by the mind. Kant, however, does not touch on something that is at the core of Croce's account, namely that it is frustrating and painful, perhaps intensely so, to be on the receiving end of this meaningless bombardment. We want to organize it in order to rid ourselves of that distress. Wordsworth speaks in the "Ode: intimations of immortality" of our early years as a time of

> . . . obstinate questionings
> Of sense and outward things,
> Fallings from us, vanishings;
> Blank misgivings of a creature
> Moving about in worlds not realized,
> High instincts before which our mortal nature
> Did tremble like a guilty thing surprised.

Croce, too, believes that there is often something we cannot make clear to ourselves that is troubling. We are driven to organize it and we do this by creating a representation that imposes a form. Think of an artist whose attempt to organize visual reality in a picture won't come right. Think of feeling that there is something one wishes to say, but not being able to find the words, and how frustrating that can be. Think of the search for the lost chord. Not being able to say it, picture it, compose it, is, even in the most mundane circumstances, a burden. When one finds the right expression, there is a sense of relief. In Virginia Woolf's great novel, *To the lighthouse*, Lily Briscoe cannot find the last touch that will allow her to complete a picture on which she has been long embarked. Then "she looked at her canvas; it was blurred. With a sudden intensity, as if she saw it clear for a second, she drew a line there, in the centre. It was done; it was finished. Yes, she thought, laying down the brush in extreme fatigue, I have had my vision."

Croce made such experiences central to art:

> Individual A seeks an expression for the impression he feels, or of which he has a presentiment but which he has not yet expressed. See him trying out different words and phrases which might give him the expression he seeks, which must be there, although he has not got hold of it yet. He tries a combination, m, and rejects it as inadequate, inexpressive, defective and ugly: he tries combination n, with the same outcome. He cannot see at all or he cannot see clearly. The expression still eludes him. After other vain attempts, in which he now draws near, now draws away from that towards which he strains, of a sudden he finds the form of the expression sought – (it almost seems that it forms spontaneously in him) – and *lux facta est*. He enjoys for an instant aesthetic pleasure or beauty. The ugly, with its corresponding displeasure, was that aesthetic activity that did not succeed in conquering the obstacles that lay in its way: the beautiful is the expressive activity that now triumphantly unfolds itself. (Croce 1992, p. 132)

Croce's use of "expression"

It is essential to understand Croce's precise use of the term "expression". An example will clarify this. Suppose there to be an out-of-work adolescent, imperfectly loved, living a life of frustration with the anger that frustration breeds. Come Friday he collects his unemployment benefit and, to numb the hurt, gets drunk. At night he walks home through the bright city, the barred windows of its shops offering him visions of consumer desirables he can never have. Then a rage surges up and he kicks in a window and goes on his way.

There is a sense in which that act expresses anger. This is not what Croce has in mind. For now imagine that having kicked in the window the youth looks at it and thinks "the glass is not jagged enough here", and "the hole should be further over", and makes careful arrangements of the glass until he can say "that's it! that's how I feel". That for Croce is how expression works in art. In the first case someone was in the grip of emotion, but in the second the emotion was in his grip because an expression has been found for it, which allows the kind of self-understanding arrived at when one can say "*That's* how I feel!".

Such an account of expression illuminates our thinking about art and the aesthetic in a rich variety of ways. Firstly, it will be noticed that expression is neither rule-governed nor reducible to recipes. When the adolescent thought that the fractured window did not express his inner life, there were no rules to tell him what to do about it. It was a matter of trying this and trying that until it looked right, a matter to which we shall have to return, if only because the question might arise: can it look right and not be right?

This point becomes far-reaching when we realize that not only are there no rules for creating expressions, there are no rules for judging them either. This has implications for critical practice. It enables what many of my students tell me is a richly appealing model of what criticism might be. When Lily Briscoe found the right line, when the abused adolescent found the right configuration of glass, they could say "That's what I was after". Here we have achieved expression. To judge this is to grasp that expression, to see that these paint marks and these glass cracks express something. Croce says that to do this we have to recreate the expression in ourselves, and that is like what we saw Wittgenstein and Tilghman saying about the necessity of seeing the world from the point of view of the work. It is related too to what Wollheim meant when, in a supplementary essay to the second edition of *Art and its objects*, he spoke of criticism as "retrieval".

On Croce's view, the first question is always "what state is articulated and expressed in this work?". So when we discuss individual works of art that is what we look for. Thus if what we are discussing is Picasso's *Nude dressing her hair*, I want to help others to *see* the torment and self-loathing of the figure *in* the claustrophobic, harshly lit yet sombre chamber of the picture-space. I want them to see also how every part of that picture – colour, posture, use of multi-perspective, the vile toenails, the large posterior and the like – has been put there by the artist to produce that effect. But I want them also to ask what attitude is expressed by the picture towards the woman depicted. Is the gaze tender? angry? is it enjoying it all too much? This expression is what we have to grasp if we are to understand the picture.

Next, suppose we take these lines by David Middleton, which were once quoted to me as a typical example of a certain sort of Victorian poetry:

> Man proposes, God disposes.
> So I wandered up to where you lay,
> A little rose among the little roses,
> And no more dead than they.

Isn't an education in taste just seeing the quality of mind articulated through these words?

Music, too, invites this approach. What is the way to characterize the mood of the third of Strauss's *Four last songs*, which regularly enchants unsuspecting students who think that such music is not for them. Can they see that every detail counts towards the overall effect? Isn't all this a training in taste and awareness?

Students not only appear to love doing this, they ask why they don't do this sort of thing in studying the literary, musical and visual arts, since this is what they wanted to study those subjects for. We shall be seeing some of the reasons why they do not in Chapter 6, these reasons having to do with erroneous theories about criticism and the kinds of proofs possible in criticism.

By way of illustration of just how radical the implications of Croce's views are it is worth noting that students are sometimes asked to do precisely what his theory renders unintelligible. We need first to note two possible directions of criticism. One is to try to grasp the articulated expression in the work, as I tried to do with the Picasso painting. Having grasped this, and only then, we can ask how the elements of the picture contribute to that articulated expression. One can now say " the choice of colours contributes importantly to the effect", and simply mean a different set of colours would have marred the effect. Having grasped the sense of the precarious equipoise that characterizes Keats' *Ode to autumn*, I can now say that even the absence of a comma at the end of the line "And sometimes like a gleaner thou dost keep" in the second stanza contributes to that expressed mood. Everything can be treated this way. Having noticed Sinatra's distinctive effects we can see how his particular phrasing contributes to them. An Annie Lennox performance has an effect to which such things as the hairstyle and manner of dress contribute.

Having grasped the effect, and only then, we can look for what might be called *critical explanations*, accounts of how the details contribute to the effect. (It is compatible with this that we should first attend to the details and wait to see if an overall effect emerges.)

Croce laid stress on (though he did not invent) what was to become the enormously influential notion of organic unity. That means no more than that all the parts contribute to an effect that emerges from them. But merely to list the parts is not to capture that effect, no more, he thinks, than to separate and lay out the different parts of a human body is to lay out a human being embodied in them.

Croce, therefore, writes "It is in the overall result, in the distinctive effect that everyone admires and that determines and bends to its service all the individual parts, and not in these individual parts, detached, and abstractly considered in themselves, that . . . a work of art . . . resides" (Croce 1992, p. 3.), and he adds that "division destroys the work, just as dividing a living organism into heart, brain, nerves and muscles and so on changes a living thing into a corpse" (*ibid.*, pp. 21–2).

Contrast that now with an opposite direction of movement. Without grasping the overall effect one draws attention to a list of features: litotes, oxymoron, alliteration, verse form, colour, compositional form, minor key, marble, and then one attempts to derive a knowledge of the overall effect of the work from these. Croce is rightly emphatic that this cannot be done. In this he is the precursor of a famous paper in which Frank Sibley distinguishes two classes of comments. One class uses what Sibley calls "nonaesthetic" terms, terms like "red", "square", "made of marble", "alliterative". The other uses what he calls "taste" or "aesthetic" terms, terms like "graceful", "garish", "delicate" and the like. And his point is that a knowledge that a work of art or anything else possesses features of the first kind could never allow us to deduce that it possesses features of the second kind. For though it is true that this picture is balanced because it has a red patch in the left corner, the next picture might be unbalanced for that very reason. Like Croce he would argue that one must first see the aesthetic quality before one can start asking what nonaesthetic qualities it depends on.

Against genres

The line of approach that I have attributed to Croce leads to further things of great interest.

The first is his controversial attack on genres, that is, on the grouping of works of art into paintings, statues, music, literature, and within these into tragedies, landscapes, sonatas and so forth. Croce allows that we can do this, but he asks about the point of so doing. For, just as knowing that there is an alliteration in a poem will not tell one whether that poem is an achieved expression, so knowing that something is a landscape will not tell one whether that is an achieved expression, nor help one to see the achieved expression.

Croce need not deny two things. One is that knowing the category into which something falls may open the way to its proper appreciation. Knowing that Swift's searing condemnation of the treatment of the Irish in *A modest proposal* falls into the category of parodies makes all the difference to appreciation. That, however, does not avoid the point that knowing that something that is to be classed as ironic *is* an achieved expression is something more than knowing how it can be categorized.

Nor need Croce deny that different genres may make different aesthetic effects possible. It might be that one can do things with music that one cannot do with architecture. But again, to know how to classify by genres is not to know whether a particular instance within a genre comes off.

We can certainly endorse Croce's central claim that there is something unhealthy about a criticism that asks how things are to be classified ("is Pope's *Rape of the Lock* a mock epic?") without asking how and why Pope's *Rape of the Lock* is worth studying. In fact that whole way of proceeding is often intellectually dishonest. It simply assumes that certain things are worth studying ("in the canon" as they put it) and then performs various classificatory dances round them. But the question for appreciation is how those things deserve to be in the canon.

Biography and history

Croce's theory yields sensible answers to questions about the relevance of biographical and historical studies to the appreciation. His point is one later to be made in the influential work of Beardsley and Wimsatt. One can study the history of literary works of art, say, but one can only do this if one has some way of determining which things are literary works of art. Hence literary history is secondary to the judgement of taste. (Ask any one why the history of Pope's literary works is studied with more zest than the history of the effusions of Ebenezer Eliot and the answer has to be that Pope's works are works of art.) We study Wordworth's biography because we know, independently of and prior to that study, that Wordsworth's poetry is great art. That makes such studies dispensable when appreciation is what we are after.

However, one can also study literary history in order to retrieve and reconstitute the object of study, as Dover Wilson reconstituted the text of *Hamlet*. It may even be that to understand the achieved expression of Spenser's *Fairie Queene* that I may need to reconstitute myself historically. So if the answer to the question "Why are we studying the history of art?", is "In order to get into a position to grasp the achieved expression of the work", then that is an entirely relevant part of the study of art.

The work as internal

Insights can lead to error as well as sense and there is one case in which something Croce sees that is true leads him to say something that looks obviously wrong. For Croce, notoriously, claims that the work of art is always internal and that what we call the external work of art, the painting on the wall, for example, is never the real work of art. That looks simply bizarre. Paintings are on walls and not in heads.

Croce writes that "the work of art (the aesthetic work) is always internal, and what is called the external work is no longer the work of art" (1992, p. 57).

The context of this passage is important. It occurs as part of a demonstration that artistic expression is independent of morality, a matter to which we return in Chapter 9. This is simply because, for Croce, morality involves choices, as when I choose to lie or steal. Croce, I think rightly, says expression is not a matter of choice. The youth who stayed to arrange the window in order to express himself certainly chose to do that. He was, too, acting voluntarily when moving the pieces of glass. But there is a good sense in which the resulting expression was not chosen. Firstly, the youth did not choose what he felt the need to express. Secondly, until the expression was achieved the artist could not have known what it was going to be, and so could not have chosen in advance to produce that. Croce next allows that there *is* one way in which art becomes involved with morality. For although one cannot choose in advance what an adequate expression of one's life will be, one can choose, once one has expressed it,whether or not to publish that expression, and one might decide on moral grounds not to do so. This suggests to him that the work of art is something internal that awaits public airing. That is further suggested by cases like that in which Wordsworth composed the "Lines written above Tintern Abbey" in his head during the walk home. When he got home he wrote them down. That is one sense of "make public". He then chose to publish them. That is another sense of "make public".

I think that Croce had his eye too firmly fixed on the Wordsworth case. That shows that a poem can be kept in the head, and I think he felt that all art was like that. But it is wholly unclear that a painting could be in the head in the way in which a poem could be in the head. I do not mean by this that someone, Mondrian perhaps, could not completely imagine a painting in advance and decide not actually to paint it. I mean for anything less schematic than a Mondrian the very imagining cannot be done. If you are tempted to think that Constable could have envisaged *The cornfield* in advance, ask if he could have envisaged the effect that serendipitously emerged when the palette knife slipped as he was painting.

There is a more interesting, and correct, thought that tempts Croce to claim that works of art are internal. This is the thought that we have not said anything about a painting *as a work of art* when we have simply listed its physical features: say the colours on its surface, described if you will by mathematical formula so exact that another person could exactly reconstruct the picture, as the great eighteenth century gardens at the University of Keele were reconstructed by George Barnes from the original plans. I think Croce thought this meant that the work of art was not a physical thing. But all he needed to say, and what he often did say, is that observation of a mere collection of physical features is not enough. One has to see what emerges from these physical constituents. He is emphatic that if artistic monuments are destroyed, "all the riches of aesthetics, fruit of the labours of many generations rapidly dwindles or disappears" (*ibid.*, p. 108). But although the physical is where the aesthetic vision is embodied, it is not reducible to the physical.

Here the following, often neglected, passage is exemplary:

> It could be objected: that the artist creates his expressions in the act of painting and sketching, writing and composing; and that, therefore, physical beauty, rather than coming after, can sometimes come before aesthetic beauty. This would be a superficial way of understanding the procedure of artists, who, in fact, do not make strokes of the brush without having first seen by means of the imagination; and if they have not seen, make brushstrokes not to externalize their expressions (which do not then exist) but as if to try out and have a simple point of support for their internal meditations and contemplations. The physical point of support is not physical beauty ... but what one could call an heuristic device. (Croce 1992, pp. 114–15)

His point is that painting is physical actions *informed by thought*. From this it follows that the work of art is not simply a physical object and that painting it is not simply a physical activity.

Scientific aesthetics

This bears on an important implication of Croce's aesthetics. For if a painting cannot be reduced to a matter of colours in spatial arrangement, if poetry cannot be reduced to combinations of words, and music to structures of sounds, although these can all be informed by expression, then in one important sense a scientific treatment of aesthetics is impossible. Since expression transcends its mathematical and physical base, those sciences that operate only on that base cannot touch it. Some, spurred by spurious dreams of importing into aesthetics the prestige of science, have tried to do the impossible. They have sought some physical, observable, measurable fact about objects from which inferences might be made as to the presence of art in them. One common candidate is the so-called Golden Section, a ratio endemic in nature from the shells of snails to the spiral nebulae. Some believed that the presence of this ratio is an index of the presence of aesthetic quality. Quite apart from the fact that there are great works that do not seem to exhibit the ratio of the Golden Section and awful works that do, one might ask how the correlation between the presence of the Golden Section and the presence of aesthetic quality was established. Presumably the investigator first found that some work had merit and then found that when it did the Golden Section was present. But then the judgement of merit can be made independently of detection of Golden Sections. The passages in which Croce deals with this tomfoolery, which he calls the *astrology* of aesthetics (*ibid.*, pp. 121–3), still alas with us, are, in their biting simplicity, a joy to read, and I commend the reader to them.

Problems
Croce offers a powerful account of art and its appreciation. But the account has its difficulties – difficulties that haunt all aesthetics – about subjectivity and objectivity, about art, truth and morality, about the often proclaimed death of the artist. These will be discussed from Chapter 6 onwards.

I begin, however, with what may seem a fundamental problem. Croce's account has this in common with many others. It tries to find characteristics that define art. To find these is to have found the essence of art. These characteristics will be necessary conditions: art will *have* to have them; and sufficient conditions: *only* art will have them. Croce's account then seems immediately suspect. For it offers one condition as the essence of art, namely expression. But it does not seem necessary for art to be expression (what of music that is just nice to listen to?); nor is it sufficient, since expression does not have to be art (what of the simple expression "I love you"?). This brings us to contemporary philosophy and philosophical aesthetics. There we are told that Wittgenstein has given a proof that all attempts, such as Croce's, to define art in terms of essences are ill-conceived. That would be a severe objection to Croce's story, so I now turn to that matter.

Guide to reading

L. Tolstoy's *What is art?* is now available in paperback (London: Duckworth, 1994). I repeat that it is a worthy read, if only because of the passion it brings to aesthetics. This was recognized by that severe judge of the frivolous, Ludwig Wittgenstein. C. Barrett (ed.), *Wittgenstein: lectures and conversations on aesthetics, psychology and religious belief* (Oxford: Blackwell, 1966) bears all the marks of a close engagement with *What is art?*. R. Wilkinson offers a good clear standard discussion in his contribution, "Art emotion and expression" to Hanfling's *Philosophical aesthetics*. Tom Sorrell also adds trenchant criticisms on pp. 314–20 of the same volume. There is a book on Tolstoy's account of art by T. Diffey, *Tolstoy's What is art?* (London: Croom Helm, 1985). M. Budd, *Music and the emotions* (London: Routledge, 1985) has criticisms to which I have tried to respond. A side note: Tolstoy's account arguably influenced the theatrical theories of Stanislavsky and, through him, Lee Strasberg and the Method school. So, out of Tolstoy came Brando, for which Tolstoy may be forgiven much. See R. Hughes, "Tolstoy, Stanislavski and the art of acting", *Journal of Aesthetics and Art Criticism* 51(1), 1993, pp. 39–48.

In discussing Tolstoy I made a distinction between what is expressed by characters in a work and what might be expressed by the work. For some interesting recent work on the way a composer might appear in a work see, for example, Justin London, "Musical and linguistic speech acts", *Journal of Aesthetics and Art Criticism* 54(1), 1996, pp. 49–46

Croce's 1902 *Estetica* has been translated by me as *The aesthetic as the science of expression and of the linguistic in general* (Cambridge: Cambridge University Press, 1992). The introduction gives an overall picture of Croce's philosophical project and how aesthetics fits into it. A slightly out of date but accessible work on Croce is

G. Orsini, *Benedetto Croce* (Carbondale: Southern Illinois University Press, 1961). Croce had 40 more years of aesthetics in him after the publication of *The aesthetic* in 1902. They culminate with *La poesia* (1943) translated by G. Gullace as *Poetry and literature* (Carbondale: University of Southern Illinois Press, 1981), the introduction of which, though taxing, is an authoritative guide to Croce's aesthetics. I find, rightly or wrongly, similarities between Croce's work and the work of Richard Wollheim, similarities to which I shall return in later chapters. See Wollheim's *The mind and its depths* (Cambridge, Massachusetts: Harvard University Press, 1993), notably essay IX, "Correspondence, projective properties, and expression in the arts". I also noted similarities between some of Croce's thoughts and those of Frank Sibley. The latter are best seen in his classic "Aesthetic concepts", *Philosophical Review* **68**, 1959, pp. 421–50, and "Aesthetic and non-aesthetic", *Philosophical Review* **75**, 1965, pp. 135–59. The latter introduces the notion of two directions of criticism and of criticism as explanation.

Croce's attacks on genres have had a mixed reception, being trenchantly criticized by both A. Quinton, "Tragedy", *Proceedings of the Aristotelian Society*, supp. vol. **34**, 1960, pp. 145–64 and Richard Wollheim in *Art and is objects*. There is a very good guide to their objections with a most judicious reply in M. Paton, "Getting Croce straight," *British Journal of Aesthetics* **25**, 1985 pp. 252–65. R. G. Collingwood's version of the view that the work of art is internal is discussed by Wollheim in *On art and the mind*.

That brings me to Collingwood, who is thought to give the nearest version of Croce's thinking in English. Certainly he claimed not to differ in any essential respects from Croce. (See the letter reprinted in A. Donagan, *The later philosophy of R. G. Collingwood*, Oxford: Clarendon, 1962.)

I have my doubts about this, which are crystallized by Merle Brown's admittedly demanding *Neo-idealist aesthetics* (Detroit: Wayne State University Press, 1966). The last chapter of this seems to show how Collingwood's aesthetic is an uneasy melange of incompatible elements of Croce, Gentile and some of his own views. But that is for more advanced study. Certainly Collingwood's *The principles of art* (Oxford: Oxford University Press, 1938) merits examination and is a vigorous and entertaining read.

Finally two books at an intermediate level that make important contributions to discussions of expression in art. One is A. Tormey, *The concept of expression* (Princeton: Princeton University Press, 1971). The other is Guy Sircello, *Mind and art* (Princeton: Princeton University Press, 1972).

Expression in music is, and always has been, a vigorously debated topic. Edvard Hanslick's views are worth discussion, and R. Wilkinson's comments in Hanfling's *Philosophical aesthetics* (pp. 207–20) are a good introduction to them.

Peter Kivy has written a series of challenging books on musical expression, of which *The corded shell* is one to begin with; now reprinted as Part 1 of *Sound sentiment* (Philadelphia: Temple University Press, 1989). See also *Music alone* (Ithaca: Cornell University Press, 1990). More advanced is Malcolm Budd's *Music and the emotions*, which is thoroughly worth reading if only for its demolition jobs on certain thinkers who have tried to make music a language of the emotions. More recently still there is A. Ridley, *Music, value and the passions* (Ithaca: Cornell University Press, 1994). If you want to know what everyone has ever said about music and the emotions try Stephen Davis, *Music, meaning and expression* (Ithaca: Cornell, 1994). For examples of how well philosophers can write about music see J. Levinson *Music, art and metaphysics* (Ithica: Cornell University Press, 1990), his *The pleasures of the aesthetic* (Ithica: Cornell University Press, 1996) and L. Goehr, *The imaginary museum of musical works* (Oxford: Clarendon Press 1993).

Chapter 4

Tales from the Vienna Woods: after Wittgenstein in aesthetics

Against essences

Some, as we have seen, believed it made sense to ask whether some common feature could be found in aesthetic responses that would give the essence of the aesthetic. That brings us to the claim, which has dominated much of the discussion of aesthetics in the second half of this century, that this whole approach is flawed. That brings us, in turn, to Ludwig Wittgenstein, a figure who looms over the philosophy of this period.

Two portions of the legacy of Wittgenstein's thinking enter this present work. Firstly, I have already invoked his view that language gets whatever sense it has from the way it is woven into the lives and practices of those who use it. Secondly there is the matter that concerns us now. For Wittgenstein introduced into philosophy the term "family resemblances", a term that, misunderstood, exerts a baleful influence on recent aesthetics.

Wittgenstein introduces the notion of "family resemblances" in his posthumously published *Philosophical investigations*. Those

Investigations begin with a quotation from St Augustine's *Confessions* in which Augustine characterizes his acquisition of language as a matter of connecting the noises and gestures made by his parents with objects in the vicinity. For example, one of Augustine's parents might have uttered the sound "dog" while gesturing to an object. He then made the connection and learnt what was meant by "dog".

Part of the first part of the *Investigations* is a demonstration of the woeful inadequacies of this account. For consider: the account is meant to explain how a child *acquires* an understanding of *meaning* by following pointing gestures. But in order to grasp what it is to do when this pointing ceremony occurs, the child must *already* have an understanding of the meaning of the gestures.

Concurrently with this demolition job, Wittgenstein sketches an alternative view. Our lives take various forms. One form our life takes is an interest in stories. Another is an interest in colours. Another is a propensity to judge the behaviour of others. Another is to express doubt and certainty. The central thought is that words like "lovely", "red", "lifelike", "wicked", "doubtful", "mind", "know", "meaning", get their sense from the various forms that our lives take and are only to be understood in the forms of life that are their home. There are the words we use in aesthetics, to be understood by their place in a certain set of practices. There are the words we use in physics, also understood in terms of another, different set of practices. So it might be a mistake to suppose "right" as used in the practices of endorsing someone's comment on a film, is used in the same way as it is used in the different practices of assessing a scientific theory.

Throughout the *Investigations* appears an alter ego, usually marked off by inverted commas, who raises problems and difficulties. At paragraph 65 this alter ego bursts out with the comment that even if Wittgenstein has said something about how words might get meaning in this or that segment of lived practices, he has not told us the *essence* of language. The objection is that the terms that we use in aesthetics *might* be called the aesthetic language, and likewise there is a scientific language, a moral language and a religious language. But Wittgenstein has not told us what makes them all *languages*.

In reply, Wittgenstein simply denies that language has an

essence and in that context introduces the notion of "family resemblances". Consider some members of a family. There is the grandmother, Maud, who has blue eyes, fair straight hair, a prominent jaw, and a rolling gait. There is her daughter Priscilla who has her mother's eyes and gait but has brown curly hair and large lobed ears. She is married to Derek who has black curly hair, a hooked nose, prominent teeth and grey eyes. They have a daughter, Kirsten, who has her grandmother's hair and jaw and her father's nose and teeth. See them all together and, because of that shared pool of resemblances, they can be seen all to belong to the same family. But Kirsten and Maud, taken in isolation, need not look alike. What the family has is an overlapping series of resemblances with nothing necessarily in common between any two people in that series. So, it is argued, a set of things can all be languages, even though there is no common feature that they all possess. They may merely have family resemblances. And, so the argument goes on, it is wrong to suppose that all works of art must have something in common. Hence it follows that it is a mistake to attempt to distil, from the various aesthetic objects and aesthetic responses with which I began, some essence of the aesthetic.

Weitz

Lest it be thought that we are dealing with straw men, let us turn to Morris Weitz, who made his name by subscribing to the family resemblance account and attacking the view that art has an essence.

Weitz's argument is in two parts. The first part claims that art simply cannot be defined by singling out one or a few features as the essence of art. The second part invokes Wittgenstein's term "family resemblance" as giving us a better picture of the matter. These parts hang together, since one only needs to invoke the Wittgensteinian position if the claim that art cannot be defined in terms of essences is true.

The argument against essentialist definitions is simply that art is what Weitz calls an "open" concept. Take the notion of tragedy. Aristotle collected all the tragedies produced in Greece and distilled common features shared by them. For example, all seemed to involve disaster befalling an important person. That seemed to him to heighten the tragedy, since the spectacle of someone big biting the dust is likely to be more awesome than the fall of some lesser mortal. But, and here Weitz is right, although we may get from this a definition of *Greek* tragedy, we cannot foreclose on future developments in that art form. Indeed, we know that Arthur Miller deliberately took Willie Loman, a salesman, as his tragic hero to show that tragedies could enter the lives of lesser people with no less an exemplary force.

So Weitz claims, firstly, that art is open. No matter what we know about art so far, we have no basis for concluding how art will develop. It is given to creatively transcending its present state and any account we might give of the essence of that present state. Secondly, an insistence on essentialist definitions will not only misunderstand art, but will have pernicious practical consequences. Suppose someone claimed that Aristotle's definition, which is at best a definition of Greek tragedy, was a definition of tragedy as such. The temptation would be to insist that people make only that sort of tragedy. This would close down creativity. That indeed happened. Aristotle was supposed to have said that good tragedies must observe "the unities". One (superbly castigated by Doctor Johnson) is unity of place, since, it was thought, audiences would be disturbed by being at one moment in Athens and the next in London. Didn't this lead, in practice, to the slavish mechanical observation of rules to the detriment of drama?

We can now ask two questions: one is whether art is an open concept in a way that defeats any attempt to state its essence. The other is whether family resemblance accounts do any better.

As to the first, an initial problem is that it is never entirely clear what Weitz means by art being open. One thing he says is that new works of art continually appear. This is entirely unhelpful as support for the claim that art works have no essence in common. New garden peas appear on the stalk without that preventing the belief that garden peas have defining features. Moreover I am tempted to argue that the fact that we call new things "art" shows that they share something with their predecessors. Why else call them that?

Weitz also says that new *types* of art arrive. The mobile, the novel, the film and earth art transcend the art we already have. Any attempt to limit art to existent operative genres is, indeed, foolish. Art is, in that sense, open. Again, this does nothing to establish the claim that art has no essence. When mobiles appeared, they were called "art" because people saw that they did what things already called "art" were doing.

Weitz has two replies. One is to ask what feature is thought essential and then, for any candidate, show it isn't. If the feature is representation, he might ask about music. Such a reply forces the person offering that feature, as it recently forced me, to ask whether it is possible properly to extend the notion of representation in order to make the account work. That possibility is not excluded by anything Weitz says.

The other strategy is to claim that although new works and types of work may have something in common with what went before, this does nothing to show that they and their predecessors share one common feature. For, Weitz can argue, Wittgenstein has shown us that these new works may merely have family resemblances to previous works and may have no one common feature with *all* their predecessors. To deal with this let us look closer at what Wittgenstein did say.

Let us first note that Wittgenstein says *nothing* that supports attribution to him of the view that within that form of life called the aesthetic there is nothing shared by the objects and responses that we call "aesthetic" or "artistic". In fact his practice, as shown in *Culture and value*, was to make expression central to art. All he says in the *Investigations* is that the different linguistic forms of life (aesthetics, science, religion) need have no one thing in common. He appears to be denying that activities (doing aesthetics, doing science, being religious) have to share one common feature but appears not to be talking at all about the objects dealt with in these activities, such as individual works of art.

But doesn't Wittgenstein take "game" as his example of a family resemblance term. So doesn't he say that even *within* an activity, say playing of games, or art, one should not look for common features of individual games or individual works of art.

Note, however, the alter ego objected that Wittgenstein does not say what all the forms of language life (religion, art, science, morality, for example) have in common that makes them all forms of language. In order to be an answer to that objection the games example must treat each type of game as a different form of life. But then it looks as if Wittgenstein is saying that each game is a self-contained practice, so that rugby union stands to blackjack as art stands to morality, such games being related to other games only by criss-crossing and overlapping features. That does look right. But from that it does not follow that there is nothing that games within the practice of rugby union games have in common that makes them rugby union games.

The notion of family resemblances, then, is not meant to show that individual works of art do not have something in common. It is introduced to show that the various forms of linguistic life do not share a common feature. Those forms of life, as the family resemblance image suggests, do, of course, share features. The ways in which we talk about sunsets aesthetically might be like the ways we assess scientific theories in terms of elegance and simplicity. That is the force of saying that there are family resemblances between different forms of life. It is compatible with this that just as what are loosely classed as games may include many different forms of activity, so our dealings with the aesthetic may have subdivisions between which there is little in common. An interest in sunsets might differ from an interests in paintings. That still allows our dealings with paintings, and indeed, works of art generally, to have some unifying characteristic.

On my account, therefore, the notion of family resemblances allows no room whatsoever for Weitz to eliminate the possibility of there being common features of the objects in which we take an aesthetic interest or of the interest that we take in them.

Seeing the resemblance

There is, however, another aspect to the notion of seeing family resemblances that establishes shortcomings in certain kinds of definitions of art, notably, as we shall see, those offered by the so-called "institution" account of art.

It is possible to be told that there is a family resemblance between a mother and daughter, to believe this, and yet not be able to see it. Similarly I might be told that Duchamp's *Fontaine* is art because it shares a feature with Rodin's *The kiss*, take this on trust, and yet not *see* it. This is why definitions can seem unhelpful. I might accept that art is expression, but unless I can see how *this* work is expressive, the definition may be no use to me.

Further, here there is a sense to talking about openness, a sense in which many of our concepts are open ones. When we learn to use a term like "dog" we do not learn it as the name of the particular dog in whose presence learning took place. That is why Wittgenstein rejected Augustine's account. How is the child to know that the sound "dog" is meant to be applied to all dogs as opposed to just this one? We are creative in the projection of terms that we learn, so that, without further guidance, the term "dog" learnt in the presence of a spaniel is then applied to dachshunds. Language would not be possible if we could not do this. We *can* do this because we *see* that this new case is like the old ones, although nothing can guarantee that we will do so. Stanley Cavell expresses this perfectly:

> We learn and teach words in certain contexts, and then we are expected, and expect others, to be able to project them into further contexts. Nothing ensures that this projection will take place (in particular not the grasping of universals nor the grasping of books of rules), just as nothing will ensure that we will make, and understand, the same projections. That on the whole we do is a matter of our sharing routes of interest and feeling, modes of response, senses of humour and of significance and of fulfillment, of what is outrageous, of what is similar to what else, what a rebuke, what forgiveness, of when an utterance is an assertion, when an appeal, when an explanation – all that whirl of organism Wittgenstein calls "forms of life". Human speech and activity, sanity and community, rests on nothing more, but nothing less than this. (Cavell 1966, p. 160)

Sometimes, indeed, we divide in our projections. Some of us see a resemblance between what Cleese is doing and what Wilde is doing and may even think that they are funny in the same way. Others cannot see this. That kind of disagreement will figure prominently in our later discussion of subjectivity.

The institution of art

So far we have looked at the way in which the name of Wittgenstein was invoked to undermine the task of defining art in terms of a common feature. However, strikingly, the work of Wittgenstein has also been used by supporters of what is called the "institution account of art", to argue that a condition *can* be stated that defines and marks off what is art from what is not.

The account rests on the correct notion that art is a social institution, this being no more than the previously stated view that a complex set of ways of responding to art and nature is a form that life takes. It may be that different societies, different subgroups in a society and even the same society over time, may have very different interests in nature and made things. The interest taken by the devout in the representational figures that decorate Hindu temples may be quite different from the interest taken by a European voyeur. The interest in the altar pieces in Italian medieval churches taken by worshippers in the twelfth century differs from the interest taken by a contemporary itinerant connoisseur. To know what these interests are we have to internalize the lives of other cultures. And since the meaning of a word is determined by its use in a set of practices, there may be no word in another culture that means what we mean by "art". It is quite unclear, for example, whether the Greeks had any word meaning what we mean by "art".

In our culture there is what Arthur Danto has called "the art world". It includes galleries, concert halls, art schools, the institutions for trading art, collecting art, studying its history, restoring and commissioning it. It involves also the myriad of verbal and other expressions that different but overlapping groups use to express an interest in art.

Why did that interest those who proposed the institution account? Although the eventual definition covers all art, those who offer it initially had their eyes on the avant-garde, that is, the often baffling new art. Many of my readers will understand this bafflement. They may have no problem in accepting that the works of Rembrandt, Constable, Rodin, Mozart, Beethoven and Shakespeare are art, even if not sure why or not caring particularly for them. But then there are objects that defeat any understanding of them as art. Some of them have become iconic problem cases.

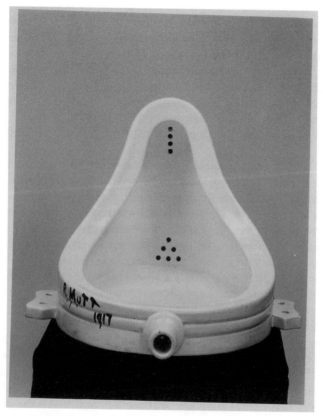

Duchamp, *Fontaine,* 1964. Centre National D'Art et de Culture, Georges Pompidou, Paris.

Duchamp's *Fontaine* is a urinal signed "R. Mutt, 1917" and bearing the title *Fontaine*. His *Bottle dryer* is simply a bottle dryer found in the street and exhibited unaltered in a gallery. Carl André's *Equivalent VIII* is 120 bricks arranged symmetrically in a two-brick-high rectangle. A pianist performs John Cage's *4'33"* by simply sitting at a piano for that period of time. There is no let up. There, pickled in formaldehyde, hangs half a cow, hailed in Minneapolis as brilliant British art. And the question rises up irresistibly: "Is it art?", to which the institution account offers a simple answer.

91

To understand that answer, begin with this odd question: does a newly christened baby *look* different before and after the christening? Give or take a few drops of water, the answer is "no". What makes the baby a christened baby is not the way it looks but the fact that a ceremony conferred membership of an institution on its unwitting head. Analogously, a work of art need not look any different from something that is not art. It is a work of art because membership of an institution has been conferred on it.

So Dickie, to whom much of this is due, wrote: "A work of art . . . is (1) an artefact (2) a set of aspects of which has had conferred upon it the status of candidate for appreciation by some person or persons acting on behalf of a certain social institution (the art world)" (Dickie 1974, p. 34). This is meant to solve the problem of avantgarde art. For a work to be accepted by the art world, into a gallery for example, is to have the status of art conferred on it. So *Fontaine* simply is art. Dickie adds that this will not guarantee the thing is good art, no more than baptism guarantees saintly comportment. But art it is, in a classificatory sense.

Much sport has been had with this account, one aspect of the analogy with other ceremonies causing much concern. Thus a christening is not legitimate if someone snatches the baby and says "I baptise thee Babe the Sheeppig", no more than a nuclear submarine is named if someone leaps out from the crowd and says "I name this vessel Rainbow Warrior VI" and kicks the chocks away. The candidate must be inducted by a properly authorized person. Some, therefore, have asked who is authorized to allow things into the art world – who, that is, corresponds to the vicar in the christening service. Others have asked whether this makes it impossible for something to be a work of art if kept under wraps by its maker. Some have smelled a rat in the notion of candidate for appreciation. For since appreciation may be based on a number of different grounds (as when one appreciates a coin when begging) we need to know what sort of appreciation Dickie has in mind. If the answer is "the kind of appreciation appropriate to art" we merely go round in circles. To all of these Dickie, in successive refinements of the theory, has offered replies that the curious will find documented in the guide to reading. I want to take a different approach.

I note, first, that there is something right about the account. An object is a work of art if those who can see some point in using the word "art", who therefore participate in the art world, *see some point* in using it of that thing.

Next, many who encounter avant-garde art and do not understand it are quite prepared to make the charitable assumption that if a thing is in a gallery, then there is some point in its being there, and so it must be art. So Dickie is right that, if you can get the thing into the art world, then it acquires an art status.

However, although those who worry about *Fontaine*, say, may not be worried about whether it is art, even the most ignorant knows that to call it "art" makes a claim on behalf of the value of the thing. What they then want to know is nothing other than what someone who does not understand why people rhapsodize about Botticelli wants to know: what value does it have. Here the institution account is simply useless. It assumes that people who ask "Why is that in the gallery?" are asking "Is it art?" whereas they are asking "Why is it art?" People don't put things in galleries just so they can call them "art", but because they see some point in doing so. To know the point is to know what value the object is thought to have. That is what the puzzled want to know about all art, and since the institution account is silent about that it tells us nothing about art.

Levinson

A different version of the institution account is offered by Jerrold Levinson who writes: "*A work of art is a thing intended for regard-as-a-work-of-art*: regard in any of the ways *works existing prior to it have been successfully regarded*" (Levinson 1979, p. 234).

To understand this approach ask what *would* help someone who cannot see why Duchamp's *Fontaine* is art. Here there are two cases. One is the person who can see why *The hay wain* has value as art but can't see why *Fontaine* does. The other is the person who doesn't know why either is art and simply wants to know what the claim of art is. To answer the first person one could try to show that Duchamp's *Fontaine* has the sorts of things that make *The hay wain* art. Even if, as Ben Tilghman has argued, this simply can't be done for the Duchamp, that is still the only strategy that could work.

This lies at the root of Levinson's account. Something is a work of art if it is intended to be appreciated in the ways in which art has hitherto been appreciated. That is also an institution theory, in that the ways in which people have appreciated art constitute our institution of art.

There is something right about this. One way to solve people's puzzlement about what is going on in avant-garde art is to get them to see that the same thing is going on as is going on in the art that they do accept.

However, this definition is as unhelpful as the original institution theory. It helps someone who knows about previous art but it does so not by saying what art is, but by assuming a knowledge of that. It is of no use to anyone who wants to know why people praise art, because it does not say what art is. How then can it be a definition?

All these institution accounts founder on a confusion between two senses of the question "what is art?". One sense is "Under what conditions would something properly be called 'art'?". To that one can rightly give the answer "If it gets into the art world" or "If it is intended to do what art has always been intended to do". But the other sense of the question, the question that expresses a common bewilderment about the avant-garde, and much else that is established in the art world, is "Why are things which are called 'art' valued?". On that central question the institution account is silent.

Guide to reading

The very best way to get interested in Wittgenstein is to read Ray Monk's biography, *Ludwig Wittgenstein: the duty of genius* (London: Cape, 1990) which you will put down with difficulty. Try also Norman Malcolm's shorter and equally compelling *Ludwig Wittgenstein: a memoir* (Oxford: Oxford University Press, 1958). A flavour of Wittgenstein's thinking about particular artists and art is well obtained from snippets assembled from his notes by Peter Winch and published as *Culture and value* (Oxford: Blackwell, 1980). I enjoyed B. Tilghman, *Wittgenstein: ethics and aesthetics* (Basingstoke: Macmillan, 1991) which seemed to me to capture much of the spirit of Wittgenstein's thinking. A central Wittgenstein work is *The philosophical investigations* (Oxford: Blackwell, 1953). If you are determined to read it, you may find helpful O. Hanfling, *Wittgenstein's later philosophy* (London: Macmillan, 1989) and N. Malcom, *Nothing is hidden* (Oxford: Blackwell, 1986). Eventually you will graduate to the monumental exegetical work of Baker & Hacker, for example the *Analytical commentary* (Oxford: Blackwell, 1983).

Weitz's co-option of Wittgenstein's notion of family resemblance definition occurs in the seminal "The role of theory in aesthetics", *The Journal of Aesthetics and Art Criticism* **15**, 1956, pp. 27–35. This is quite beautifully criticized in a miniature by Frank Sibley, "Is art an open concept?", *Proceedings of the 5th International Congress in Aesthetics*, Athens, 1960, pp. 545–8. A definitive review of all definitions of art is to be found in S. Davis, *Definitions of art* (Ithaca: Cornell University Press, 1991).

The notion of the "art world" was introduced in Arthur Danto, "The art world", *Journal of Philosophy* **61**(19), 1964, pp. 57–87. It is an influence on the institution account that gets its main airing in the work of George Dickie. The early version is to be found in his *Art and the aesthetic* (Ithaca: Cornell University Press, 1974), the latest (with a good, readable, collection of critical material) in G. Dickie, R. Sclafani & R. Roblin, *Aesthetics* (New York: St Martins, 1989). There are good, not always easy, comments by Wollheim (in suppplementary essay I to the second edition of *Art and its objects*) and T. Cohen, "The possibility of art", *Philosophical Review* **82**, 1973, pp. 69–82. Levinson's account is to be found in "Defining art historically", *British Journal of Aesthetics* **19**, 1979, pp. 232–50. The most recent and interesting work that grapples with the institution theory is R. J. Yanal (ed.), *Institutions of art* (Harrisburg: Pennsylvania Sate University Press, 1992). See also M. Rollins (ed.), *Danto and his critics* (Oxford: Blackwell, 1993).

If you are interested in the avant-garde try reading Robert Hughes, *The shock of the new* for a start. It is deliberately provocative and, even where contestable, informative. Browsing in Harrison and Wood, *Art in theory* is not a bad way of finding out what some of the artists involved *said* they were up to. Ben

Tilghman has also written critically about *Fontaine* in *But is it art?* (Oxford: Blackwell, 1984), to which we may add Ian Ground's, *Art or bunk?* (Bristol: Bristol Classical Press, 1989), commended to me by many students. There are many useful remarks about Duchamp in P. Humble, "Duchamps ready-mades: art and anti-art", *British Journal of Aesthetics* **22**, 1982, pp. 52–64.

Chapter 5

Ne'er so well expressed (II)

There is, then, no reason not to look for definitions of art in terms of necessary and sufficient conditions. The question becomes whether any plausible candidate is forthcoming. To illustrate the strategies for testing definitions I take Croce's definition of art in terms of expression.

Art defined as expression

In the second chapter of *The aesthetic* Croce equates art and expression. Works of art, such as paintings, in which artists order the stimuli they receive by creating expressive representations, are paradigm cases of products of a power we all possess to impose a form on the world by creating expressive representations from our sensory stimuli.

Croce's claim is that being an expression is both necessary and sufficient for being art. To say it is necessary is to say that if something is art, it necessarily must be expression. To say it is sufficient is to say that if something is expression, then that suffices to make it art. We falsify the former claim by finding something that is art and not expression. We falsify the latter claim by finding something that is expression and not art. (An interesting problem for philosophy in this connection is that to do this testing we have already to know what art is. The problem of definition presumably arises because, as I said in the introduction, we have some sort of problem in making clear to ourselves what we know, see Lyas 1971.) That aside, and since it seems obvious that there *are* things that are expressions without being art, I start with questions about the sufficiency of the condition.

Sufficiency

To subvert the claim that art simply is expression we have to show that some expressions are not art. To show this is to show that there are two classes of expressions which differ in kind: those that are art and those that aren't. Croce's claim is that this cannot be shown. All that can be shown is, firstly, that expressions differ in degree and not kind, and secondly, that although we call some expressions "art" and withhold that title from others, this is not rooted in any real difference.

Let us begin with the thought that the difference between artistic expressions and ordinary expressions lies in the fact that artistic expressions have a greater intensity. But it is unclear that artistic intuitions are more intense than those of ordinary life. A simple declaration of love can be as intensely felt as that sentiment expressed by a great poet.

What distinguishes expressions we call "art" from more ordinary expressions is what Croce called the greater "range" of the expression enshrined in, say, a great poem. Think first of someone with deeply and sincerely felt passion breathing the simple words "I love you". Those words can be as replete in feeling as any written by the greatest poet's pen. Then consider Auden's *Lullaby*:

> Lay your sleeping head my love
> Human upon my faithless arm
> Time and fevers burn away

Individual beauty from
Nature's children and the grave
Proves the child ephemeral.
But in my arms till break of day
Let the living creature lie
Mortal guilty but to me
The entirely beautiful.
          (*Lullaby*, 1937 from *Collected shorter poems* 1927–57.
                              London: Faber, 1966)

Although this poem does not differ from a humbler expression in intensity, it does so in *range*. There is more language in the poem, and so the range of reverberations, resonances and associations of the words will be immeasurably greater. The poem shows us that faithlessness, and time, and beauty, and the grave and guilt are involved with this particular speaker's love. So Croce is right to say that humble words from humble mouths can be perfect in the intensity of their feeling and yet more limited in range than the "complex expression" enshrined in a complex poem.

To see that this does not establish the difference in kind between the ordinary and the artistic expressions consider this: there is a technical distinction that philosophers mark by using the words "intension" and "extension", where the intension of a term corresponds roughly to its meaning and the extension of a term refers to the range of cases to which it is applied. Thus the terms "the morning star" and "the evening star" differ in meaning or intension but, somewhat surprisingly, have the same extension, since they both refer to the same object, Venus. What Croce claimed is that the term "art" and the term "expression" have the same intension or meaning but that, because of accidents of language, the range of cases to which we apply the term "art" happens not to coincide with the range of cases to which we apply the term "expression", the latter ranging over a wider range of cases. "Art" and "expression" have the same intension but a different extension.

If so, we have as yet found no difference in kind between artistic and ordinary expressions. There are only differences in degree between their ranges. Though we call the poem I just quoted "art", we do not dignify simple statements like "I love you" with that title. But they are both expressions and both belong in the same class.

It is a question for empirical linguistics where, on a scale of gradually increasing complexity in expression, we put the dividing line between what is called "art" and what is not. Our question is what the common nature is of the things on that common scale. Indeed the decision as to where we draw the line between what is called "art" and what is not may come to seem purely arbitrary. If an expression in the form of an epigram belongs with art, why not a simple word? If a landscape painting is art, why isn't a simple topographical sketch?

Croce was well aware that as a matter of empirical fact the term "art" is applied in his language to a narrower range of cases than the term "expression". But that fact does not establish that, when we look more closely into this linguistic difference, we will find a difference in kind between artistic and other expressions. That is why the fact with which I began, that we call only some expressions "art", is a shaky basis for claims that such expressions differ in kind from others.

It is tempting to think that complex expressive works of art must differ in something essential from lesser expressive utterances. But now consider: in the Jewish cemetery off Mile End Road in London lies a stone to a two-year-old child with the simple inscription "Peace to his dear soul". The inscription has its own expressive perfection. As with the best poetry, each word does its job. "Peace to his soul" would have lost something, as would "May his soul rest in peace". It does not seem to me too far-fetched to claim that we can see in such small-scale expressions just what we see in the greatest, the difference between them being not one of kind but of degree.

To make the distinction between artistic and other expressions one only of degree has profound implications. The tendency to put artistic expressions a cut above supposedly more humble expressions is one of the reasons why aesthetics and the arts are sometimes thought of as what Croce dubbed an "aristocratic club" to which humble folks are denied entry. To be inclined to claim a distinction in kind between artistic and ordinary expressions is to be tempted to think that what happens in art is unconnected with what happens in ordinary life. This, Croce says, is one of the "chief things that has prevented the aesthetic from reaching its real roots in the human soul"(1992, p. 15). Hence, too, the sadness that I feel when I see so many people who, as children, showed capacities for intense aesthetic delight, debarred from access to art by an education system that has failed to exercise and develop their native capacities for joy.

Croce's belief, which I share, is that the highest artistic expressions are rooted in the same soil as the humblest. Wittgenstein, too, asserted that our concepts, however lofty they may seem, have their roots in ordinary activities. Aesthetics, for example, although it may involve us with works of grandeur and complexity, and with grandiose concepts like beauty and sublimity, has its roots in the kinds of things that we do when, for example, we reject a jacket because the lapels look too wide. If this were not so we could not learn aesthetic terms. That we can talk of a complex symphony as moving, a complex painting as balanced, rests on the rootedness of such talk in spontaneous reactions displayed when as children we move with music and find shapes pleasing.

Further evidence of the continuum between the expressions that are called art and those that are not is the way in which great artists can reveal us to ourselves. A work of art may give us a means to express ourselves. Someone reading *The love song of J. Alfred Prufrock* may of a sudden think "that is how I am" and thereafter think "there's a bit of the Prufrock in me". So, too, one may come, after reading Kafka, to see the situation in British universities as Kafkaesque, or, after viewing a Turner painting, to see a sunset as Turneresque. Works of art give us ways of organizing and expressing our thinking about ourselves and our worlds. But how could an artist speak to us unless there were a common nature between us? It is because of a community between what the great artist does and what we all do that we can share the intuitions of the great artists and make them our own.

Necessity

We can make a plausible case that expressions that are not called "art" are not different in kind from those that are. What, though, of the claim that there are works of art that are not expressions?

Wilkinson, for example, argues that minor pieces of music, listened to for the mild pleasure they give, are not thought of as expressions yet are nonetheless thought of as art.

Let us first ask about these minor pieces, said to be art without being expressions; why are they art? Not, presumably, because they sound pleasant to the ear. That would make the flutings of nightingales art. They are art because they involved a complex kind of making.

Consider someone producing a piece of music that is an expression. A composer, starving in a garret, is commissioned to produce a requiem for a deceased monarch. The piece is lugubrious, moves the audience to tears, and becomes a classic often played on occasions of public lamentation. There can be no requirement that the composer feel grief while composing. The feeling may be joy at getting a commission. During the writing the composer might think with glee "this will get them", and may, during the rites, watch from the gallery smiling broadly when it has the desired effect. The music can be expressive even though it does not express the emotions of its composer, just as the melancholy attributed to the face of a bloodhound requires no assumptions about its visceral states.

Does this mean that the requiem is not an expression in Croce's sense? Not in the least. The composer, though happy to receive the commission, had to execute it, and probably had some idea of how he or she wanted it to come out. But it might have been a struggle to get it so to come out.

We must not assume that when Croce says that a work of art is an expression he has to mean that it expresses only such things as joy and grief. One can as well seek to express one's ideas of how, say, a requiem should sound, or how a hard-boiled San Francisco detective might behave. When one solves one's problem by making the work as one wanted it, then that is achieved expression in Croce's sense.

Now we can handle Wilkinson's counter-examples. If these are music, they are so because someone had a conception and then worked to give it the appropriate embodiment. That the conceptions were slight and the problems of expressing them not demanding, does not mean that that process did not occur. How else is it to be thought about and assessed as *music*. This is more than a matter of it merely sounding nice. It requires that we can make some assessment of the worth of the conception that the musician had and the degree of success in finding a solution that expresses that conception. Moreover in that working out the personality of the artist is expressed, as when we delight in the ingenuity with which Mozart resolves a musical problem.

Definition again

Let us return to the claim that the differences between the most ordinary expressions that we utter and the finest artistic expressions are differences not in kind but in degree. Here may lie a radical answer to some perennial questions about the definition of art. I beginning with a quotation from Tolstoy: "Art in all its forms is bounded on the one side by the practically useful, and on the other by unsuccessful attempts at art. How is art to be marked off from each of these?" (Tolstoy 1994, pp. 18–19).

Now if, as we do, we call only some things "art", then, although there will always be borderline cases, we must have a principle that will allow us to divide the furniture of the universe into things that are art and things that are not. But Tolstoy does not put it as I just did. He says that the problem is how to divide *the things that human beings make* into those that are art and those that are not. Dickie does the same. He sees a vast array of made objects, from urinals to carved marble. Some, he supposes, are art and some aren't. So he seeks a way of sorting the humanly made objects that are art from those that are not.

For at least a hundred years powerful minds have spent huge amounts of time trying to find such a way. Given the power of the minds, it is striking that no way has been found. Suppose now we conjecture that the problem is not to find a way of dividing *made* things into those that are art and those that are not. Suppose we said (as the Latin origin of the word "art" suggests) that *all* made things are art, so that the only division that we need is between things that are made and things that are not, art and nature. This is the implication of Croce's claim that the difference between what is art and what is not is a matter of degree and not kind.

Not every culture would have found this odd. If we look at Greek culture, for example, we find that the notion of art as a subset of humanly made things seems not to be there. Rather there is the notion of making, simpliciter (a notion also underlying the fact that for us terms like "artisan", "artefact", and "artificer" are all cognate with "art"). The question was more about the different things that can be done with things people make.

Croce's proposal does not entail that there is no difference between what is art and what is not. Willow leaves are not art, though they may, as in the remarkable work of Andy Goldsworthy, be components of art. Explosions of rage are not art, though dramatic renderings of them might be. Nor does it entail that we cannot, among things that differ only in degree of expression, have reasons for calling some things "art" and some things not, no more than the fact that temperatures differ only in degree stops us calling some things hot rather than cold. We might single out from the varieties of ways in which we express ourselves those where something complex and powerful is successfully achieved and call that "art". But this will not mark a difference in kind among expressions.

One advantage of this proposal is that we can simply stop the unending and futile search for a way of distinguishing in kind between those things we make that are art and those that are not. Instead we will have the general notion of making something and a variety of interests in what is made.

Another advantage is that we stop any tendency to elevate art into some sort of aristocratic club by hinting that that activity is confined to the making of high art, where that has nothing to do with rave dancing, Dire Straits, *Batman* comics, *Reservoir dogs*, body piercing and the play acting of children. As Tolstoy remarked in a passage quoted earlier "It is all art" (*ibid.*, p. 59).

Croce's suggestion has a deeper aspect. Richard Wollheim has correctly, to my mind, laid emphasis on the way in which our interests in art are bound up with expression. That, he rightly argues, can only be understood if we see expression as related to the place of projection in the general mechanisms of the mind's economy. Strange then that one should ever have thought that expression in art could be isolated from its place in a whole life. That suggestion of the place of expression in a more general picture of the mind, which is clearly related to what Croce has said, suggests a source of the power of art. Projections are rooted in the terrible storms of infantile adjustment. They are no less than the way in which we come to live with the demons of our wish to lose what we hate and possess what we love.

I have come close to saying that all our makings are expressive.

One reply is that not everything that we do is expressive in Croce's sense. To that I am inclined to reply, that not everything that we do (think here of routine work and talk) is something that *we do*.

Again it might be said that I ignore the difference between art, where what is made is not only consciously made but made in order to get something clear that is in one's mind and heart, and crafts, like making door frames, which are consciously made but not for that reason.

That, I think, simply underestimates the way that our whole lives are shot through with the effort to articulate what is inchoately in us. Artisans who think a chair looks wrong and fiddle with it until they can say "that's it" are doing something continuous with what the greatest artist does. Workers who simply churn out MFI furniture to pattern aren't in some full sense active at all, a fact that underlay much that Marx had to say about alienation.

The suggestion that all made things be thought of as art and as expressive is meant to start a discussion, not end it. It invites the attempt to reinstate a difference between the made things that are art and those that are not. One difference, suggested to me by Bob Sharpe, and involved in some versions of the institution theory of art, is that to classify something as art is to open it to a distinctive approach, which is to invite the activity of interpreting it. That suggestion is certainly worth exploring. One drawback to it, to which I return in a later chapter in which I discuss the work of Derrida, is that it is unclear that any of our utterances are exempt from the kind of interpretation that we hitherto thought special to art. (That, indeed, is the burden of a notable article by Richard Rorty on philosophy as a kind of writing, referred to in the guide to reading to Chapter 8.)

Illuminations

Beuys

The suggestion I have been exploring is one that has implications for our understanding of the often deeply puzzling art of our time. I begin with Josef Beuys, one of the most interesting figures in the avant-garde. Although many think him simply a charlatan we might get deeper than merely name-calling by considering this problem: what would be a suitable memorial to the victims of a concentration camp? It would not be a triumphal arch or a Whitehall Cenotaph. Then ask why Beuys made the memorial that he did. Again, if I asked you to produce a work entitled *The end of the twentieth century*, what would you do? Then meditate, as my students did with increasing understanding, what Beuys did. Wollheim says somewhere that confronted with what floors us in art, we always have to ask why making *that* at *that time* seemed to someone the only possible way to make art. But of more interest to me in the context of the present discussion is that we may understand why Beuys persistently claimed that we need to elide the difference between what is art and what is not among our human products. In this he is simply arguing, as Croce argued, that the attempt to distinguish within the products of humanity between those that are art and those that are not, and to distinguish between the producers of those products who are artists and those who are not, has been both socially pernicious and intellectually suspect.

Duchamp, Beuys and Cage

Mention of Beuys leads me to ways in which a conception of art as expression helps, much more than institution accounts have ever done, with puzzling cases of avant-garde art. Here are some examples:

Duchamp

Of each of the elements in a work of art we can ask "why that and not that?", "why there and not there?" "why that word, colour, keychange?". Duchamp's *Fontaine* is not just a urinal, randomly put where it is. It is cunning. So we can ask these questions: Why a urinal? How is it mounted? Not any old way, but in a position that renders it quite useless. It is signed. Why signed and not unsigned? It is signed with the name of a cartoon character. Why? Why not sign it "Duchamp"? It has a date, 1917. Why 1917 and not 1913 or 1812? It has a title, *Fontaine*. Why?

I start, as all good appreciation starts, in letting my imagination engage in a play controlled by the work. What do fountains suggest to me? I think of the great monumental fountains of Versailles, paradigms of the taste of a culture whose political system erected into a system of government a simulacrum of God's kingdom hierarchically conceived. In that culture the king owned the people, the magnate owned the workers, the father owned the family, the ego repressed the id, the author owned the work and God owned the world. Then I meditate on 1917. What was happening around that time? Then the world lived in the immediate aftermath of massacres of the First Battle of the Somme, and was even then living through the battles of Ypres, including Passchendaele. These atrocities, or so the avant-garde, and many others, believed, were not simply accidents. Their seeds lay in a culture, the very culture of the fountains of Versailles, and that culture nurtured them into fullness. A certain kind of art was implicit in that culture and that crime. That culture must be swept away. The people are to be liberated from possession by the king, the boss, the family, and, in a battle that is still being fought, from the father conceived as God and from God conceived as father, king or factory boss. And, of a piece with this, artists are no longer to be the dictators of the meaning of their work. Then I remember that 1917 is also the year of the Russian Revolution in which all culture, including all art, is to be made new. What, then, were the fountains of Versailles worth as emblematic of the culture that produced the terrified human beings atomized, dismembered, castrated and lobotomized as they marched towards the enemy? Nothing more than urinals. Who owns the work? Not Duchamp. Who then? Anyone or no-one. You are now free to make it yours, as you are free to make the world yours. And now I can begin to think: was there a better way to express all this?

Beuys again

In a brightly lit, spacious and parqueted room of the Pompidou stands a grand piano. But it is a piano with a difference. It is sewn into a suit of grey felt with such manic precision that every contour of the piano can be seen. So I set my mind free to play and start asking: Why a grand piano? Why grey felt? Why grey? Why felt? Felt muffles, so the piano is silenced. Grand pianos suggest to my imagination, in its controlled free play, the accoutrements of grand culture. Grey felt is the material of the German field uniform. So here high culture is silenced by that. But by a deft trick, the piano fits its suit perfectly. They were made for each other. Which is to say that the culture asked for it. I could express this by simply saying that a certain culture bred its own discontents. But this image expresses it with a deeper and more unsettling power.

Cage

A pianist comes on stage and sits at a piano for 4 minutes and 33 seconds and does nothing. (It is too common to hear talk about this piece by those who haven't sat through it. My students have on occasion staged a range of avant-garde pieces, in the proper formal setting of a music room. These are immensely enjoyed by audiences who are unused to being shaken up, intrigued, made to laugh and encouraged to act informally in music rooms. The Cage piece, which, Cage's first producer in Britain tells me, received a storm of applause at its premiere, never fails to reach them.)

I ask why *4'33"*? (*4'33"* is 273 seconds and 273 is absolute zero on the Kelvin thermometer – nice little joke here, but even the most minimalist comedian wouldn't be happy with just that.) Why no score? Why no conductor? Why no structure of sound? I think about conductors. They tell people what to do as scores tell performers what to do. Together they control the audience. So *4'33"* is an exercise in anarchy. You are on your own. All you can do is listen to whatever comes into that silence. For the first time, perhaps you become attentive to sounds. Then Zen thoughts may enter, or thoughts of the pulsing life of the world of which you and the sounds your body makes in that silence are all part. So the experience may be religious. Is it music? Cage says that if it isn't we may feel free to call it something else. Who cares about the label? Is it art? That is the question whether it successfully brings something to articulated expression. Ask, then, whether this does.

There is a belief that much of the avant-garde cannot be art because it is not pleasurable to look at, as if a Grunwald crucifixion were a thing to hang in the bedroom; or because it is too easy to come up with, as if Picasso found any great difficulty in drawing or everyone at the time of Duchamp were coming up with *Fontaine*. What people really worry about is that they cannot see the point of these things. I have argued that to see their point is to understand and be taken by what they express. I can now never see the glorious fountains of Versailles without my mind being troubled by the images of *Fontaine*. I do not find that the fountains delight the eye less, no more than I want to deny that one reason for seeking out art is that it delights the eye (which is why impressionists are so valued). But Duchamp once said that art is not merely retinal, else why not settle for the beauties of nature. The mind is expressed there, too.

Expression and horror

That Beuys felt able to design a monument to the victims of the concentration camps suggests a way in which the claim that art involves expression bears on a problem raised in an earlier chapter. I reported that some have said that in the face of the Nazi death camps art must be silent. They must feel that to make art out of that suffering is to make an object for aesthetic enjoyment out of it, and that seems as obscene as the activities of the emperor Heliogabalus who slaughtered slaves on the lawn because the red blood went so nicely with the green grass. So Sylvia Pankhurst looked into the eyes of the dispossessed of east London and realized that she must give up her art. For she could not any more capture those suffering faces so that the Bloomsbury Group might indulge their taste for the purely aesthetic delights of significant form.

It would, indeed, be wrong to use the forms of the suffering to produce objects for the delight of viewers interested in compositional and other aesthetic features. But if saying that art about suffering causes unease, as much unease is occasioned in me by the suggestion that art has nothing to say about suffering. That is counterintuitive. Those in the camps who produced art did not think so. And Auden, at least, thought that the old masters were never wrong about suffering.

If, however, we replace the conception of art as simply a matter of producing things, the contemplation of which will be in some narrow sense aesthetically enjoyable, with the conception of art as expression, we may come to a better understanding. Those who produced art in the camps wished to articulate how it was with them, partly to get that inchoate burden clear. I, too, have my burdens, inchoate and struggling to be born into clarity, about those horrors. I need artists to articulate these. When that happens the pain of these things will not be eased, but the burden of the inchoate will be lifted by that expression. Even to say "In the face of the camps art is silent" is to articulate and to express a possible feeling about those events.

Moreover, unlike the view that art is to produce pleasurable contemplation, the view that art is a matter of articulating and expressing how it was, gives a motive for what those did who, in the horrors of the camps, produced their art and what I, too, might do in writing about them. What was done was done not merely to lift the burden of the unarticulated, but done also that others could know how it was. That motive is movingly summed up by Dr Rieux's determination at the end of Camus's *The plague* – that partial analogy of the Nazi occupation of Europe – to write the chronicle of those events so that some record be left of the injustice and violence that had been done to those plague-stricken people.

The art of others

We are often told that art fits differently into different cultures. What the Siennese did with their altar pieces is not what we do with van Gogh's *Sunflowers*, and the interest of Hindus in their erotic temple art is different from any interest we might take in the erotica of Schiele. The place the *Iliad* had in its Greek culture was, Tilghman tells us, quite different from the place it has in ours.

If all this is so, I wonder why we call it all "art", unless we mean by that that we can, imperialistically, treat the artefacts of other cultures the way we treat certain of our own. That is dangerously close to saying that we are the only people who have the concept of art.

However, if art is bound up with expression, we see not differences between cultures, which make it unclear why we use the term "art" of them all, but similarities that make it plausible to do so. Siennese art sought to articulate a feeling about God, and doubtless gave its viewers a way of recognizing their own inchoate feelings about that. So too for the arts of other cultures. To be sure, I may not be able to empathize with what is expressed in a Siennese altar painting. Shorn of that I have to settle for things like colour, form and the like. (Although it will, like any art, express its author's problems and solutions to problems about the representation of such things as body and space.) The art of another culture, the music of Harlem, for example, may be inaccessible to me because I do not share the culture that would allow me to comprehend what that art expresses. But that does not stop me from thinking that it is art because it is expressive. Cultural imperialism will show itself in the demand that others express what one's own culture thinks to be important, so that, for example, certain parts of the body must be concealed by conveniently falling leaves. Salman Rushdie has been on the receiving end of that kind of attitude. But it need not show itself in ignoring the fact that the art of others is art like our own because expressive.

What next

I have been looking at the stories we tell about the power of art and I have suggested that the notion of art as expression points us in the direction in which an account of that power can be found. But even if that is right much remains to be done. If we make art expression, whose expression is it? Can we ignore the artist in talking of expression, as many have argued we must. Again some expressions seem questionable. *Mein Kampf* may perfectly express its author's crazed views, but is none the better for that. That suggests that questions about the truth and morality of what is expressed may enter. How do they? And if, as I say, some expressions are more impressive than others, what right have I to such judgements? Aren't such judgements about art purely subjective? Since that last question sums up a very widely held view I shall begin with that.

Guide to reading

The core of Croce's definition of art as expression is to be found in the last sections of Chapter I and the early sections of Chapter II of *The aesthetic*. Wilkinson's criticisms of that are to be found in his "Art, emotion and expression" in Hanfling's *Philosophical aesthetics*. I have to say that they are expressed with some hesitancy. Wilkinson quite correctly asks whether the expression account is refuted by finding only minor art that is not expressive. On the relation between expression and the more general mechanisms of projection see Wollheim's *The mind and its depths* (1993) and *The thread of life* (Cambridge: Cambridge University Press, 1985). The great attempt to distinguish art from craft is made in Collingwood's *Principles of art*. The attempt, to which I return in a later chapter, merits close scrutiny. For more on Beuys see H. Stachelhaus, *Josef Beuys*, trans. D. Britt (New York: Abbeville, 1991). Since I have mentioned Andy Goldsworthy you might like to look at the book *Stone* (London: Viking, 1994). Goldsworthy is represented at the Grizedale Sculpture Park, a venue I commend for your aesthetic enrichment.

Chapter 6

The proof of the pudding

The terms "objective" and "subjective"

The terms "objective" and "subjective" seem easy to characterize.
The world, it is said, contains two classes of things. There are
objects out there: trees, stones and clouds, which have properties
like weight and shape. Then there are subjects that have a psychological life: me, your dog, their hamster and her pig. An objective
assertion refers to a property out there, in the object. A subjective
assertion expresses some state of the psychological life of the subject. To say a strawberry has a certain mass is to say something
objective. To say one likes the taste of strawberries is to say something subjective.

One might, as Idealists do, query the distinction embedded in
that world picture. This, as Gentile's *The philosophy of art* shows,
leads to striking conclusions about the alleged subjectivity of aesthetics. A more recent querying of the distinction is to be found in
Merleau-Ponty's phenomenology. Here aesthetic questions inter-
twine with deep philosophical issues. If, however, the distinction is

accepted, then to claim that aesthetics is subjective is to claim that judgements that a work of art is feeble, elegant, brilliant, or dire, do not refer to properties it has. It is to describe the effect of the object on the judger.

Hume, in a classic essay, writes:

> All sentiment is right; because sentiment has a reference to nothing beyond itself, and is always real whenever a man is conscious of it. But all determinations of the understanding are not right; because they have reference to something beyond themselves, to wit real matter of fact ... No sentiment represents what is really in the object ... It exists merely in the mind that contemplates ... and each mind perceives a different beauty. (Hume 1969, p. 117)

If aesthetic judgements are subjective, then if two people make different claims about a work, the claims do not conflict. If I say, "It's grand" and you say "It's trite", what I am really saying is "It impresses me" and what you are saying is "It irritates me". Both assertions can be true, as they could not be were you to say "that is a cube" and I say "it is a sphere". Hence the Latin tag – *de gustibus non disputandem est*. In matters of taste there is no disputing.

This whole problem, then, only arises, on the natural-seeming assumption that we can divide up reality between subjects and objects. Anyone who does this immediately runs into a problem. Any access to objects has to be through experiences of subjects. But aren't these, as experiences of *subjects*, simply subjective? How, as Bishop Berkeley pertinently asked, can I be assured that there is any objective world beyond my experiences, since all I have is the experiences? But then aesthetic judgement is no worse off than any other judgement.

This matter goes beyond aesthetics into the theory of knowledge. Here I adopt a more limited strategy. I shall simply point out that, Berkeley to the contrary, all of us assume an ability to talk about how the world is, as when a witness says "The traffic-light was red when Bugs Bunny rocketed through it". Then I shall simply point out that aesthetic talk is like that sort of objective talk and entitled to the same status. It will be open to someone to reply that, on deeper inspection, no judgements are really objective. But then aesthetics will not be, as is usually supposed, especially subjective.

A presupposition guides my thinking. If ways of speaking have emerged and continue to have a role in our practices, an initial presumption is that they have a point. In those practices, as Kant noticed, there simply is a difference between saying a painting has grandeur and saying that one likes it. If the judgement that a thing has something good about it always reduces to the assertion that one likes it, it remains quite mysterious that we should have two ways, with apparently entirely different implications, of saying one and the same thing. There *can* be two ways of saying the same thing. "You'll find it tough when you graduate" says the same thing as "soon you'll be sliding down the razorblade of life". But in the case we are dealing with we don't have two variations on a common theme, but two entirely different-looking claims.

That aesthetic judgements don't simply reduce to assertions about likings is suggested by other things. We feel we grow in our powers of judgement. When 17 I may like Take That. When 23 I may simply wonder how I could have liked anything so banal. I don't express this by merely saying that my likings have changed. This can happen, as when someone comes to like Donne's later religious poetry more than his earlier love poetry without thinking any the worse of the earlier. But in other cases one thinks an earlier judgement mistaken. That would be hard to explain if all we had were merely transient likings. This suggests that we mischaracterize our lives in some as yet unexplained way when we say, of aesthetic preference, that it is all subjective.

Sibley and objectivity

I want now to deploy an argument, developed out of remarks by Frank Sibley, that undermines a common proof of aesthetic subjectivity.

Two things about subjectivism need to be explained. Firstly, the assertion "aesthetic judgement is subjective" is seldom a neutral observation. It is a derogatory comment about some supposed deficiency of aesthetic judgement. Odder yet, the people who say this sort of thing need have nothing against subjectivity elsewhere. "Love is a subjective matter" seems not to import the same opprobrium. Indeed that subjectivity is often celebrated rather than sneered at. So one question is why aesthetics attracts *sneering* accusations of subjectivity. One reason is that the ignorant, unable to exercise taste, deny it. But there is more to it than that.

Secondly, *why* do people think that aesthetics is a subjective matter?

A first argument

One argument, as puerile in aesthetic contexts as it is in moral ones, is this:

P1: There are massive disagreements in aesthetics

So aesthetic judgements are subjective.

This is a wretched argument, no better than another perennial favourite:

P1: Criminals break the law

So they should go to prison.

Someone who presents us with an argument says to us, "If you accept this premise, then you should accept this conclusion". About an argument, therefore, we can ask at least two questions: firstly, should I accept the premise(s) upon which the conclusion is based? And, secondly, if I did would the conclusion follow? Both conditions have to be met. I may grant you that *if* I accepted your premise, then I should accept your conclusion. But if I don't accept the premises why should I accept what follows from them? Alternatively, I may concede that your premise is true, but that the conclusion simply doesn't follow from it. The first subjectivist argument is heir to both of these ills. It is simply untrue that there is massive disagreement in aesthetic matters (or even moral ones come to that). Indeed what impresses me is the amount of agreement. What distracts people from seeing this is concentration on such avant-garde extremes in art as *Fontaine*, and in morality as Hannibal Lecter, and even there there is more agreement than is often supposed. But even if it were true that there are widespread disagreements, the conclusion that aesthetic judgements are subjective does not follow. Disagreements need not be evidence for subjectivity. Were I to ask any large group of people mentally to do the sum $768 \times 654 \div 397$ in the next minute, I would get a fairly hefty disagreement between the answers of even those prepared to have a go. Do I assume that mathematics is subjective? Creationists and Darwinians have had fierce disagreements about evolution. Does that establish that biology is a subjective matter? From the fact of disagreement nothing whatsoever follows about anything (except that there is disagreement), least of all about subjectivity.

A second argument

The reply is likely to be that mathematics and science have an objectivity that is lacking to aesthetics because they have methods and proof procedures for settling these disagreements. If there is disagreement as to whether the angles of a triangle add up to 180 degrees, we can give a deductive proof. If there is dispute as to whether areas of low pressure over Iceland are a reliable indicator of rain within days in Lancashire, then we can call on the evidence of past experience to establish the degree of probability that this is so.

This suggests the following argument for the subjectivity of aesthetic judgements:

P1: A type of judgement is objective if methods exist by which disagreements on such judgements can be settled.

P2: Mathematics and science meet this test.

P3: The methods they use are induction and deduction

P4: Aesthetics does not use these methods to settle disagreements in aesthetic judgements

So, C1: It has no methods for settling disagreements

So, C2: Its judgements are subjective

I could create trouble for the early stages of this argument. Thus, in P1, is the requirement that the disagreement actually be settled by the methods? If so we don't yet know whether or not biology is objective since the creationists haven't agreed with their opponents yet. Again, it is not clear that the methods of scientists and mathematicians are so easily reduced to a couple of proof procedures. But let us grant P1, P2 and P3.

117

That brings us to P4. P4 is true, but it is important for a proper understanding of criticism to be absolutely clear why it is. In order to show this I need to lay out the structure of criticism. We can think of this as having three levels, which I first indicate, then annotate.

Level 3
Overall aesthetic verdicts

Examples: This work is brilliant, magnificent, pathetic

Level 2
Aesthetic judgements

Examples: This line is elegant, the colour is vibrant, this composition is balanced

Level 1
Nonaesthetic judgements

Examples: there is a red patch in the corner, this line is curved, there is an alliteration in line three.

At level 3 we make overall judgements of works of art. Having found out about all the components of the work, we put everything together and give a verdict. At level 2 we are still dealing with elements of the work. Even to say that a work as a whole has an elegance, say, is not to claim that it is, overall, a satisfactory work of art. For the elegance might be at odds with some other element of the work, say its subject matter. At level 1 we have the features of the work upon which its aesthetic qualities depend and from which they emerge. That the work is balanced depends on there being this patch here and this mass there, for example.

Often when we cite a remark at a higher level we link it to something at a lower level using the word "because". We might say that "It is a great work of art because of the sheer strength of the composition, and astonishing vibrancy of the colour". And we might say "It is balanced because this colour patch here is off-set so exactly by the positioning of that colour patch there".

If aesthetics is to use deductive or inductive methods in any significant way, then they must have an important role in conducting us from the first level to the second level or from the second level to the third. This is not so.

Let us take the move from level 1 to level 2. Suppose first that we can all see a red patch in a certain position or an alliteration in a poem and we would like a proof that this makes the picture balanced or the poem witty. Deduction won't help. We simply can't deduce that because there is an alliteration in line three the poem is witty. For alliteration is compatible with witlessness. Indeed the very same colour patch that makes one work balanced may make another unbalanced.

Induction fares little better. We are not given to arguing that, because the last 27 pictures in which there was a red patch in the left corner were balanced, so probably this one which has that feature will be. It would also be unhelpful for those seeking to develop capacities for appreciative experience. What they want is not proofs that would bring them to *believe that* a work has a certain value feature. They want to *see and enjoy* that feature. Being told, as they often are, that most works by Rembrandt are good, may lead them to infer that this work, being by him, is probably good. Not only is this unreliable, since not all Rembrandt's works are necessarily good, but they still can't experience those features wherein the excellence of Rembrandt lies.

What of the move from the value features of a work to judgements about its overall merit? Induction fares no better here. Being told that most works that have wit in them have turned out to be good overall, one might infer that this work, which has wit, is probably good. But that is no help to someone who wants to experience the goodness. Lest it be thought that this is to attack a straw man, that seems to be the way in which one prominent aesthetician, Monroe Beardsley, proceeded. For he seemed to suggest that from the presence of unity, complexity and intensity, we can safely infer merit. We can't. A work can have an overall unity of tone and be simply tedious in the intensity of its complexity, as seems to be the cases with the bizarre structures of Lyly's *Eupheues* and the Byzantine wanderings of *Dynasty*.

When we come to the deduction of an overall judgement from the possession of merit features, the case is more complex. We are entitled to say that if a work possesses elegance, then there is something good about it, so that if I were to say that what makes a play so bad is its elegant plot, or its wit, I would have to give some special explanation. For to say a work is elegant, without qualification, is to say that there is something good about it. This is not, however, to show that one can deductively establish that a work has an overall merit. For works of art, unlike kitchen knives, are not such that one can say the more merits the better. In art the merits have to fit together. Thus, humour is a merit feature. But it can be out of place, as some have argued it is in the porter scene in *Macbeth*. Elegance is a good-making feature, but its presence might be damaging if the overall effect being sought is rough force. In assessing a work of art we need not merely to know that a collection of merit features is present. We need to know that they go together in the right way. I know of no method of induction and deduction that could demonstrate for any particular work of art that this is so.

We see, then, the truth of P4 as well as the truth of P1–3. From this the first conclusion is drawn, namely that aesthetics has no methods for settling disagreements. From that it follows, given the first premise, that aesthetics is subjective.

But that first conclusion simply does not follow from P1–4. We can concede that a subject is objective if it has methods for settling disagreements. We can allow that science has such methods, induction and deduction, and is therefore objective. We can allow that aesthetic judgements are neither deductive not inductive. But it simply will not follow from that that aesthetics is subjective. This is because nowhere does the argument say that the *only* methods by which to settle disagreements are induction and deduction. This leaves open the possibility that aesthetics is objective. For though it does not use induction and deduction there is another method it does use.

All that will follow from P1–4 is that in not using deduction and induction to settle its disputes, aesthetics is not like science and mathematics. That begins to explain why a sneer attaches to the assertion that aesthetics is only subjective. For mathematics and science have, or had, prestige in our culture. Since aesthetics does not use their methods, its claims are ill-grounded. Some feeble minds impressed by the genuinely marvellous achievements of science, have supposed aesthetics ought to be reformed along scientific lines. One way to do this would be to eliminate any inclination to make value judgements and to confine oneself to talking about the observable facts about the physical properties of works. But since works of art are nothing if not objects of value, this is not to reform aesthetics but to kill it off.

The other alternative is to try to find scientific laws of taste. These are usually inductive. One looks for things that are simply observable (this is usually dressed up as "empirically" observable): patches of colour, figures of speech, sound tones. Then one tries to infer value conclusions from these.

Again I ask Croce's question: how is the correlation between the physical feature, say a patch in the right corner, and the merit feature, say balance or overall brilliance, to be made. One presumably has to make a correlation by noting that whenever value is present this feature is present also. But then the presence of value has to be ascertainable independently of ascertaining that the physical features are present, else there would be nothing to correlate with anything. But if value can thus be ascertained directly, why is the induction needed at all?

The best comment on all this is Trotsky's swingeing comments on those Russian Formalists who tried to scientize literary appreciation:

> Having counted the adjectives, and weighed the lines, and measured the rhythms a formalist either stops silent with the expression of a man who does not know what to do with himself, or throws out an unexpected generalization which contains five per cent of Formalism and ninety five percent of the most uncritical intuition (Trotsky 1957, p. 172).

Aesthetic proof

It is one thing to say that aesthetics may have methods, unlike those of the sciences and mathematics, for settling disagreements, and so have some claim to objectivity. What, though, is that method? Consider this: You come in and say "It's raining". I reply, "Surely not". We don't now trot out inductions or deductions. You can simply say, "If you don't believe me go and look". There is a vast area of our lives where disagreements are settled by simply looking.

That that is true in aesthetics is suggested by two things. Firstly, aesthetics is importantly to do with perception. We have to see the grace of a painting, hear the plaintiveness of the music, see the expression emergent from a statue. This is why induction and deduction can seem so inapposite in aesthetics. At best they can be used to get us to *believe that* a work has a certain property but do nothing to help us *perceive* it.

Secondly, bringing someone to a work in order to settle a disagreement about it is simply what we do. If I say that parts of D. H. Lawrence's writing are pretentious, I can go with you to the novel and point out the exact passages that seem to support my contention.

Imagine the case of an accident at a traffic light. There is a dispute as to whether the light was red or green. Here the defendant, asked in court why he went through the red light, would be ill-advised to reply that colour is a subjective matter. That may well, in some philosophical theorizing, be true. In the traffic of life and the M6, however, it is nonetheless the case that lights are red, yellow and green, and that people can be right or wrong, with tragic consequences, in saying which of these they are. This by itself is enough to establish the possibility of the kind of rightness and wrongness about the lights that enables us to treat that as an objective matter, even if, when philosophizing, we may come to doubt this.

What gave rise to our practice of saying that traffic lights, say, are truly red or green? Nothing scientific. Wave lengths may attach to different colours, but we had our colour words long before we knew that. What underlies our present practice is our biological emergence as colour-sighted beings. A survival value became attached to a shared capacity to sort things in certain ways by the use of the eyes, and this capacity continues to be useful to us in a wide range of ways. Talk about colours, then, reflects our capacities and practices. Colour discrimination need not, in fact, be something that a majority of us possesses. Colour discrimination could be a minority skill, those not possessing it learning by experience to rely on those who do (for example, when camouflage is needed). Those who do not have the capacity can infer that others do, but the inference will not give them that ability to see, an ability of which they may keenly feel the lack. Moreover, even where all have the capacity, some may have it in a more developed form, may discriminate more shades and subtleties of colour, an ability that they notice grows with practice. There is, too, the possibility of a physical defect, so that people can, perhaps curably, be affected in their capacities to discriminate colours by the condition of physical organs like the eye. Other factors, too, they may learn, can affect discrimination and cause disagreement: factors such as lighting conditions, haste and tiredness.

What lies at the root of all this is those *agreements in our judgements* employed in our exercise of our evolved capacities and the practices, like taking a colour sample into better light, that emerge from those evolving agreements.

What I have said about colour discrimination suggests a way of thinking about aesthetic objectivity that is far from certain scientific models. We have developed as creatures that have the capacity to group things together in certain ways. We simply do, even as children, naturally find things funny, music martial, compositions balanced, certain animals pleasing in their movements. Those groupings, naturally expressed in cry and gesture, are augmented as we learn the words like "balanced", "elegant", "graceful", "funny" and the like. We find agreements that deer are graceful, colours vibrant, movements dynamic and so forth. So, if that sort of agreement is enough to establish some objectivity in colour discrimination, why does it not establish a case for that in aesthetic discrimination?

One answer is to suggest disanalogies between the two cases.

A first is that there is more disagreement in aesthetics that in colour cases. At the level at which fairly basic sortings of colours and aesthetic features are made this is not obviously so. Most people find spectacular sunsets pretty rousing and Torvill and Dean pretty elegant. True, fewer people seem able to make the finer discriminations in aesthetics. But then the analogy with colour discrimination is maintained. For fewer can see the differences between BS2100 and BS2101 on the colour chart. Finer discrimination takes practice, as witness the case of wine tasting. We should not confuse the fact that some don't develop their aesthetic capacities with the claim that ineliminable differences are rifer in aesthetics than elsewhere.

This same line of reasoning would deal also with the claim that a relevant difference between aesthetic and colour discrimination is that a small minority has the former and a large majority the latter. In fact, minorities are neither here nor there. The colour language could perfectly well survive if most of us lost that capacity.

Another important disanalogy between the cases of aesthetic and colour discrimination is sometimes thought to be this: we think a colour to be either blue or red, say, so if one person says it is red and another says it is blue, one *must* be right and the other *must* be wrong. But, the argument goes, that does not seem to be so in the aesthetic case. Two experienced people, who agree about Brahms and Mozart, might simply agree to differ about Mahler, with not the least inclination to think that the other *must* be wrong. It is as if they agreed which things are red and which things are blue but agreed to differ on which things were yellow. But again the analogy holds, since even in colour judgement there is some slack. To my surprise I find that although people in full possession of well-working visual apparatuses agree that grass is green and Paul Newman's eyes are blue, for a wide range of judgements they cannot agree whether certain things are green or blue. That does nothing to incline us to the belief that there is *no* right and wrong about colour attributions. Why should it do so in aesthetic cases?

More interesting is this thought: both aesthetic and colour judgements can be disqualified because of defects in the organs of perception and in the viewing conditions. A colour-blind person or one dazzled by the sun is be trusted neither in their judgements about red and green nor about the colour harmonies in a Cézanne. The interference factors in the case of colour discrimination are physical. What makes us tend to think of reports of aesthetic discriminations as more subjective is the fact that they are affected by *psychological* as well as physical interference conditions. Jealousy, for example, can affect one's judgements.

If the claim is that being in certain psychological conditions can make our judgements suspect, then that supports what I have been saying about aesthetic objectivity. The force of saying that a matter has a right and wrong about it is that there can be reasons for ruling out certain claims, as we rule out some of the colour judgements of those who are colour-blind. If I am now told that we question some aesthetic judgements not merely on physical grounds but on psychological ones, that supports the analogy. That we can and do rule out judgements because of perceived deficiencies in the psychological apparatus of the judger makes no difference as long as we retain some notion of *ruling out*. For that is what imports the ascription of objectivity. To say that someone is too ignorant or too prejudiced to make a fair judgement of a work is simply to say that that person's judgements are likely to be wrong, and that, far from undermining the notion of objectivity simply serves to strengthen it.

Beyond objective and subjective

Let us review our progress. The first step was to say that if objectivity goes with finding a use for the terms true and false, right and wrong, then there seem to be grounds for attributing objectivity to remarks about the colours of things. Secondly, that possibility rests on a certain agreement in judgements, displayed in their practices by people possessed of certain capacities. Thirdly, that same sort of agreement seems also to pertain in cases of aesthetic discrimination. From this it follows that those judgements too have a claim to objectivity. The difference between the two cases, to which we have to return, is that our judgement that a thing is red seems not to be conditioned by our emotional or other psychological states as aesthetic judgement seems to be.

This kind of account accords with our inclination to say that willow trees are graceful, deer elegant, colours garish, sounds mellifluous, paintings balanced, lines dynamic and tints delicate. This is to say that such aesthetic judgements are as objective as any judgement of colour.

I once thought that that was a sufficient refutation of subjectivism in aesthetics. It is not, and the reason it is not is because someone might see that a colour is garish, a picture balanced, a dance elegant, a movement graceful and still not *like* any of those things, saying, perhaps, "I'm not much into the delicate". That looks damaging. For as I set the problem up, objectivity went with settling disputes by showing that one of two conflicting judgements could be ruled out. That is certainly possible when the dispute is, say, as to whether a thing is or is not delicate or graceful. We look and see. But now another dispute arises in which, although two people agree on the aesthetic qualities of a thing, one person expresses a liking for it and the other does not. Since what might seem to us to be important in aesthetics is how in the end we respond to a work, and since that response expresses itself in expressions of liking or disliking, which are subjective if anything is, we seem forced to the conclusion that aesthetics is at heart subjective.

Here we may add, too, that our judgements about works of art seem inevitably conditioned by factors other than the purely physical variations in physical organs and viewing conditions. These factors have to do with the personal history of those who make such judgements, their special emotional constitutions, their interests, their idiosyncratic selves as they are conditioned by individual psychological histories. Since we are unavoidably different in these respects, so our judgements are conditioned by our subjectivities and, so, are radically subjective.

One attempt to deal with this is Kant's. He asks what might disqualify my judgement about a work of art from having a claim on others. His answer would be "its being involved with interests which are particular to me", as when an interest in bowls leads me to overrate a picture of Drake finishing his game as the Armada heaves into sight. Kant may have thought, therefore, that his proof that aesthetic judgement is disinterested shows that aesthetic judgement rests on no interests personal to me alone and so is objective. It has a universality rather than a particularity of appeal. A jealous man who, because of conditions idiosyncratic to himself, thinks that *Othello* is a fine play because Desdemona gets killed is not making an aesthetic judgement by this test.

We can concede that if partial interests enter into judgements we are likely to feel that the judgement is subjective. Kant is right that a disinterested, nonpartial judgement is not going to be open to that accusation. The question is what exactly it is for a judgement to be thus disinterested. Here it has been felt that Kant defines this in unhelpfully negative terms. We can be told that a disinterested judgement is one that does not involve private financial interests, personal vanity, spite and the like. This says what it is not and not what it is.

Might we say that the objective nonpartial judgement expresses an interest that all share rather than one private to me? An objection to this is that it seeks to make illegitimate what is perfectly legitimate, which is to let one's personal life enter into one's dealings with art. That is reflected in the fact that we are tolerant of ways in which differences of temperament affect aesthetic judgements. I am more intellectual and like Bach, you are more passionate and like Rachmaninov. So we let subjectivity enter our aesthetic judgements in a way in which we do not let it enter our colour judgements. It is time now to rethink this whole matter.

The problem arises because we are presented with a choice between saying that something is objective and saying that it is subjective. This choice is not offered in a neutral way. The clear implication is that it is somehow better if a judgement be objective, where that means in some sense demonstrable in such as way as to settle disputes. The alternative is, it is thought, a welter of personal opinions, each of which simply expresses a liking. One thing that inclines some to this is the brilliant success of the physical sciences that become the model to which any well-founded discipline must aspire. Influential too is the kind of thinking that Bernard Williams claims originated with Descartes, the tendency to divide what there is between an objective physical world which exists and has its properties independently of us, and the inner subjective world.

To expose the assumptions that drive the tendency to divide what there is into the objective and the subjective would be, as the wrestlings of Heidegger demonstrate, a tortuous task. For it would be to lay bare the models of thought that dominate and shape our thinking, and then to ask whether these are more than local effects of the kind of interests we happened to have had at a particular time in our history. Here my task is the more modest one of showing that we are simply not forced to choose between the terms "subjective" and "objective" in describing our aesthetic comments. Assent to the necessity of such a choice would indeed force on us demands as to how aesthetics must be if it is to be acceptable as a "proper", "objective" discipline. And since aesthetics manifestly does not meet those demands, it will be *dismissed* as subjective.

Let us begin by noting a common force of the word "subjective" in these characterizations of the aesthetic. The claim that aesthetics is subjective often represents aesthetic claims as egoistic. Aesthetic judgements are characterized as "I like Barry Manilow", said with a defiant air and with an arrogant tone that refuses discussion.

This, however, is not how assertions that one likes something are typically made. One leaves the cinema with someone one loves and says, "Good, wasn't it?". One says to a friend, "I liked the part where Cleese did the silly walk" or "I liked the way she played the *adagio*". These are not subjective remarks, if to be a subjective remark is to be offered in a way that brooks no argument. These remarks are attempts to engage with another. They invite replies like, "Yes, wasn't it good?", or "I couldn't see much in it. What did you like about it?"; "No, I thought Brendel did it better. Too much right hand". In these contexts the question whether our remarks are objective or subjective simply does not arise for us. Indeed, when asked to characterize them, using these terms, we might simply fumble. Since we are talking about what we liked, we might think that they are subjective. Yet we were talking about the film or music.

If we do not find a natural use of the terms "subjective" and "objective" in these contexts, then these contexts are not its home. Why then demand the remarks be one or other? Why not look and see what happens here?

What happens when we make these remarks is that we reach out in an effort to establish community. To find that someone else finds that particular thing funny is to find one is not alone. To find that another does not share one's reaction is to have a rift open up. Objectivists seem to want it to be the case, when such rifts open up, that we have some argument, as we do in mathematics, that is *guaranteed* to close the rift again and to bring us into unity. We have no such arguments, least of all deductive and inductive ones. It does not follow from that that we have nothing at our disposal. What we do is try to get someone to see what we think we see, much as one tries to get someone else to see a face in a puzzle picture. In so doing we place ourselves at the risk that they may instead get us to see it their way.

Sibley has a compelling picture of the kinds of things we might do in such cases. Someone cannot see the joke in Brueghel's *Fall of Icarus* and we say, "Did you notice the tiny splash in the corner?": for a failure to see or hear or understand what is there to be heard, seen and understood makes a difference. Sometimes we simply point to what we want the other to see (as we do when the question might be about a traffic light): "Look at the graceful line", "Listen to the quiet resolution", "See the impudent wit". We use metaphors and analogies: "It is as if the paint had been thrown at the canvas", "as if birds were flying up". We invite "what ifs": "If you want to understand why it is so solid, imagine the figure moved to the right a little; the effect would be lost". We gesture with hands, face and body, as a conductor might who wished to get the orchestra to see the effect that was being sought. And sometimes the other says: "yes, now I see it", "now I begin to see", "of course", "right", as we might be brought to say these things by others. And then delight rises in us. Since it is my delight, it is subjective, if you really want to use that term. But because the delight is referred to the work as its object, it is also objective, if you want to use that term. But neither really fits.

It is a mistake to think that when I say "I don't like it", that is an end. It is a beginning. It invites "Why don't you like it?". And what I say may get you to see it, too: a remark like "Its humour is sophomoric" might do the trick.

Aesthetics is dismissed as subjective (in a way in which love, significantly is not) because what I say about something is conditioned by how it is with me. I bring my whole life to the work. But that fact, although it may be a reason for dismissing some of my judgements (I'm given to overhaste and violent and short-lived enthusiasms), can't be a reason for dismissing all my judgements, especially when others spontaneously share them.

Although my judgements express my likings, I am inclined to say that there is the possibility of a right and wrong in aesthetics. I say this because we simply do say "That's right" as a response to the judgement of another. That means "I see it as you do". These judgements are revisable (see Chapter 9) as I am revisable. As my life changes I might come to see why you saw it a certain way. And then I will say "That's right". Kant was right so far as this: any tendency to think of our aesthetic talk as objective talk rests upon interests that are not partial but shared. What I think he failed to see was that there is not one sharing but an extraordinary range of cross-cutting, patchy and nonpatchy sharings.

Conclusions

Firstly, some say that aesthetics is objective if aesthetic properties are "in" objects. It is, however, wholly unclear what it is for properties to be in objects, where the spatial term "in" suggests that they are stuck in objects like currants in a pudding. Some have argued that any property is a disposition or power of an object to affect us, and if that account worked, we would have as much right to say that aesthetic properties are in objects as to say that any other of their properties are.

Here we have to remind ourselves continually that the colour language exists because objects affect sentient human beings with certain capacities in certain ways. This is entirely compatible with our having evolved a way of talking about the colours of things that admits a true and false, a right and wrong. So it is with the aesthetic, including the aesthetics of our likings.

Secondly, doubts arise about the real properties of things because we make an absolute rift between a world of objects and a world of selves. Some, Idealists like Kant and Gentile, simply refuse to start there. Whether or not Idealism is defensible, there are models of our dealings with the world that spoil that simple bifurcation. Consider the way in which we say of a landscape that it is melancholy or smiling. Here there is some sense in saying that we project these properties on the world. The mechanism of this and the way these projective capacities fit into the economy of our psychological lives is a matter to which we shall return when we come to our final answer to the question wherein lies the power of art. But the phenomenon of projection reminds us that it is not always a simple question: is the quality in the work or in us? We refer an inner life to an object fitted to receive it.

I suppose there will be a worry about whether the fact of projection is compatible with there being a truth and falsity, right and wrong about such assertions as the assertion that an object is melancholy. The answer is that we do use these terms in these contexts: we are inclined to agree that it is right to say that a winter landscape is melancholy and a balmy summer evening is tranquil. The question is not whether these comments can be right and wrong, true or false. The question is what makes that possible. What makes that possible is that we agree in the judgements that we make. These agreements need not be universal, can be changeable, can alter as our lives alter, can be affected by the lives we have had and will have. But that there are these agreements is all that underpins this language. There are those who would like there to be something that underpins these agreements, so that the reason we say that a landscape is melancholy is that there is some property, being melancholy, tranquillity or whatever, that it possesses independently of our judgement that it is so. Certainly there will be qualities that a melancholy landscape will tend to have – darker colours for example. But these can never entail that it is melancholy, as opposed to dreary. But as far as melancholy goes there can be no such property in a thing over and above the one assigned to it in encounters by sentient beings.

All this has profound implications for educational practice, particularly an education in the arts. The teacher cannot, in one sense, be an authority. When teachers do have an inclination to ascribe a property to a work, the job is not to *tell* people that it has that property but to try to get the others to see, hear, understand or feel what the teacher sees, where that is to put oneself at risk that the others may get one to see it their way. I have indicated some of the ways in which that can be attempted. But honesty is required of the others, too. For in the business of the spinning of words often the most persuasive image-maker can get people to say they see what is not really seen. The only safeguard against that is honesty and courage, the honesty to realize that one hasn't yet seen and the courage to say so. The child who said the emperor had no clothes could do this out of innocence. More is usually required of us.

Guide to reading

A more detailed version of some of the remarks in this chapter can be found in my contribution to Hanfling's *Philosophical aesthetics*. The best place to start on prime source material is with Hume's delightful and influential essay "Of the standard of taste" in Tillman & Cahn (eds), *Philosophy of art and aesthetics*. It will be apparent that his whole account rests on the subject–object distinction. For a demonstration of how an aesthetics might look that didn't start with that, try Gentile's passionate (though often very obscure) *The philosophy of art*, trans. G. Gullace (Ithaca, NY: Cornell, 1953). For a contemporary example of how philosophy might look without that assumption try acquainting yourself with Merleau-Ponty, to whom Hammond, Howarth & Keat's *Under-*

131

standing phenomenology contains a good guide. Bernard Williams has traced many of the features of objectivism to Descartes in *Descartes: the project of pure enquiry* (London: Penguin, 1978). Sibley's work on objectivity is largely contained in "Colours", *Proceedings of the Aristotelian Society*, 1967–8, pp. 145–66 and (in a symposium with Michael Tanner) "Aesthetics and objectivity", *Proceedings of the Aristotelian Society*, supp. vol.42, 1968, pp. 31–54. Other useful essays are G. Sircello, "Subjectivity and justification in aesthetic judgements", *Journal of Aesthetics and Art Criticism* **27**, 1968–9, pp. 3–12 and, more advanced, David Wiggins's "A sensible subjectivism?", in his *Needs, values and truth* (Oxford: Oxford University Press, 1987), pp. 185–214.

   Sibley's remarks on criticism and its structure, which, so Nick MacAdoo tells me, have often been found of great use by practising teachers, can be distilled from the second, usually more neglected, half of his "Aesthetic concepts" and from his "The generality of critical reasons" in *Essays in aesthetics*, J. Fisher (ed.) (Philadelphia: Temple University Press 1983), pp. 3–20. The latter contains a full account and criticism of Beardsley's inductivism. Mention of Trotsky in the text leads me to commend his *Literature and revolution* (New York: Russell and Russell, 1957), if only for the vision of aesthetics in the redeemed classless society with which that work ends. My sketch of aesthetic judgement as a search for community is ultimately traceable to Stanley Cavell. A good way to begin a study of this very important and often very difficult writer is via Stephen Mulhall's splendidly achieved labour of love, *Stanley Cavell: philosophy's recognition of the ordinary* (Oxford: Clarendon, 1994). The introductory material to a series of essays dedicated to Cavell, T. Cohen, P. Guyer & H. Putnam (eds), *Pursuits of reason* (Lubbock: Texas Tech Press, 1993), gives further help. The essay in that volume by Ted Cohen "Some philosophy, in two parts" (pp. 385–401) argues directly that criticism goes with the notion of seeking community. In that essay he refers to an earlier essay along those lines, "Jokes" in Eva Schaper (ed.), *Pleasure, preference and value* (Cambridge: Cambridge University Press, 1983), pp. 137–57. Many of the articles in that book, for example John Macdowell's "Aesthetic value, objectivity and the fabric of the world", are germane, in a more advanced way, to the present topic. Ultimately some of the concerns in this chapter will link up with wider concerns that presently engage philosophers, of a kind to be found in Crispin Wright's *Truth and objectivity* (Cambridge, Massachusetts: Harvard University Press, 1992) and John McDowell's, *Mind and world* (Cambridge, Massachusetts: Harvard University Press, 1994).

Chapter 7

The empty tomb
and the resurrection
of the artist

In much of the foregoing I have spoken of artists as present in their works. I spoke of the way in which, in Picasso's *Nude dressing her hair*, one might admire the way the representation had so been arranged that each detail contributed to the overall effect. In something like Scorcese's *Casino* one might admire the judiciousness of the cutting, aware that different decisions would have produced a less impressive effect. In music one admires the artistry with which an effect is achieved, as when Helen Schlegel noticed the effect of the key change in the last movement of Beethoven's *Fifth Symphony*. We speak, too, as if an artist's qualities manifested themselves in the work: the distinctive irony in Jane Austen's novels, the mawkishness Dickens can show, the discrimination shown by Mozart in his development choices, the characteristic wit of Wilde, the scatological interest Swift and Picasso can display, the pretentiousness sometimes shown by Peter Greenaway.

What is so striking, given the familiarity and ubiquity of these ways of talking, is that virtually the whole of this century has been characterized by the attempt to eliminate any reference to the artist.

Today, as the century draws to an end, we still hear talk of "the death of the author" and, from Derrida, that the work is "cut off from any father", a remark reminiscent of Beardsley's and Wimsatt's remark that the literary work of art is "cut off from the author at birth".

Strategy

Attempts on the person of the artist vary. Some, Beardsley, Wimsatt, Barthes and Derrida, for example, attempt to show that reference to what an artist *intended* is not necessary when what is at issue is determining the meaning of a work of art. There is also, in Beardsley and Wimsatt, the more general attempt to show that no reference of *any* kind to an artist has any bearing on the critical *appreciation* of a work of art. If the latter thesis is true, the former will be true. For, if no reference to artists is legitimate, then no reference to their intentions is legitimate. Let us therefore begin by examining the general thesis.

Descartes

Over all these discussions, in both the Anglo-American and the continental European traditions, hovers the influence of Descartes. This influence interestingly differs in the two traditions. Beardsley and Wimsatt seem to subscribe to his world-picture and deduce the irrelevance of the artist from that, whereas stark opposition to that picture fuels the work of Derrida, Barthes and Foucault. I begin, therefore, with Descartes and what is called the "Cartesian" picture.

That picture posits two kinds of substances, the mental and the physical. Our bodies are modes of physical matter, our minds are modes of mental substance. Hence what is called "Cartesian dualism". Given that picture, how am I to know the mind of another? Whereas I can directly observe a body I cannot directly observe the mind that is yoked to it. The former is public, the latter private. The Cartesian account, therefore, gives rise to the vigorously debated problem of knowledge of other minds.

Dualism, and its attendant problem of the privacy of the mind, figures prominently in writings of Beardsley and Wimsatt, whose influential article "The intentional fallacy", and whose many subsequent writings, denied the relevance to criticism of knowledge of and reference to the creators of works of art. There we find an inclination to rule such references out because of a Cartesian-like belief that they involve a reference to the private and so unknowable mind of the artist. Thus Wimsatt writes:

> Let us say that an art work is something that emerges from the private, individual, dynamic, and intentionalistic realm of its maker's mind and personality . . . In the moment it emerges, it enters a public and in a certain clear sense an objective realm. (Wimsatt 1976, p. 131)

He talks of those critics who see the art work "as mainly a token of its source, a manifestation of something behind it, that is, the consciousness or personality of the artist" (*ibid.*,p. 117). Speaking jointly, Wimsatt and Beardsley speak of an intention as something "in the author's mind" (Beardsley & Wimsatt 1976, p. 4), a sentiment repeated by Beardsley in his book *Aesthetics* (Beardsley 1958, pp. 18–19).

In such utterances we find the view that there is a private place called "the mind", inhabited by the private mental life of an artist, which lies "behind" the public world of the work. The use of such spatial prepositions as "in" the mind, "behind" the "objective" world, and the use of terms like "private" show the grip of the Cartesian picture.

Having accepted such a picture, two approaches clearly tempted Beardsley and Wimsatt. The first lays stress on the notion of privacy. They were tempted to argue that although there is indeed a private, mental world, it can be known neither by the critic nor anyone else. Consequently what goes on there cannot be a consideration for interpreters and critics of literature. Hence they claimed that knowledge of intention is not "available".

But although there is an inclination to dismiss references to the artist's mind as unverifiable references to an unknowable entity, what we more often find in Beardsley's work is a second approach in which the argument rests not on the unknowable privacy of the mind but rather on the dualistic Cartesian picture of mind and body. I shall call this the "two-object argument". It runs thus:

> *P1: A work of art is one object, existing in a publicly observable way in an "external" world, whereas the intentions, emotions and more generally the mind of its creator, is another, entirely separate object, existing in another, separately existing "internal", private world.*

> *P2: It is self-evident that the proper object of study for those who study art is the work of art itself. If those who undertake this study divert attention to any other, discrete and different object, then they deviate into irrelevance.*

> *But, P3: The mind of the artist is a discrete and different object from the public work of art itself.*

> *So, C: To turn one's attention to that object is to divert one's attention away from the proper object of study, namely the public work of art itself. Hence, even if one can know about minds, and thus about the minds of artists, to refer to those minds is to deviate into irrelevance.*

Evidence that Beardsley subscribes to what I have called the two-object view is readily found. Thus, in his *Aesthetics*, having quoted a passage in which Edmund Wilson comments on a novel by Malraux, Beardsley comments: "The clauses in italics are about the novel, the rest about the novelist; and the paragraph passes from one to the other as though there were no change of subject" (Beardsley 1958, p. 19). More generally:

> In the case of aesthetic object and intention, we have direct evidence of each: we discover the nature of the object by looking, listening, reading, etc., and we discover the intention by biographical enquiry. But also, what we learn about the nature of the object itself is indirect evidence of what the artist intended it to be, and what we learn about the artist's intention is indirect evidence about what the object became. Thus, when we are concerned with the object itself, we should distinguish between internal and external evidence of its nature. Internal evidence is evidence from direct inspection of the object; external evi-

dence is evidence from the psychological and social background of the object, from which we may infer something about the object itself. (*ibid.*, p. 20)

This passage makes it clear that although work and artist are to be treated as discrete objects, inferences between them are possible. However, if the inference is from the artist to the work, then it is eliminable. For that inference will first have to ascertain some fact about the private mind of the artist and then infer from that that the publicly observable work has a certain publicly observable feature. If that is so, then the reference is eliminable. If the work indeed has the public property in question, it ought to be possible to detect that property in the work by direct inspection without firstly having to discover facts about the artist and inferring the presence of that property from them.

Suppose, alternatively, that the inference is from a perceived property of the work to some conclusion about the artist, as when one infers from *Hamlet* the presence of some mental perturbation present in its author at the time at which the play was written. In that case the inference to the artist is irrelevant to criticism (although, as Beardsley and Wimsatt noted, it may not be irrelevant to literary biography, "a legitimate and attractive study in itself" Beardsley & Wimsatt 1976, p. 10). For the inference has taken us away from what we should, as critics, be talking about, the public work of art itself, to something separate from that work, the private mind of its artist. This is to deviate into what is, from a critical point of view, irrelevant. Thus we have a proof that, if artist and work are discrete entities, between which inferences are possible, those inferences, and the knowledge of and reference to the artist that they presuppose, are either eliminable or irrelevant. Either way reference to the mind of the artist is otiose.

A certain view of the process of interpretation and criticism emerges from Beardsley's arguments. A work of art is a publicly observable object with publicly observable properties, some of which are relevant to its status as a work of art. The job of the interpreter, and critic is to establish the presence of such art-relevant properties. All that interpreter or critic needs to refer to in carrying out that job is the public work of art and its publicly observable properties. True, that work of art exists because it had a cause, that cause being the productive agency of an artist possessed of intentions, emotions and beliefs. But the cause is one thing, namely the private mind of the artist, the effect is another, to whit, a public work of art, and the effect can be studied independently of its cause. Thus Beardsley writes: "Literary works are self-sufficient entities, whose properties are decisive in checking interpretations and judgements. This is sometimes called the Principle of Autonomy" (Beardsley 1970, p. 16).

The artist-in-the-work

The two-object account derives support from the fact that, for many of the terms used in talking about works of art, we *can* make a distinction between using those terms of the work and using those terms of its creator.

Thus, take, first, such terms as "elegant", "delicate" and "graceful", as they might be used of the lines and colours of a painting. Our ability truly to assert that a painting, or a component of a painting, possesses one or other of these features rests not upon the discovery that its creator intended it to possess, or believed it to possess, such a feature, but upon an examination of the painting itself.

The same seems to apply to what might be called the "expressive" qualities of a work, as when we call a painting "cheerful" or a piece of music "sad". Again we can make a distinction between saying that a piece of music is sad and saying that its creator is, or was, sad. For it is not, as we saw in an earlier discussion of the composition of a *Requiem*, an essential precondition of something's being a sad piece of music that its composer had been sad when producing it. To discover that music sounds sad, we listen to the music.

To take a final example, to which we shall return for a lengthy discussion, we can distinguish between talking, on the one hand, about the meaning-properties of the words of a text and, on the other, about an authorial intention to mean something by those words. Beardsley writes (1958, p. 25), that we can ask two questions about any utterance, "(1) what does the speaker mean by those words? and (2) what do the words mean?". The latter is determined by examining the words of the work, utilizing what

Beardsley calls the "public conventions of usage that are tied up with the habit patterns in the whole speaking community" (*ibid.*) and which exist independently of the will of any particular speaker or author. So again the two-object account finds support. We can distinguish between asking about the meaning of the work of literature and about the meaning intended by the artist.

If the categories of terms so far mentioned embraced all the terms used in describing and praising art, then the demonstration that a general distinction exists between talking about artists and talking about properties of works, the two-object argument, would be complete. However, if other art-relevant terms exist, for which it is not true that we can always distinguish between the use of these terms to refer to works of art and their use to refer to the creators of those works, the argument fails.

Take, then, the following terms, which I shall call the "personal quality" terms, all of which I have taken from actual writings of critics about works from all branches of the arts: mature, intelligent, sensitive, perceptive, discriminating, witty, poised, precise, self-aware, ironic, controlled, courageous, simple-minded, shallow, diffuse, immature, self-indulgent, pretentious, gauche, glib, smug.

The problem for the two-object argument presented by these personal quality terms is that the question: "Is that term being used of the artist or of the work?" does not always admit a clear answer. When a novel is called "self-indulgent" and we are asked: "Is it the *novel* that is self-indulgent or the *novelist*?", we might refuse to choose. Instead we might claim that the reference is to some composite entity that we might call the-work-conceived-as-a-performance-of-its-creator, a performance in the public record of which the artist displays the quality in question. We are talking about an artist-in-the-work. *Lady Chatterley's lover*, if Wayne Booth's *Rhetoric of fiction* (1961) is right, manifests a pretentiousness. But the pretentiousness is Lawrence's pretentiousness as it is displayed there, in the novel.

We have found a set of critical terms that resists the two-object analysis. These are terms which, when used by the critic, involve a reference to the work that is inseparable from a reference to the creator of the work. Reference to the artist then becomes an integral part of criticism.

On Beardsley's account what I have called the personal quality terms will have to be given a two-object analysis. There will, for example, have to be one instance of, say, perceptivity, which will be a property directly discernible in the public work of art, reference to which implies no reference to any perceptivity possessed by the private mind of the artist. It is the task of the critic to concentrate on the instance of perceptivity present in the publicly observable work.

One clear way to show the coherence of this would be to show that it is possible for it to be true that a work is perceptive and false that its creator is. Such a demonstration would immediately subvert my contention that to say that a work is perceptive is necessarily to say that the artist there displays a perceptivity. Then, even for the personal quality terms, we could get rid of reference to the artist.

Isn't such a demonstration easy to give? For it is commonplace that sensitive and perceptive works can be produced by boorish artists. Think of the hostess who invites an author to dinner on the basis of the wit of that author's works, only to be treated to boring and egocentrically monopolizing displays of the writer's true mentality. In these cases the perceptivity of the work is distinguishable from the perceptivity of the artist. So the personal qualities of the work and the personal qualities of its creator seem easily distinguishable.

The argument is unconvincing. It is true that if a work has a certain personal quality, say perceptivity, then the inference that its creator has the disposition regularly and commonly to display that quality in life is a shaky one. But when I say that in calling a work of art "perceptive" we are referring to a perceptivity displayed *there* by its creator, I do not license any inference to the conclusion that the artist possesses a disposition regularly to display that quality. An artist may be perceptive only when writing or painting or composing. What I do assert is that whatever the artist's general disposition, that creator *there* displayed perceptivity, and that in calling the work "perceptive" I am referring to that performance. Thus, Leavis was right to claim in that Hardy's poem "After a journey" displays Hardy's sensitivity, and wrong to infer from that that Hardy could be expected generally to display that quality.

Imitation again

A more interesting approach is prefigured in a remark in the "The intentional fallacy". Beardsley and Wimsatt write:

> The meaning of a poem may certainly be a personal one, in the sense that a poem expresses a personality or state of soul rather than a physical object like an apple [sic]. But even a short lyric poem is dramatic, the response of a speaker (no matter how abstractly conceived) to a situation (no matter how universalized). We ought to impute the thoughts and attitudes of the poem immediately to the dramatic speaker, and if to the author at all, only by an act of biographical inference. (Beardsley & Wimsatt 1976, p. 5)

Given this account, the two-object view can be reinstated. The personal quality terms, when used of the public work, refer to a speaker *in* that public work. Their use in referring to that speaker can and must be distinguished from their use to refer to the artist.

Beardsley later developed from this a general attack on the tendency to identify the qualities of the speaker in the work with the qualities of the creator of the work. All those later developments rest ultimately on the view that the creation of works of art involves a kind of acting or imitation. Thus, in *The possibility of criticism* he says:

> The so-called "poetic use of language" is not a real use, but a make-believe use . . . The writing of a poem . . . is the creation of a fictional character performing a fictional illocutionary act. The utterance . . . takes on the character of being an appearance or a show of living language use. (Beardsley 1970, p. 59)

This is to say there is an analogy between what an author does in creating a literary work of art and what an actor, mimic or impersonator does. The work of art is an imitation, and we should no more assume that its properties, including its personal qualities, are those of the person doing the imitation than we should assume that the qualities of the French lieutenant's woman are the qualities of Meryl Streep.

Take, then, the case in which one person, the imitator, intention-ally exhibits behaviour characteristic of another person or thing, the imitated, and ask if we can construct upon this an argument for distinguishing between the personal qualities of the work itself (thought of as an imitation) and the personal qualities of its creator (thought of as the imitator).

Literature presents us with the strongest case for Beardsley's thesis, for there authors do, as Browning did, adopt voices. If the thesis fails to work there, we need go no further with it.

The first difficulty is a factual one. Beardsley would have us believe that in every work of literary art there is an intention to engage in imitation. Sometimes, as in Tennyson's "Northern farmer" or Browning's dramatic monologues, this is so. But not every literary work of art is like this. It is not obvious, for example, that Mrs Browning was intending to imitate an expression of love in her *Sonnets from the Portuguese*. The attempt to make it a defin-ing condition of something's being a work of art that its maker must have intended it as an imitation thus runs immediately foul of the fact that many artists who produced paradigm cases of art did not have such an intention. Van Gogh, I suspect, would vehemently have denied any intention to engage in some kind of imitative play. Henry Miller writes of his Tropic sequence: "The theme is myself, and the narrator, or the hero, as your critic puts it, is also myself . . . If he means the narrator, then it is me . . . . I don't use heroes, inci-dentally, nor do I write novels. I am the hero, and the book is myself" (cited in Booth 1961).

The second problem is the coherence of Beardsley's account. He asserts that all works of literary art are imitations. He asserts that when critics address themselves to works of art, they must focus only on the work itself and must not import into their activities any knowledge of the creator of the work or that creator's intentions. For: "It is not the interpreter's proper task . . . to draw our atten-tion off to psychological states of the author . . . His task is to keep our eye on textual meaning" (Beardsley 1970, p. 74).

Can one assert, without a knowledge of an artist's intention, that a work is an imitation and is to be appreciated accordingly? No. If I put on the radio and hear what appears to be a recording of the flutings of a nightingale, I have no way of knowing, just by attend-ing to the sounds themselves, whether or not this is an imitation.

To know that it is an imitation, and so to appreciate it properly, I have to know something that the sounds themselves cannot tell me, namely that they were or were not produced by a person with a certain intention. If I have only the sounds, I have no right to assert that they are an imitation. And, similarly, if my task is to attend only to the words of Elizabeth Barrett Browning's effusion that begins "How do I love thee? Let me count the ways", I have no right to assert that they are an imitation of someone lovelorn. To have that right I have to go away from the words themselves and find out something about the intention of their production. And this is just what Beardsley forbids me to do. On Beardsley's own account, a work of art is an imitation. In order, therefore, for me to know that, I must know the intention with which it is offered. But since, on his account, I am also forbidden to enquire into intention, it is not clear how I can know this.

The full and relevant critical description of a text can only be achieved with the aid of a knowledge of its surroundings, where this knowledge may include a knowledge of the intention with which it is offered. The clearest case is presented by ironic writings. It is possible to imagine Swift's *A modest proposal* to have been so convincingly done that, if all we had was a knowledge of the words of the text, we would be forced to take it as a genuine (albeit horrific) proposal. So to take it would be to misdescribe it. Truly described, and the description would have to refer to the intention with which it is offered, it is a piece of irony, and nothing that omitted reference to this fact could count as a proper and full description of it. This immediately falsifies the view that a full description of a text can be achieved without reference to the surroundings of that text, including a reference to the intention with which it was written.

But to see the fundamental incoherence of Beardsley's account we need to ponder on his remark that "the so-called 'poetic use of language' is not a real use". Behind this lies a comparison between what a writer does in producing a literary work of art and what the actor does in performing a role, where what is produced in the latter case is what Hamlet calls a "fiction" or "a dream of passion". Beardsley's claim is that in the literary work a character, a dramatic speaker, is imitated. Such characters may be described as turbulent, distracted, intelligent, crafty, noble, deranged, pretentious and so forth. The authors, actors or impersonators who produce simulacrums of such a character may indeed also be these things, but if they are, that is a coincidence that is of no interest to the critic. So, Beardsley says:

> Once we learn from the work itself the character of the speaker we can, if we wish, ask how similar he is to the author. When we ask, "Is *Stephen Hero* an autobiographical work?", we invite this comparison. But to compare Stephen Hero with Joyce is to compare two different people. (Beardsley 1958 p. 238)

So the two-object argument survives. To talk about the personal qualities of the work is to talk about those qualities of the imitated characters in it; and this can be distinguished from talking about its author.

A crucial observation now has to be made about imitation, a point obscured by Beardsley when he says that the poetic, that is the imitative, use of language is "not a real use". For although *what* is imitated need not be real, the act of imitation is a real act. Even though there is no real Watson who speaks to us in the Holmes stories, there is such a real thing as *A study in scarlet*. This is the deposit of a real act of someone's assuming the *persona* of Watson in order to present a literary work of art. From this follows the collapse of the imitation theory as support for the claim that reference to the creator of a work can be eliminated.

For real acts of imitation, can, like any actual performance, display the mental and personal qualities of their agents. They may be clumsy, clever, perceptive, glib, slick, ill-judged, subtle, brilliant, unfortunate, callous and the like. When these terms are applied to such performances, it is an agent's qualities in those performances and not the personal qualities of the imitated agent that is being judged. If, then, a novel is an imitation, it is a real act of imitation and invites the application to it of such terms. The referent of such terms is the author as displayed in that imitative performance. The notion of imitation, far from reducing the possibility of references to the creator of a work, has actually increased the scope for such references. If the work just is, as Beardsley says, an act of imitation, to talk about its qualities seems inevitably to be to talk about it as an act of its presenting agent.

It will not do to reply that one can always detect *in the work itself* evidence of its creator's ironic intention. Not only is this not self-evidently the case, for example where the imitation is particularly well achieved, but the reply concedes that authors are, contrary to the two-object argument, detectably and relevantly present in their works.

It is no help either to suggest that, perhaps, the qualities of the imitator as evidenced in the work are themselves the qualities of some further imitation. This falls foul, first of a danger of infinite regress. For the new imitation will itself be a real act with its personal qualities. Secondly, there is a more awkward difficulty for Beardsley in such a proposal. For some personal qualities cannot be imitated, if that means that the agent, although lacking such qualities, produces a successful imitation of someone who possesses them. For suppose the quality to be perceptivity. We are then asked to imagine that a writer lacking such a quality might produce a whole work that successfully imitates a perceptivity that writer does not possess; whereas such a performance would in fact establish that the writer actually did possess that quality and has manifested it in the work. Many of the mental personal qualities seem to have this property: they cannot be successfully imitated by producing a performance that actually displays them.

To summarize: if Beardsley is to use the notion of imitation to make a general distinction between referring to a work and referring to its creator, he has to do two things. Firstly, he has to establish that the imitated speaker in a work can be distinguished from the imitating speaker who creates the work; that is, he has to distinguish the speaker in the work from the speaker of the work. This he indeed does, using as an example the distinction between Conan Doyle, the creating speaker of the Holmes stories, and John Watson, the speaker in those works. This is a special case of the general fact that we can, in any imitation, distinguish between the qualities of what is imitated and the qualities possessed by the imitator. The imitation of the song of the nightingale may be mellifluous, but this is not true of the act of imitating it.

Given that we can distinguish, within the total act of imitation, both what is imitated and the imitating of it, Beardsley has, secondly, to show that the imitative work of art must be identified with only one of these, namely, with what is imitated: with the speaking voice of Watson for example. If he could do this, then given that the personal qualities of the author doing the imitating can be distinguished from the personal qualities of the imitated speaker, it would follow, from the facts firstly, that the work is identical with the imitated speaker and, secondly that the critic and interpreter must concentrate only on the work itself, that reference in criticism to the personal qualities of the author is irrelevant. The only reference to personal qualities that is possible is reference to the personal qualities of the imitated speaker.

It is, however, this second step, the identification of the total work of art with that component of the total act of imitation, which is the thing imitated, that is illegitimate. The proof is simple. If, to use Beardsley's example, we identify the Holmes stories with the imitated response of John Watson, who speaks them, then it follows that the personal qualities of John Watson are the personal qualities of the work itself: and since he is obtuse, slow, bluff and over-hearty, it would follow that the Holmes stories are obtuse, slow, bluff and over-hearty. Since this is absurd, it follows that the personal qualities of the work are not identical with those of the speaker in the work. They are, rather, the qualities of the other component in the total act of imitating, the imitating speaker: and who is that if it is not the creator of the work? (It is no use invoking, as Catherine Belsey does in her elegant reading of the Holmes stories, the fact that the presenting speaker shows evidence of a nonunitary mind, not always aware of what it is doing. That does not show we are wrong to refer to the artist's mind as present in the work. It shows only that we would be wrong in assuming any manifested mind must be a Cartesian unified one, always fully aware of what it is doing.)

Beardsley, then, quite clearly shows that the personal qualities of a speaker in a work cannot simply be attributed to its author. He offers no proof, however, that the personal qualities of the work are not those of its creator. He writes:

Clearly Conan Doyle's use of the word "I" in the Sherlock Holmes stories does not give this pronoun a reference to any actual person . . . Why, then, must we assume that when Keats or Shelley uses the pronoun he is always referring to himself? (Beardsley 1958, pp. 239–40)

The answer is, "We don't." When, in "The cloud", Shelley writes, "I bring fresh showers for the thirsting flowers", it would be a form of insanity to think that Shelley himself was claiming to do this. But when Shelley writes, in "Ode to the West Wind", "I fall upon the thorns of life, I bleed", then in the absence of any evidence of imitative or ironic intent, the responsibility for any emotional inadequacy expressed in the line rests with him. The difference is that in the first case we feel ourselves to be referring to a speaker in the work, in the second to the speaker of the work.

There is an important implication of this distinction between the speaker in the work and the speaker of the work. It is sometimes asked whether the correct way to respond to a work of fiction is by identification with a speaker in the work (so that one might try to see the way things are going from Lear's point of view) or whether one ought to take a spectator view, that is to make one's own response, which may be pity and sorrow for Lear (which is not incompatible with an adverse judgement of his behaviour). There is, that is, a choice between seeing or not seeing the work from within, or, as some have put it, between empathy and sympathy. If what I have said is correct, then an appraisal of the work requires one not to see it from within, or, even if one takes that viewpoint, not to remain there. For the evaluation of the work is the evaluation of it for the qualities that it has, and these are not identical with the qualities possessed by any speaker we might identify within it: nor are its judgements necessarily the judgements of any speaker in the work. To deny this is to fall into the absurdity displayed by the prosecutor in the trial of *Lady Chatterley's lover*, who was unable to distinguish between the behaviour of Constance Chatterley and the beliefs of Lawrence.

One loose end remains to be tidied up. I claimed that certain personal qualities of the artist, notably those exemplifying positive mental qualities, cannot be imitated. For I could imagine it being said that, even if these positive qualities are beyond pretence, negative personal qualities, such as mawkishness, pretentiousness, smugness and glibness are not. One *can* successfully pretend to have these kinds of qualities.

If someone does produce a work that successfully pretends to be mawkish, or pretentious, this is a successful act of imitation. However, it is then unclear that the work itself has these negative features. For the discovery of certain facts about such a work might entitle us to redescribe it more accurately as a brilliant parody of, say, a low-grade romantic novel. Our original claim that it is mawkish was, in fact, false: what it is is the successful imitation of a mawkish work. The imitated content of the work is mawkish: the work as the act of imitating mawkishness is not. Here we have another case, in which the correct description of a work requires us to know something about the way in which its creator conceived it.

To assert the foregoing is not to deny that an author may deliberately give a work the appearance of possessing defective personal qualities. This can be done as an act of imitation, which in turn may be undertaken for a variety of reasons; perhaps to make money out of a gullible reading public, perhaps to cock a snook at art. But although we may begin by attributing these defective qualities to the work, once the full story of the work is known, our description must be changed. We must stop thinking of it as a defective work with negative personal qualities and consider it instead as a more or less adequate imitation of such a defective work undertaken for this or that purpose.

There is an important corollary of this for criticism. If we are in genuine doubt as to whether a work is the brilliant pastiche of the display of a defective set of personal qualities or merely the really defective display of such a set, if, for example, we cannot determine whether a novel is the ravings of a chauvinist pig or the ironic representation of such ravings, criticism is stultified. We have cases, of course, where we have reason to believe that we are deliberately being left in doubt which way to take a work. But then we have reasons to believe that we know the intention and can judge the work accordingly.

Freedoms

There is a version of the argument about the legitimacy of references to the artist that focuses less on the possible relevance of such references and more on the question of their desirability. That argument seeks, rightly, to query the authority of the artist over the reader of the work.

Thus Beardsley and Wimsatt deny that what authors *say* about their finished works of art, and about their prior intentions in writing them have any special authority over the critic, interpreter or reader. For:

> The poem is not the critic's own and not the author's (it is detached from the author at birth and goes about the world beyond his power to intend or control it). What is said about the poem is subject to the same scrutiny as any statement in linguistics or the general science of psychology. . . . In Eliot's "The Love Song of J. Alfred Prufrock" . . . occurs the line: "I have heard the mermaids singing each to each", and this bears a certain resemblance to a line in a Song by John Donne, "Teach me to heare Mermaides singing", so that for the reader acquainted to a certain degree with Donne's poetry, the critical question arises: Is Eliot's line an allusion to Donne's? . . . There is . . . the way of biographical or genetic enquiry, in which, taking advantage of the fact that Eliot is still alive . . . the critic writes to Eliot and asks what he meant . . . Our point is that the answer to such an enquiry would have nothing to do with the poem "Prufrock"; it would not be a critical enquiry . . . Critical enquiries are not settled by consulting the oracle. (Beardsley & Wimsatt 1976, p. 5, 17–18)

Later Beardsley wrote:

> Of course we must admit that in many cases an author may be a good reader of his own poem, and he may help us to see things in it that we have overlooked. But at the same time, he is not necessarily the best reader of his poem, and indeed he misconstrues it when . . . his unconscious guides his pen more than his consciousness can admit. And if his report of what the poem was intended to mean conflicts with the evidence of the poem itself, we cannot allow him to make the poem mean what he wants it to mean, just by fiat. (Beardsley 1958, p. 26)

All this is true but gives no grounds for any general elimination of references to artists. Time and again writers in this area, in all traditions, confuse the claim that we can ignore what artists *say* about their works and the claim that we can ignore artists altogether.

151

Evidence that works exhibit personal qualities of their makers is tested by reference to the works. Their artists may not have intended and may not even know that this or that quality of their mind is exhibited there, no more than I may intend or know that my present remarks are trite and banal. But, for all that, these are qualities the artists show in the works. Further, even if statements by artists about their intentions are unreliable, it does not follow that reference to their intentions are irrelevant where that knowledge may come from other sources (including the work itself) than the artists' statements. As well argue that because politicians are often unreliable sources of information about their intentions, we should not try to discover and take into account what their intentions really are.

It is true, secondly, that artists may not be the best critics and interpreters of their works and may be mistaken as to what is important or significant about them. Composers, for example, are not always the best conductors of their compositions, and playwrights are generally not the best people to direct their own plays. Even if artists are right in believing that the features they intended to put in a work are indeed there, there is still the possible error of believing that the features one succeeded in putting in a work are its most important ones. Again, however, this, although it denies a special authority to the artist, does nothing to show the irrelevance of references to artists or their intentions. The evidence of the intention to be ironic may not be the professed statement of the intention of an ironist, but I need to know that that intention existed if I am properly to characterize the work. Again, artists may believe and assert that their work is perceptive when it is merely pretentious, but that does not stop the reference being to their pretentiousness as displayed in their work.

That we deny the authority of the author over the work does not entail that we have to deny a place for references to the author of a work. This may neatly be illustrated from Beardsley's and Wimsatt's own practical criticism. Both discuss the question whether Housman's Jubilee Ode "1887" is or is not ironic, given that Housman denied any ironic intention. Beardsley writes that Housman may not be the best reader of his poem and may misconstrue it "when his unconscious guides his pen more than his consciousness can admit" (Beardsley 1958, p. 26). But although that casts a doubt on the relevance of considering *statements* of intention, it does nothing to eliminate reference to intention (albeit unconscious). Wimsatt says of Housman's disavowal of ironic intention that "it stands in sharp contradiction not only to the cunning details of the poem in question but to the well known and sceptical cast of the poet's canon" (Wimsatt 1976, p. 131). Not only might we ask whose cunning and scepticism is being referred to, if not Housman's, but there is a clear implication that the "cunning details of the poem in question" are a better guide to Housman's intentions than his avowals are. And that is a strange proof of the irrelevance of references to authorial intentions.

There is, however, a different and more radical argument as to the desirability of ignoring artists in the work of Sartre, an argument, as we shall see, present also in the work of Barthes, Derrida and Foucault. Here the undesirability of referring to the artist is argued on the grounds that to give an artist authority is to undermine the *freedom* of the reader, viewer or listener. To allow the artist into criticism and interpretation is to give house room to a dictator. That the artist is thus conceived is easily established. Writing, disparagingly, of Mauriac, Sartre says that this novelist "is to his own creatures what God is to his . . . What he says about his characters is Gospel . . . The time has come to say that the novelist is not God" (Sartre 1955, p. 14).

The same image of the divine dictator is used by Barthes, Derrida and Foucault. For example, as we shall see in the next chapter Barthes asserts that "it is the language that speaks, not the author; we know that the text is not a line of words releasing a single 'theological' meaning (the 'message' of the Author-God)" (Barthes 1977, pp. 143, 146).

I spoke in Chapter 5 about a broad movement of twentieth century thought in which there is a rejection, in the interests of human liberty and fulfilment, of authority figures, including God, fathers, bosses, kings and even the ego that represses the id. The enthronement within the family of the father as God curtails the free development of the children, so that the throne must be toppled. The owner of the means of production is the God over the workforce who alienates them from their labour. He too must go. Kings inhibit the full development of the free life of their subjects and must be overthrown. And God, too, must die that his people can take to themselves the responsibilities for their own lives. So Nietzsche wrote: "Who is the great dragon which the spirit no longer wishes to call Lord and God? The great dragon is called 'Thou shalt'. But the spirit of the lion says 'I will!'" (Nietzsche 1961, p. 55).

The philosophers of the arts can now add their contribution. The artist, conceived as a god, a dictator over the work, must go the way of all gods and all dictators. Then the reader, viewer or listener is turned free by the literary theorist as, for Nietzsche, for example, the religious believer was turned free by the death of God. The death of the author, Barthes asserted, is the birth of the reader (1977, p. 148). Artists, too, joined in. Hence, as we saw, Cage's *4'33"*, which requires an instrumentalist to sit doing nothing for that length of time, thus eliminating the composer as a kind of dictator who tells the musicians what to play, and the conductor as what Cage calls a kind of "policeman". One should, he writes, "give up the desire to control sound, clear his mind of music and set about discovering means to let sounds be themselves rather than man-made theories or expressions of human sentiments" (Cage 1966, p. 10). For traditional music:

> . . . controls a human being [giving] the alarming aspect of a Frankenstein monster. This situation is of course characteristic of Western music, the masterpieces of which are the most frightening examples, which when concerned with human communication only move over from Frankenstein monster to dictator. (*ibid.*, p76)

Does the passion for liberty justify the conclusion that reference to the artist in the work ought to be eliminated? Here the question is not whether the attempt by artists to dictate to their audiences how their works are to be taken is wrong. To show that such attempts are wrong we need only to see, as Beardsley and Wimsatt point out, that artists are not necessarily the best authority on their works. The question is whether reference to artists as they show themselves in works entails a subordination to any dictatorial inclinations that they may possess. I doubt that it does.

I have argued that artists show themselves in those works which it is the task of critics to characterize and judge. This fact, in a sense, does indeed put a restriction on the critic. For if critics are properly to characterize works they cannot say whatever they want. That restriction on freedom is not one to which Sartre is in any position to object. For consider the following statement he makes in talking about literature:

> The literary subject has no other substance than the reader's subjectivity; Raskolnikov's waiting is my waiting which I lend him. Without this impatience of the reader he would remain only a collection of signs ... On the other hand the words are there like traps to arouse our feelings and to reflect them towards us. Each word has a path of transcendence; it shapes our feelings, names them, attributes to them an imaginary personage who takes it upon himself to live them for us and who has no other substance than these borrowed passions. (Sartre 1950, pp. 31–2)

This passage makes it clear that readers are *not* absolutely free, when reading, to make what they wish of a work. There are elements in works of art, for example, words, colour patches and sounds, that work on readers,viewers and listeners, which shape their feelings and responses, and which dictate how the work should be characterized. To characterize the work according to the dictates of the elements in it is to say what is true about it. The fact that we must be true to what is in the work does not constitute an illegitimate limitation of our freedom. How could it? What worthwhile freedom is it that would require us to shut our eyes to the truth about a thing? But, now, I have argued that the mind of the artist is there in the work, as much as any word, sound or colour patch. And if my freedom is not improperly circumscribed by a recognition of such elements in the work as words, notes and colours, which shape my response to the work, it is not illegitimately circumscribed by the recognition that the elements of the work include qualities that the author displays in it.

Moreover, it simply does not follow from the fact that I recognize authors in their works, that I have to take those authors at their own estimation. Indeed I may, as a free reader, be a better judge of the qualities displayed by an author in the work than is that very author. Samuel Johnson believed himself to have found Shakespeare's faults in Shakespeare's plays, faults on the presence of which Shakespeare was not the best authority. But he could do so only because he was free, having made the free choice to attend to the work, to say what is true about it. To ignore the artist's dictates about the work is not to ignore the artist in the work.

Sartre would be on stronger ground if he could argue, as Beardsley and Wimsatt are inclined to argue, that the artist is not detectably present in the work. For then the artist would come upon the scene only as a possibly dictatorial commentator. But he argues the exact opposite. On his account the work is the residue of a set of choices which itself shows the artist's hand. So for example, making the time span of a novel a day, rather than an hour or a minute, is a choice made by the artist, and in making that choice the artist shows him or herself and is present to us in the work. Here is a crucial passage.

In giving up the fiction of the omniscient narrator, we have assumed the obligation of suppressing the intermediaries between the reader and the subjectivities – the viewpoints of our characters. It is a matter of having him enter into their minds as into a windmill. He must coincide successively with each one of them. We have learned from Joyce to look for a second kind of realism, the raw realism of subjectivity without mediation or distance. Which leads us to profess a third realism, that of temporality. Indeed, if without mediation we plunge the reader into a consciousness, if we refuse him all means of surveying the whole, then the time of this consciousness must be imposed upon him without abridgement. If I pack six months into a single page, the reader jumps out of the book. This last aspect raises difficulties that none of us has resolved and that are perhaps partially insoluble, for it is neither possible nor desirable to limit all novels to the story of a single day. Even if one should resign oneself to that, the fact would remain that devoting a book to twenty four hours rather than to one, or to an hour rather than to a minute, implies the intervention of the author and a transcendent choice. (Sartre 1950, p. 229)

If artists are thus inevitably in the work the only threat to our freedom comes from those who would forbid us to refer to them, and that is an offence not merely against freedom but against truth-telling.

So far, we have found no argument for the general death of the artist, where that means the elimination from criticism of all references to them. That, however, leaves the possibility that some less general claim might be true. An example would be the claim that whatever the relevance of references to the personal qualities of artists, references to their *intentions* can at least be excluded when we are interested in the *meaning* of their words. I deal with the extraordinary ramifications of that claim in my next chapter.

Guide to reading

Details of writings in the continental tradition will be given in the next chapter, which largely deals with them. Beardsley & Wimsatt's "The intentional fallacy", to be found in D. Newton de Molina (ed.), *On authorial intention* (Edinburgh: Edinburgh University Press, 1976), is the seminal article that, in 1946, started things off. It is however, not the best introduction, being unduly rambling and discursive. Better is Beardsley's *Aesthetics* (New York: Harcourt Brace & World, 1958). His later thoughts are to be found in *The possibility of criticism* (Detroit: Wayne State University Press, 1970). This contains a stormy rejoinder to Frank Cioffi's now classic "Intention and interpretation in criticism" reprinted in a very good collection of material in C. Barrett (ed.), *Collected papers in aesthetics* (Oxford: Blackwell, 1965). Wimsatt separately published "Genesis: a fallacy revisited", to be found in the Newton de Molina volume. One of their targets is E. D. Hirsch's *Validity in interpretation* (New Haven, Yale: Conneticut University Press, 1967). The most up-to-date thing in this still flourishing field is G. Iseminger's much praised collection of new essays entitled *Intention and interpretation* (Philadelphia: Temple, 1992) which is thoroughly discussed by G. Dickie & W. Kent Wilson, "The intentional fallacy: defending Beardsiey", *The Journal of Aesthetics and Art Criticism*, **53**(3) 1995, pp. 233–50. Catherine Belsey's interesting remarks on the Sherlock Holmes stories are to be found in her *Critical practice* (London: Methuen 1966). The remarks by

Sartre are dealt with in a splendid and accessible discussion in W. J. Harvey, *Character and the novel* (London: Chatto and Windus, 1965). Much of that is related to the equally important discussions of the inexcludability of authors in Wayne Booth's highly informative, tightly reasoned and highly readable *The rhetoric of fiction*, 2nd edn (London: Penguin, 1991).

Chapter 8

The structures of the self-sufficient word

I shall look at three sources of the claim that the intentions of artists are irrelevant to the determination of the meaning of their works. These are: Beardsley and Wimsatt, whose article "The intentional fallacy" began Anglo-American debate; structuralism; and the poststructuralism of Derrida.

Beardsley and Wimsatt

This is the view to which Beardsley and Wimsatt, Barthes and Derrida are opposed:

> Almost any word sequence can, under the conventions of language, legitimately represent more than one complex of meaning . . . A determinate meaning requires a determining will . . . Verbal meaning is whatever someone has willed to convey by a particular sequence of linguistic signs. (Hirsch 1967, pp. 250, 266)

Against this Beardsley writes: "It is not the interpreter's proper task, then . . . to draw our attention off to the psychological states of the author" (Beardsley 1970, p. 34).

In a similar vein Barthes writes that "it is the language that speaks, not the author" (Barthes 1977, p. 143). This, as we shall see, is a thought that will be more fully exploited in the writings of Derrida.

All objections to any attempt to assert a connection between meaning and intention implicitly oppose Cartesianism. The Cartesian philosopher, we saw, maintains that there are two kinds of substance: the mental and the physical. With this goes a certain view of language. There are, on the one hand, physical entities, for example, sounds and ink marks. Of themselves these are merely brute and mute elements of physical reality. If they have a meaning, it is because behind them lies a mind that wills meaning onto them and dictates that they shall have that meaning. Wittgenstein, much of whose later philosophy undermines this view, characterizes it thus:

> We are tempted to think that the action of language consists of two parts; an inorganic part, the handling of signs, and an organic part, which we may call . . . meaning them . . . These latter activities seem to take place in a queer kind of medium, the mind. (Wittgenstein 1958, p. 3)

The Cartesian mind might be said to "transcend" the physical, in the sense that the physical world does not contain it and, additionally, in the sense that it gives the physical world any meaning that it might have. When, as they often do, Derrida, Barthes and Sartre attack the notion of the transcendent self, they are attacking this Cartesian self, which as meaning-giver to the world, can also be described, as they often describe it, as a kind of God or sovereign or father who dictates a meaning to things.

The anti-Cartesian argument used by Beardsley, by structuralists and by poststructuralists, demonstrates that the attempt to link meaning to an intending Cartesian mind would make communication impossible. This crucial central argument can be explained by reference to the procedures of an arch-Cartesian in the field of meaning-determination, Lewis Carroll's Humpty

Dumpty. At the conclusion of a more than usually specious piece of reasoning, Humpty Dumpty remarks, "There's glory for you!".

"I don't know what you mean by 'glory,'" Alice said.
Humpty Dumpty smiled contemptuously. "Of course you don't –
till I tell you. I meant 'there's a nice knock-down argument for you!'"
"But 'glory' doesn't mean 'a nice knock-down argument'," Alice objected.
"When *I* use a word," Humpty Dumpty said, in a rather scornful tone, "it means just what I choose it to mean – neither more nor less". (Carroll, *Through the looking glass*, Chapter 6)

Humpty Dumpty's attitude is Cartesian. A speaker wills a meaning onto otherwise meaningless marks or sounds.

This is incoherent. Suppose the speaker wills onto the sound or mark "glory" the meaning "a nice knock-down argument". How is the speaker to make it clear what he has done here? For suppose Alice had asked, "And what do you mean by the marks or sounds 'nice knock-down argument'?". On his own account the speaker will have, by a further act of will to intend a further meaning, say "dog", onto those marks or sounds. But then he can be asked, "and what do you mean by that mark or sound?". There are two possible outcomes. One is an infinite regress of intentional acts of meaning-assignment, so that that meaning is never assigned. The other is that the regress ends with the speaker appealing to public meaning-giving structures of syntax and semantics, and that is to give up the claim that the speaker's will determines meaning.

Beardsley and structuralists agreed in their belief in a meaning-determining structure of public rules. Beardsley is emphatic that a text has a determinate meaning, but is equally emphatic that a determinate meaning does not require a determining will. Instead, the determinate meaning of an utterance is readable by anyone possessed of a knowledge of the structure of rules of meaning and grammar in the public language. That is also a structuralist claim. Hence the similarities between Beardsley's assertion that "it is in its language that a poem happens. That is why the language is the object of our attention and of our study when its meaning is difficult to understand" (1970, p. 34) and Barthes's claim that "It is the language that speaks, not the author".

So the meaning of a text depends upon a structure of rules of grammar and meaning and not upon the will of an author.

Central to Beardsley's argument is the belief that any words used by a writer have a meaning independently of that writer's will. Whoever uses a word uses it as already having a meaning, a meaning it had before its speaker was born, and which it will still retain when the speaker is dead. If I wish to know the meaning of a word I do not understand in a poem, I go to the dictionary of these public uses. Beardsley further asserts that when individual words are combined together, using public grammatical rules, a further "textual meaning" emerges. We can determine this emergent textual meaning without reference to authorial intention. "Textual meaning", he asserts, "is not reducible to authorial meaning". For the question, "What does a sentence or combination of sentences mean?" is not the same as the question, "What did a speaker mean by that combination of words or sentences?" (Beardsley 1958, p. 21). The meaning of a sentence, or a combination of sentences, in a text can be determinate or unambiguous and that determinate meaning can be known without appeal to an intention to mean something determinate by it. It is the structure of rules of meaning and grammar that determine the meaning of utterances, not the utterer's intentions.

What of ambiguity? If my remarks are ambiguous don't you have to ask me what I meant in order to understand me? Beardsley writes: "An ambiguous text does not become any less ambiguous because the author wills one of its possible meanings. Will as he will he cannot will away ambiguity" (Beardsley 1970, p. 29).

The argument here is this: suppose a form of words, to take Beardsley's example, "I like my secretary better than my wife" could be used to say either that I like my secretary better than my wife does or that I prefer my secretary to my wife. It would be a mistake to believe that in such cases one can make this set of words mean one of these things rather than the other, by some prior act of intention. For it is a condition of having such an intention that one be able to represent one's intended meaning to oneself. This presumably means bringing before one's mind a form of words that does have the meaning one wishes to express. This cannot be "I like my secretary better than my wife", for that is the very phrase whose meaning is indeterminate. Whatever phrase one does bring before one's mind, if it has a determinate meaning, one must immediately concede the impossibility of willing this as the meaning of the ambiguous phrase with which one began. For that original phrase was genuinely and in its own right indeterminate in meaning, whereas the one before one's mind is not. How, then, can the latter be willed as the meaning of the former? Thus Beardsley says that "an ambiguous text does not become less ambiguous because its author wills one of its possible meanings".

So when the meaning of an utterance is determinate, what gives it its determinacy is not the intention of its speaker but the structure of rules of grammar and meaning of the public language. And when the meaning of an utterance is indeterminate, it is so by those public rules and no intention of its utterer can make it anything else. From this it seems to follow that the intentions of writers are irrelevant to questions about textual meaning.

I begin my reply to this argument by noting something said by Beardsley and Wimsatt in "The intentional fallacy":

> One must ask how the critic expects to get an answer to the question about intention . . . If the poet succeeded in doing it, then the poem itself shows what he was trying to do. And if the poet did not succeed, then the poem is not adequate evidence, and the critic must go outside the poem – for evidence of an intention that did not become effective in the poem. (Beardsley & Wimsatt 1976, p. 4)

This looks contrary to the conclusion of the argument I have just outlined. For the way that Beardsley and Wimsatt put the matter suggests that when a speaker succeeds in saying something determinate, it is possible to see *in* that utterance an intention to say some particular determinate thing. For "the poem itself shows what he was trying to do". This is connected to a curious passage from Wimsatt's "Genesis: a fallacy revisited" in which he offers, in words that, coming from so determined an opponent of the reference to authorial intentions, have a certain piquancy, the following gloss on the intention behind "The intentional fallacy":

What we meant, and what in effect I think we managed to say, was that the closest one could ever get to the artist's intending or meaning mind outside his work would still be short of his effective intention or operative mind as it appears in the work itself and can be read from the work. (Wimsatt 1976, p. 136)

This passage concedes that it is possible to see the artist's intention in the work, and, read in conjunction with the passage I have quoted from "The intentional fallacy", in fact supports the intentionalist view that if we can grasp the determinate meaning of a work, it is because the utterer of the work makes clear to us in that work precisely what he or she is saying.

An intention is embedded in public activities and is recognized by seeing it embodied there. What is true of intentions, say to run for President, is true also of intentions to say something. They may show themselves in behaviour in such a way as to make it entirely clear to us what a speaker or writer intends to say. And when that happens we have determinate meaning. Indeed the possibility of determinate, communicated meaning depends on the possibility of recognitions of publicly displayed intentions.

To be sure, our ability to have intentions is bound up with our possession of a language in which we can represent our intentions to ourselves. This is why I can intend or hope to do something the week after next whereas a cat cannot. And this is why I can directly express my intentions in language, whereas a cat can, through its behaviour, at best only give us evidence on the basis of which to ascribe intentions to it. But from the fact that there has to be a pre-existent language if I am to have and express intentions it does not follow that my utterances in that language can be determinate without my intentions being manifested in those utterances.

Hirsch claimed, then, that: "A determinate meaning requires a determining will ... Verbal meaning is whatever someone has willed to convey by a particular sequence of linguistic signs and that can be conveyed (shared) by means of those linguistic signs" (Hirsch 1967, pp. 250, 266).

If this means that what makes an utterance determinate in meaning is a prior, Cartesian, private act of intending that meaning, this is defeated by the arguments that defeat Humpty Dumpty. If, however, it means that where we find a determinate meaning in an utterance it is because we see in that utterance the intention of its speaker to say a certain determinate thing, then not only have Beardsley and Wimsatt offered nothing to refute that claim, but their claim to have been interested in "operative" intentions seems actually to assent to it.

One is not required, I should add, to believe that the meaning of an utterance is exhausted by what its utterer successfully intended to say. There is more in any work of art than any maker could have intended. Reading Wordsworth will be affected by what happens subsequently, and the whole lesson of some of the best feminist criticism is that the significance of a work may emerge as something rather different from what its maker could have supposed. (It need not be the case, as some have argued, that the work changes in the light of changes in the cultural world that receives it. It may more plausibly be supposed that a greater awareness, brought about by these cultural changes, allows us better to see the work as it is.) Further, some elements of a work, for example its symbols, may have a richness that even its creator could not fully explicate. Moby Dick, the white whale, was as inexhaustibly mysterious a symbol to Melville as it is to us. But from the fact that there may be more in a poem than its creator could have known, it does not follow that what that creator meant to say cannot be or become obvious to us.

The structuralist model: Barthes's dead author

The arguments to which I now turn have some of their origins in the work of the Belgian linguistic scientist Ferdinand de Saussure. I begin with a borrowing from de Saussure by structuralists.

What de Saussure calls *la parole* is the total corpus of all actual written and spoken utterances. Some will be grammatical, some not; some will make sense, some will not. Underlying this corpus of utterance-episodes lies *la langue*, a structure of rules by which readers and listeners understand the meaning and decide upon the grammaticality of the actual utterances that they encounter. This structure of rules is transpersonal. The individual speaker enters into it at birth and it continues after any speaker dies. Given possession of the structure of rules, rules that specify the contributions that elements, such as words, can make to complexes of elements, such as sentences, we can assign a determinate emergent overall meaning to utterances.

It seems inexorably to follow that reference to the author of a literary work is unnecessary, if our purpose is to understand the meaning of a work of literature. The author issues that work to the world. But the reader brings to these words a set of rules governing the meaning of these words and their combination into utterances. These rules are the common possession of all who speak or read the language. These rules, possessed by readers, are the source of any meaning that a text has. Reference, therefore, to the author as a source of authority over the meaning of the text drops out. "The death of the author," Barthes writes, really "is the birth of the reader".

This model transcended the linguistic, in some narrow sense, to become a tool for understanding social life in all its forms. Social life is made up of meaningful episodes, and thus shares a property, meaningfulness, with language. Meaning is given to these episodes, too, by structures of meaning-giving rules. In order to see that an event is a wedding, it is necessary to understand the rules constitutive of weddings. Visitors from another culture, unacquainted with these rules, simply could not understand the meaning of what is going on. To understand the elements of social life, either within a culture or, as with myths, across a culture, is to understand the rules that give these elements their meaning. It was to the discovery of the meaning-giving structure underlying the complex web of myths across all cultures that Lévi-Strauss devoted much of his life.

The structuralist model of meaning has another implication. It casts doubt on the possibility of transcendental Cartesian individual consciousnesses that, from some point outside language and culture, give languages and culture their meaning. Rather than being the transcendental producer of meaning for a structure of words or other meaningful items, any consciousness is itself a product of such structures. For, whatever concept we have of a person, what we mean when we use that term is determined by that subset of the transpersonal rules of language which assign that term a meaning. This immediately establishes the impossibility of consciousnesses that somehow give meaning to language from some mysterious point transcendent to language. The term "I" is a function of the public, transpersonal, meaning-giving rules for that item of the language. Moreover those rules may change and with them the concept of a person. This is why Lévi-Strauss said that the "goal of human sciences is not to constitute man [by which he meant Cartesian man] but to dissolve him" (Lévi-Strauss 1962, p. 326) a project central to the work of Foucault. The corollary of all this is that artists are not individual transcendent consciousnesses that give meaning to their products. There are only the words of those products, given meaning, as are the artists themselves, by transpersonal meaning-giving structures. So Derrida can assert: "The subject . . . is inscribed in language, is a 'function' of language, becomes a speaking subject only by making its speech conform . . . to the system of rules of language" (Derrida 1981a, p. 15).

The structuralist account is one of a closed, underlying structure that is mechanically operated to give an effective procedure for the assignment of a determinate meaning. This notion, in a way that Derrida was to exploit, fails, however, to allow for the creative openness that is an essential feature of language.

Suppose I have learned the word "deep", according to the rules of the meaning-giving structures of my language, to talk of oceans and certain ponds. One day I simply say, "I felt the slight deeply". What is more, no-one seems confused or surprised by this, although I have gone beyond the rules I have learned for the use of the word "deep". So it is throughout the daily life of our talking: feelings are deep, people feel blue, notes are high or low, music is sad, and so on.

Cavell wrote:

> We learn and teach words in certain contexts, and then we are expected, and expect others, to be able to project them into further contexts. Nothing ensures that this projection will take place (in particular not the grasping of universals nor the grasping of books of rules), just as nothing will ensure that we will make, and understand, the same projections. (Cavell 1968, pp. 160–1)

This is to say that our use of language is essentially creative, and, indeed, unless it were so, it would not be a use of language. It is one thing to learn a phrase book for a foreign language so as to produce phrases like "my postilion has been struck by lightning" by rote, and another to speak a language. This is why a computer that can merely apply the rules with which it has been programmed cannot speak and why computers have such difficulty translating poetry, where the creative projection of language is especially marked.

One would have expected those who use de Saussure as their inspiration to have noted that he was well aware of the possibility that I am canvassing. He writes:

> Whoever creates a language controls it only so long as it is not in circulation; from the moment when it fulfils its mission and becomes the property of everyone, control is lost . . . A man proposing a fixed language that posterity would have to accept for what it is would be like a hen hatching a duck's egg: the language created by him would be borne along, willy-nilly by the current that engulfs all languages. (de Saussure 1959, p. 76)

This openness and projectability casts doubt on the elimination of the subject who speaks. A language would not be a language unless individual human beings constantly projected their words into new situations in ways that could not be anticipated merely by a knowledge of the rules in operation at a particular time. If the structuralist dismissal of the author depends upon the truth of the claim that it is the structure of the rules of the language that is important and not the individuals that operate them, then that dismissal is ill-founded. Indeed it would render speaking a language impossible.

Here I wish to observe that even what was appropriated from de Saussure by anti-authorial structuralists was selectively appropriated. De Saussure offered a distinction between *la parole*, the total corpus of actual speech episodes, and *la langue*, a structure of rules that underlay these episodes. The structuralist adopts this distinction but then concentrates only on *la langue*. If attention is thus focused on *la langue*, then there will be a temptation to ignore the individual consciousness, for *la langue* is the transpersonal structure of rules into which individuals are born and that survives the death of any one of them. But only an already decided determination to eliminate authors and all other individual consciousnesses could begin to explain the total attention given to *la langue* and the total indifference to *la parole*. Both are integral to de Saussure's account, and necessarily so. He writes, in a passage ignored by those who wish to use his account to substitute the impersonal structures of *la langue* for the humanly impregnated activity of speaking:

> Within the total phenomenon represented by speech we first singled out two parts: language and speaking. Language is speech less speaking. It is the whole set of linguistic habits that allow a speaker to understand and to be understood . . . But this definition still leaves language outside its social context; it makes language something artificial since it only includes the individual part of reality; for the actualization of language, a community of speakers is necessary. Contrary to all appearances, language never exists apart from the social fact . . . Its social nature is one of its inner characteristics. Its complete definition confronts us with two inseparable entities . . . Under the conditions described language is not living – it only has potential life. (*ibid.*, p. 76)

There is human language, speaking and writing, only if the rules of *la langue* are applied (and creatively applied) by individual acts of individual speakers (*la parole*), just as there are only football matches if the rules of soccer are put into effect in individual games in which individual creativity is shown. *La langue* needs *la parole* if it is to become concrete in actual utterances (including actual works of literature). But once we admit this necessity, individual consciousnesses, no matter how structured they may be by their culture, are inescapably involved in acts of language, including works of literature. No one saw this more clearly than Maurice Merleau-Ponty. Noun and verb, he agreed, may only be allowed by the rules to combine in certain ways to form grammatical sentences. But they are only combined into sentences when someone actually speaks. "Between the noun and the verb", as he put it, "lies the gap that each person who speaks and writes must leap" (Merleau-Ponty 1960, p. 30). In our capacities to project words, in ways that the system of rules could never allow us to predict, lies the possible of our freely transcending the otherwise determining structures into which we are born.

Poststructuralism

We have followed a progression of thought which begins with Beardsley and Wimsatt asserting the possibility of determinacy of meaning but denying that what gives an utterance its determinacy is the intentions of individual consciousness. Determinate meaning, rather, is possible because of structures of rules of grammar and meaning. That view is shared by structuralists. They have, however, a deeper scepticism, which we do not find in Beardsley and Wimsatt, about the existence of individual meaning-determining consciousnesses. This supports the notion that determinacy depends on the existence of structures of rules of grammar and meaning. For, in the absence of a determining consciousness, what else could give utterances determinate meaning? The next stage in this progression occurs because, just as determinacy is not given to an utterance by an individual act of willing, neither is a determinate meaning guaranteed by the existence of structures of rules of grammar and meaning, for those rules could not close down the openness of our language. But now what seems to follow is the impossibility of determinacy of meaning. Where would it come from? Not from the individual acts of willing a determinate meaning and not from structures of rules of meaning and grammar. Since these seemed the only possibilities, the conclusion seems to follow that determinacy is not to be had at all.

Such an argument for indeterminacy is powerfully evidenced in the writings of Derrida.

The first premise

Firstly, like many of his predecessors, Derrida subscribes to the premise that the intention of a transcendent Cartesian individual consciousness cannot determine meaning:

> It remains to the sign to be legible, even if the moment of its production is irredeemably lost, and even if I do not know what its alleged author-scriptor meant consciously and intentionally at the moment he wrote it, that is, abandoned it to its essential drifting. (Derrida 1981a, p. 317)

Derrida has a familiar argument, cryptically expressed, for his claim that intention cannot determine meaning. He says, first, that "my death is structurally necessary to the pronouncing of the I", then adds:

> As soon as I speak, the words I have found . . . no longer belong to me . . . Henceforth, what is called the speaking subject is no longer the person himself . . . The speaking subject discovers his irreducible secondarity, his origin that is already eluded; for the origin is always already eluded on the basis of an organized field of speech in which the speaking subject vainly seeks a place that is always missing. This organized field . . . is . . . the cultural field from which I must draw my words and syntax. (Derrida 1978, pp. 177–8)

If I am to articulate myself as a consciousness, I need to be able say things like "I am tired" or "I am in pain". My sense of myself, and the feelings, beliefs, experiences, memories and awarenesses that give me my sense of myself, can be articulated only if they can be thus articulated in the assembled elements of discourse. Suppose we ask how these utterances get their meaning. It would be absurd to suppose, for reasons already given, that, by an act of intention, I can give these utterances a meaning they would not otherwise have. That Cartesian picture would have us believe that we bring some physical and mute sound or mark before the mind and will a meaning on it. But if I am to do this, I have to bring before my mind the meaning that I am going to will on the mark or sound. To do that I will have to bring before my mind some set of words with the meaning I want the mute marks to have. How do these words get their meaning? By some further act of willing? And so on in an infinite regress? We are forced to the conclusion that if these words have a meaning, they have it independently of my willing. Hence, the very word "I", by which the pure consciousness is to express its self-awareness, is a sound or mark like any other in the language and I lose authority over what that means. The "I" ceases to be a pure consciousness standing behind language and becomes enmeshed with, and dependent for its meaning upon, the very language that it was meant to illuminate. Rather than being the giver of meaning to language it takes any meaning it may have from language. So Derrida writes: "The subject . . . is inscribed in language, is a "function" of language, becomes a speaking subject only by making its speech conform . . . to the system of rules of language as a system of differences" (Derrida 1981a, p. 15).

This lies behind Derrida's assertion that "my death is structurally necessary to the pronouncing of the I". "My death" here refers to vanishing of myself conceived as a pure Cartesian ego. That pure ego cannot give the word "I" its meaning. To be able to pronounce the word "I" and mean something by it, something other than the pure ego must give that word meaning. This can only be the language itself. This is why Derrida remarks that "the subject becomes a speaking subject only in commerce with the system of linguistic differences" (Derrida 1981a, p. 16).

The elimination of the pure consciousness is, of course, welcomed by Derrida, for, like many we have encountered, he conceives this Cartesian ego as a dictator, of a piece with an all-powerful God or a dictatorial father, seeking to impose its meaning on things. "One could say", Derrida writes, "that the 'speaking subject' is the *father* of his speech" and that to give such a speaker authority over the meaning of words is to "tie speech . . . to the master and lord". "Parricide" is needed, he writes, to open "the play of difference and writing" (Derrida 1981b, pp. 77, 164). Freed from dictatorial fiats about the meaning of the words, released from the "author God" who wills that we read words a certain way, we are at liberty to read them as we will. Then we will find in the words that confront us "the affirmation of a world of signs without fault, without truth, without origin, offered to the active interpretation" (Derrida 1978, p. 292). So, too, we have the notion of the sovereign author as a God to be deposed, so that "no transcendent truth present outside the sphere of writing can theologically command the field".

A text is on its own. Beardsley and Wimsatt wrote in "The intentional fallacy" that "the poem is not the critic's own and not the author's (it is detached from the author at birth and goes about the world beyond his power to intend or control it)" (1976, p. 3). In very much the same language Derrida writes:

> To write is to produce a mark which constitutes in its turn a kind of productive mechanism, which my absence will not . . . prevent from functioning and provoking reading . . . For writing to be writing it must continue to act and be readable even if

what we call the author of the writing be provisionally absent or no longer uphold what he has written, what he appears to have signed ... This situation of the writer or underwriter is, with respect to the writing fundamentally the same as that of the reader. This essential drift ... a structure cut off from any absolute responsibility, orphaned and separated since birth from the support of the father, is indeed what Plato condemned in the *Pheaedrus*. (Derrida 1981a, p. 316)

The second premise

The second premise of the argument for indeterminacy of meaning is that no structure of rules of grammar and meaning determine or close down the meaning of an utterance. "What I can never understand in structure", Derrida writes, "is that by means of which it is not closed" (Derrida 1978, p. 160). Of such a mark as a word he writes: "no context can enclose it. Nor can any code" (Derrida 1981a, p. 317). It is to Derrida, indeed, that we owe the most powerful image of the shortcomings of the notion that to investigate a work is to investigate the structures that determine it, an investigation that, as Stuart Sim demonstrates, can descend to a mathematical dryness in which the life of the work dies. Derrida aptly compares these probings to investigation of a city from which all life has fled leaving only its dead structures behind (Derrida 1978, p. 11).

Rules, then, do not cover every eventuality. Wittgenstein, whose work has been illuminatingly compared with Derrida's by Henry Staten (1985), noticed the same thing:

I say "There is a chair". What if I go up to it, meaning to fetch it, and it suddenly disappears from sight? – "So it wasn't a chair, but some kind of illusion". – But in a few moments we see it again and are able to touch it and so on. – "So the chair was there after all and its disappearance was some kind of illusion." But suppose that after a time it disappears again – or seems to disappear. What are we to say now? Have we rules ready for such cases – rules saying whether one may use the word "chair" to include this kind of thing? But do we miss them when we use the word "chair"; and are we really to say that we do not attach any meaning to this word, because we are not equipped with rules for every possible application of it? (Wittgenstein 1953, para.80)

But Derrida gives a further reason for asserting the openness of language and the inability of rules to determine and confine its meaning which is distinctively his own and that, again, owes something to de Saussure.

Consider chess. Understanding this game does not consist in knowing what the pieces stand for, but in understanding the different roles the pieces have and how they combine to form a system that is the game of chess. So, too, language is understood not by asking what its units stand for but by understanding the difference that using this linguistic unit rather than that would make. De Saussure writes: "Just as the game of chess consists entirely in the combination of the different chess pieces, language is characterized as a system based entirely on the opposition of its concrete units" (de Saussure 1959, p. 107).

"In language", de Saussure writes, "everything boils down to differences". A term acquires its value as a separate element of language "only because it stands in opposition to everything that precedes and follows it". Thus "boat" is different from "coat" only because the substitution of the latter for the former in the sentence "I bought a boat" makes a difference. Of the two signs "father" and "mother" he writes:

> Between them there is only *opposition*. The entire mechanism of language . . . is based on oppositions of this kind and on the phonic and conceptual differences that they imply . . . When isolated, neither *Nacht* nor *Nächte* is anything: thus everything is in opposition . . . Language, in a manner of speaking, is a type of algebra . . . Some of its oppositions are more significant than others; but units and grammatical facts are only different names for designating diverse aspects of the same general fact: the functioning of linguistic oppositions. (*ibid.*, p. 121–2)

How this might work in practice is described thus by de Saussure:

Modern French *mouton* can have the same signification as English *sheep* but not the same value, and this for several reasons, particularly because in speaking of a piece of meat ready to be served on the table, English uses *mutton* and not *sheep*. The difference in value between *sheep* and *mutton* is due to the fact that *sheep* has beside it a second term while the French word does not . . The value of a French plural does not coincide with that of a Sanskrit plural although their signification is usually identical; Sanskrit has three numbers instead of two ... It would be wrong to attribute the same value to the plural in Sanskrit and in French; its value clearly depends on what is outside and around it. (*ibid.*, p. 115–16)

So there emerges the notion of a system of differences, where the value of a linguistic unit is a function of its place in the system and the difference it makes to the utterances in which it appears. "Boat" has a different value from "coat" because substitution of the one for the other makes a difference. Users of language, in using "boat" must be implicitly aware, if they have mastered the language, of the possibility of using "coat" instead of "boat" and of the difference this would make. "Coat", we may say, leaves a trace in the implicit awareness of the user of the word "boat".

Derrida often expresses a commitment to de Saussure's analysis:

The *arbitrary character of the sign* and the *differential character* of the sign . . . There can be arbitrariness only because the system of signs is constituted solely by differences in terms and not by their plenitude . . . The elements of signification function due . . . to the network of oppositions that distinguishes them and then relates the one to another ... Every concept is inscribed in a chain or in a system within which it refers to the other, to other concepts by means of the systematic play of differences. (Derrida 1981a, pp. 10–11)

Now consider something that, for Derrida, undermines the notion of any closure to the openness and indeterminacy of meaning. "Boat" means something different from "coat" because the substitution of the one for the other in an utterance makes a difference. But it is not only the substitution of the word "coat" for

175

"boat" that makes a difference: similar effects would be produced by substituting for "coat" the words "moat", "groat", "map" and indeed any other word of the language. Hence the meaning of each word is bound up with the meaning of all other words and the meaning of all other words remains as a trace within any word of the language. Derrida writes: "Each element appearing on the scene of presence, is related to something other than itself, thereby keeping within itself the mark of the past element, and already letting itself be vitiated by the mark of its relation to the future event" (Derrida 1981a, p. 12).

The task of plotting the infinite play of these traces can never be completed, and hence every interpretation is provisional. Every word is implicated with every other word. Every combination of or relation of meaning is implicit in every text. Hence Derrida's remark that "words . . . communicate with the totality of the lexicon through their syntactic play" (Derrida 1981b, p. 129). Interpretation is not, therefore, a matter of finding *the* meaning of the text, but of taking part in and enjoying the infinite play of meanings in a text. (Puns, of course, have a special interest in this activity, autonomously and playfully reminding us of unlikely connections.) The outcome, in Derrida's words, is that in the absence of determinate meaning the traditional project of criticism, that was "to determine a meaning through a text, to pronounce a decision on it, to decide that this or that *is* a meaning" (*ibid.*, p. 245), cannot be accomplished: "the life of the signifier is produced within the anxiety and the wandering of language always richer than knowledge, the language always capable of movement that takes it further than peaceful and sedentary certitude" (Derrida 1978, pp. 72–3).

"Writing is read . . . and does not give rise to a hermeneutic deciphering, to the decoding or a meaning or truth". All we are left with is "the limitlessness of play" (Derrida 1981a, p. 329).

The conclusion

Two assertions, that neither the will nor the rules of language determine meaning, become premises that entail, for Derrida, a denial of the possibility of determinacy of meaning. Thus the absence of a determining will "abandons language to its essential drifting" (1981a, p. 317).

This belief in the indeterminacy of meaning is not to be lamented but celebrated in a Nietzschian vision of "the joyous affirmation of the play of the world and the innocence of becoming, the affirmation of a world of signs without fault, without truth, and without origin that is offered to the active interpretation" (Derrida 1978, p. 292).

In that interpretation we do not seek the meaning. For that "play of signifying references" never ends in a determinate meaning but "substitutes incessant deciphering for the unveiling of truth". The absence of the transcendental will "extends the domain and play of signification infinitely" (*ibid.*, p. 280).

Queries

I am struck by the fact that in Derrida's writing there is, on the one hand, the dramatic assertion that sweeps away much that we would unthinkingly accept as sheer common sense. On the other hand there is a subtext, which if read carefully leaves common sense intact and purges only some philosophical error. In the present case the dramatic assertion is that determinacy is not to be had. We are enmeshed in a play of words, each echoing every other word, that prevents any determinacy of meaning. The absence of a determining will "extends the domain and play of signification infinitely". There is a *limitlessness* of play. There are "calculations without end", "incessant deciphering", "wanderings of the semantic" and "there is no centre that arrests and grounds the play of substitutions" (Derrida 1978, p. 289). "Writing", in short, "does not give rise to a decoding of a meaning or truth" (Derrida 1981a, p. 329).

Such a view commits its holder to a scepticism about communication, where communication is a matter of understanding what someone wants to say, which in its turn seems to require us to grasp a determinate meaning in an utterance. That scepticism surfaces in Derrida's writing, notably in "Signature event context" in *Margins* where he speaks of "a general displacement" after which "writing would no longer be a species of communication". He speaks, too, of "my non-presence in general, for example, the non-presence of my meaning, of my intention-to-signify, of my wanting-to-communicate-this, from the emission or production of the mark" and goes on to speak of

the break with the horizon of communication as the communication of consciousnesses or presences, and as the linguistics or semantic transport of meaning . . . the disqualification of . . . the concept of the "real" or "linguistic" context, whose theoretical determination . . . is strictly speaking rendered impossible or insufficient by writing. (Derrida 1981a, p. 316)

In sum, "writing is . . . not the means of transport of sense, the exchange of intentions and meanings". It is a corollary of this that critical interpretation cannot be the task of determining the meaning of a text, for Derrida talks of "the impossibility of reducing the text as such to its effects of meaning, content, thesis or theme", and queries that notion of criticism that "tries to determine a meaning through a text" (Derrida 1981b, pp. 7, 245).

These apocalyptic passages seem radically to subvert all our assumptions about the possibility of communicating meaning in our day-to-day dealings one with another. And yet, this is arguably not Derrida's intention.

Firstly, there is, throughout Derrida's writing on the philosophers to whom he stands in opposition, a commitment to the view that one can and must, prior to any criticism, accurately represent what is said in those texts. True, this may be a prelude to showing by a close examination of the texts (by what is called "deconstruction") that those who wrote them had blind spots that led them to attempt, unsuccessfully, to exclude certain possibilities, but that deconstruction requires one truly to record what is in those texts. Here contrary forces in Derrida surface. On the one hand he tells us that when he uses terms like "Rousseau", "Hegel" or whatever, no reference is intended to the bearers of these proper names:

"The names of authors or doctrines have no substantial value. They indicate neither identities nor causes. It would be frivolous to think that 'Descartes', 'Leibniz', 'Rousseau', etc., are names of authors" (Derrida 1976, p. 99).

In practice, however, a different picture emerges. Thus we read:

As to Descartes in particular, no historical question about him – about the latent historical meaning of his discourse, about its place in a total structure – can be answered before a rigorous and exhaustive external analysis of his manifest intentions. (Derrida 1976, p. 99)

The following passage is deeply significant for it seems to say that there *is* something identifiable as the determinable authorial meaning of the text (even though the author might not be the best judge what it is) that has to be identified before critical work can be performed:

> The writer writes in a language and in a logic whose proper system, laws, and life his discourse by definition cannot dominate absolutely. He uses them only by letting himself, after a fashion and up to a point, be governed by the system. And the reading must always aim at a certain relationship, unperceived by the writer, between what he commands and what he does not command of the pattern of the language he uses. To produce this signifying structure obviously cannot consist of reproducing, by the effaced and respectful doubling of commentary, the conscious, voluntary, intentional relationship that the writer institutes in his exchanges with the history to which he belongs thanks to the element of language. This moment of doubling commentary should doubtless have its place in a critical reading. To recognize and respect all its classical exigencies is not easy and requires all the instruments of traditional criticism. Without this recognition and this respect, critical production would risk developing in any direction at all and authorize itself to say almost anything. (*ibid.*, p. 158)

This, I might say, is utterly reminiscent of, and possibly derivative from, Kant's view that the free play of the imagination is not uncontrolled by the object of its attention. If this is so, then we are not at liberty to play as we will with the words of that text.

Secondly, having argued for a disappearance of intention and an indeterminacy of meaning, Derrida writes:

> I will not conclude. . . that there is no relative specificity of the effects of consciousness, of the effects of speech . . . no effect of ordinary language, no effect of presence . . . It is simply that these effects do not exclude what is generally opposed to them. (Derrida 1981a, p. 327)

This passage seems to concede that we can, in our day to day dealings with others, make our meanings clear, and again dilutes what I have called the more apocalyptic claim that the determinacy necessary for communication is impossible.

If Derrida allows communication, it is appropriate to ask what makes possible that understanding of another's meaning that communication requires. Here it is tempting to think that when we understand the meaning of an utterance we do so by recognizing in it the intention, whether the speaker knew it or not, of that speaker to say some particular thing. That reply would not be available to Derrida, if what I have called his first premise severs the link between meaning and intention. But the premise did *not* do that, and I am not sure that Derrida meant it to. What the premise establishes is that meaning cannot be willed onto an utterance by an intention conceived as a private event in a transcendent *Cartesian* consciousness. That is incoherent. But this would be a demonstration of the lack of connection between meaning and intention only if the dualistic picture of a Cartesian consciousness were the only possible picture of the connection between meaning and intention, mind and the world.

I have argued that this is not the only picture. I sketched a view of the mind and its beliefs, emotions and intentions, as visible *in* the public world, visible *in* the acts, including the speech acts, of agents. Such a view was also expressed by Wittgenstein when, in Part II of the *Investigations*, he spoke of the human body as the best picture of the human soul. We are not obliged to think of minds as detached from the world and the bodies in it. We could think of the mind, and this would be to think of the great contribution of Merleau-Ponty, as embodied and visible.

Here again I note a tension in Derrida's writing between an apocalyptic claim and a subtext that subverts its force. Derrida takes as his target the Cartesian or Husserlian transcendental consciousness. Such a consciousness is conceived as standing apart from the words of a language upon which it imposes a meaning by an act of will, this being an emblem, and possibly the root, of all the forms of repression that have disfigured human history. Thus he remarks that his attack on this transcendental consciousness is part of an "analysis of totalitarianism in all its forms" (Derrida 1986, pp. 242–3). Arguments that undermine the claim that a transcendent consciousness can will a meaning onto mute signs seem to me to be unanswerable, from which it follows that the concept of a transcendent Cartesian consciousness is also incoherent. It is then fatally easy to mistake this for the more sensational claim that individual consciousnesses as such have been eliminated.

This is what can lead to the suspicion that there is something anti-humanistic in Derrida's writing. He can seem to have a jaundiced view of individual consciousnesses. "Henceforth, what is called the speaking subject is no longer the person himself". "One may imagine a consciousness without man". "Polysemia puts us outside humanity". "Responsibility and individuality are values that can no longer predominate here". "Play . . . tries to pass beyond man and humanism" (Derrida 1978, p. 162).

Yet, carefully read, this is not the intention of Derrida's work. He states, equally emphatically, "I have never said that there is no subject" (Derrida 1978, p. 292). What he does claim is rather different and, stripped of its rhetoric, rather unsurprising. For, closely read, the claim is not that there are no persons, but that Cartesianism cannot give a good account of them. That, however, would count as a general scepticism about persons only if Derrida could be shown to think that Cartesianism is the only possible account of persons. This he does not believe. He remarks that he is opposed "above all to the thingification of the subject, of the subjectivity of the subject as supposed by Descartes" (Derrida 1989, p. 15). That unites Derrida with Wittgenstein and Gilbert Ryle, both of whom resist the notion of the mind as a strange kind of *thing*, existing, apart from the body, in some queer kind of space. But to resist that notion is not to be committed to saying that the mind is nothing at all. "It is not a something," Wittgenstein remarked, "but it is not a nothing either" (1953, para.304). That may also be Derrida's view. He writes "the category of intention will not disappear; it will have its place, but from this place it will not be able to govern the entire scene and the entire system of utterances" (Derrida 1981a, p. 326). And I, too, have tried to sketch an account of intention that will make it relevant to refer to art without giving the artist the last authoritative word.

As to what would be a more adequate account of mind than that offered by Descartes, Derrida is less clear. I have spoken of the need to avoid dualism and to think of the mind as visible in the actions and words of human beings. Derrida too, has a view of the human mind as spread out in the words and actions of a human life. When he says that "the person writing is inscribed within a determined textual system", we can read that as a way of saying that we do not stand dualistically apart from our words, but show ourselves in them as we manipulate their pre-established meanings.

Derrida writes: "thus one comes to posit presence . . . no longer as the absolutely central form of being but as a determination and an effect. A determination or effect within a system which is no longer that of presence but of difference" (Derrida 1981a, p. 16).

Our existence, that is, is not conducted in the silent room of the disembodied mind but manifested in language, by whose effects it is known to others, perhaps better known than the agent might acknowledge. That, though, looks remarkably like the claim that the authors are not the last authority on their creations, since that created work can tell us more about them than they might know. But that is entirely compatible with a belief that writers and other artists can, to use Derrida's own term, "manifest" themselves in their works.

Postscript

The most striking example of the compatibility between the accounts that Derrida gives of the death of the (Cartesian) author and a reading of texts that pays the most scrupulous attention to the immanent authorial meaning of a text, is to be found in the reading that Derrida gives to the controversial articles written by Paul de Man in Nazi-occupied Belgium. I add that this reading seems to me to exemplify a humane process of literary interpretation in the sense that it respects the person of the immanent writer and is determined neither to conceal the truth about the text nor to lack compassion in its treatment of its writer as revealed in the textually manifested mind.

Paul de Man, a deeply loved and extraordinarily influential Yale scholar, with whom Derrida, a detester of all things totalitarian and fascist, was on the closest of terms, was discovered, shortly after his death, to have written, as a young man, a series of allegedly anti-semitic articles for a collaborationalist newspaper in occupied Belgium.

Derrida's overriding concern is to read what there is to be seen in the articles, having no time for those who in a shoot-from-the-hip witch-hunt forgot "the elementary rules of reading and philological integrity". He begins with a statement that gives the lie to anyone who thinks that his procedure is obliged to deny authorship. "Nothing permits us to imagine that the editorial was written by anyone other than the journal's editor, that is by Paul de Man". It continues with a testament to the need for respect to the text as the best evidence, regardless of its writer's opinions, for the state of mind of its author. So we must begin "precisely by listening, to try to hear what he said to us, him, de Man, already" (Derrida 1986, p. 239). What follows is a sensitive reconstruction of what the texts tell us about the manifest state of mind of their writer.

I am not concerned with whether that account is or is not correct so much as with the governing presupposition of the method that is deployed. That method traces the windings of an immanent mind. It utterly gives the lie to the belief that Derrida's beliefs commit him to ruling out a consideration of (and for) the creators of works of art as he or she is manifested in the work, or, as Derrida put it elsewhere, as they are is "inscribed in the language". That, too, is all I have wished to argue.

At the end of *Memoires for Paul de Man* Derrida responds to those who have read his work as anti-humanistic and anti-rational. Certain things he has said might seem to support the view that he is both of these things. He writes of reason as a "dictator" and of the "jailer" that is "classical reasoning" (Derrida 1986, pp. 36, 37). He speaks of trying to "pass beyond man and humanism" (*ibid.*, p. 292) and says that it is possible to "imagine a consciousness without man" (Derrida 1981a, p. 118). It is, however, possible to read this in a more charitable way. It is possible to use the terms "reason" and "humanism" as sledgehammer words never subjected to critical examination. But it is possible to ask whether the culture to which we belong, what Derrida calls "Western culture", with its "white mythology", a culture that is supposed to exemplify the cardinal virtues of rationality and humanism, has lived up to the demands implicit in the notions of rationality and humanism. Then it might emerge that what we proudly claim as our tradition of rationality in fact excludes large tracts of the human race, women, for example, from it. The humanism that is so proudly thought to underlie European civilization turns out to be compatible with a penchant for committing obscene atrocities.

Then one might want to ask whether there might not be buried in our ways of thought something that has to be purged in order to create a better humanism and a better understanding of rationality. One might ask this, not in order to abolish these notions, but in order to replace their debased forms in a corrupt culture with better ones. Hence it seems entirely proper for Derrida to ask of his more careless critics, few of whom display qualities of rationality and humanism in their invective:

> Why the charge of irrationalism as soon as any one asks a question about reason, its forms, its history, its mutations? Or the charge of anti-humanism with the first question put to the essence of man and the construction of the concept? . . . To what order are we being recalled by the sinister disciplinary counsels with their gravely intoned litanies . . . and the most brutal disregard of the elementary rules of discussion . . . (I mean differentiated reading or listening to the other, argumentation, analysis, proof). (Derrida 1986, p. 259)

The task is to restore "against a certain humanism, a profound humanism". That humanism will not be a humanism that represents the human as a Cartesian transcendental consciousness, confident in its total self-understanding. That idealized picture is less able than Derrida's alternative to account for "the windings and twistings of fear and desire, weakness and lust, sadism and masochism, and the will to power, in the mind of even the most sincere man" (Staten 1985, pp. 126–7). But it does not follow from the shortcomings of Cartesianism that there are no human beings, nor that these human beings cannot make themselves manifest in their works of art, nor even that the meaning we give those works has some relation to what their authors, knowing or unknowingly, said in them. That is to say that the artist lives still.

Guide to reading

Beardsley and Wimsatt's contributions are covered in my last chapter. The problem with Barthes is that he goes through many different stages to be classified as simply a structuralist. Structuralism is best approached obliquely, therefore. One good start is to read Stuart Sim's "Structuralism and post-structuralism" in Hanfling's *Philosophical aesthetics*. This should give a pretty clear indication of why analyses of literary structure seemed to Derrida like the explorations of the structures of a lifeless and abandoned city. Then it is worth reading at least the early parts of Jonathan Culler's *Structuralist poetics* (London: Routledge and Kegan Paul, 1975), and his *Barthes* (London: Fontana, 1983). There is also useful material to be extracted from pp. 918–86 of Harrison & Wood's *Art in theory*, especially an instructive piece by another sceptic about authors, Foucault. Those reading this material should point out to those careless enough to say that structuralists abolished authors that Barthes (p. 944) allows the author in "as a guest" (that is, as subject to the reader's judgement). Who could object to that? Foucault's windings about on this matter are well worth scrutiny in the Harrison & Wood extract. What, given that not anything goes (see p. 928), does he think about the relevance of references to authors? And could those who claim that *poststructuralists* also abolished authors have explained to them (a) that to abolish authors as Cartesians conceive them is not to abolish authors *per se* and (b) those passages I have quoted from Derrida that acknowledge authors and intentions as immanent in texts. (But then it is easier to waffle about Derrida than to read him.) For a panacea to waffle see the deliciously cool and aptly titled R. Tallis, *Not Saussure* (London: Macmillan, 1988).

That brings me to Derrida. Again the challenge is formidable and best approached obliquely. Start with Sim and with Christopher Norris, *Deconstruction: theory and practice* (London: Methuen, 1982), which is very short and, some obscurities apart, pretty clear. (Norris has also written *Derrida* (London: Fontana, 1987).) Bear in mind that Derrida is first and foremost a philosopher (though one who is also a critic and who has also influenced criticism). Part of his task is negative: to expose a tendency, running through the whole of Western philosophy, and surfacing in the most unlikely places, to posit a dualism and then elevate one term of it (man–woman, is an obvious case). This is shown by deconstructing texts in such a way as to make them own up to their own privileging deficiencies. A nice account of the utility of this for feminist criticism is given in the remarks on Derrida in T. Moi, *Sexual textual politics*

(London: Routledge, 1988). The other part of Derrida's work is an attempt to say what a better view of things might be (a frustrating task for one who thinks that communication of definite meaning has something suspect about it). Some Derrida is accessible: parts of *Margins*, for example, "Signature event context" and the *Memoires for Paul de Man*. The rest though is, I fear, a matter of chipping away a bit at a time and letting the light gradually dawn. I hope my exegesis, even if limited to a particular theme, will at least give some pointers. A important figure sympathetic to Derrida is Richard Rorty: you will find his essay, "Philosophy as a kind of writing", *New Literary History*, X(1) 1978–9, pp. 141–60 some help. I also enjoyed Hilary Putnam's fastidious engagement with Derrida's thought in *Renewing philosophy* (Cambridge, Massachusetts: Harvard University Press, 1992). A journalistic, unreliable but riveting read about the Paul de Man affair is David Lehman's *Signs of the times* (London: Deutsch, 1991). In a very demanding book H. Staten has illuminatingly compared *Wittgenstein and Derrida* (Oxford: Blackwell, 1985).

Chapter 9

Helen's Beethoven:
truth and morality

Helen pushed her way out during the applause. She desired to be alone. The music had summed up to her all that had happened or could happen in her career. She read it as a tangible statement, which could never be superseded. The notes meant this and that to her, and they could have no other meaning, and life could have no other meaning. She pushed right out of the building, and walked slowly down the outside staircase, breathing the autumnal air, and then she strolled home.

Helen Schlegel, in Forster's *Howards End*, says that Beethoven's music is important because he got something right. Here are some other cases where appraisal appears to be affected by considerations of truth and morality.

An obviously old but beautifully clear black and white film begins with a propeller-driven aircraft flying over a city. So begins what some think a masterpiece of the cinema: Leni Riefenstahl's *The triumph of the will*. Then we realize that this film contains no obvious condemnation of the Nuremberg Rallies that it meticulously records. Some will find appraisal affected by this.

David Mamet's *Oleanna* seemed to some of those who took part in the various fights that broke out during its performance to be the worse for the wrong message it contained, a similar sentiment being expressed by those who heckle the end of *The taming of the shrew*. Think, too, of the way the tradition of male painting of female nudes has come to seem suspect.

There is widespread evidence, in these kinds of responses made to works of art, of a belief that the value of a work of art can be in some way related to our opinions about the truth or falsity of the beliefs and attitudes articulated in it. Moreover, since such attitudes are often characterized using such moral terms as "offensive", "repugnant", "noble" or whatever, considerations about the relevance of truth to artistic value tow in their wake considerations about the relevance of the morality to that question.

I have to say, straight off, that I do not see how in the case of at least some of the arts, notably the arts of narrative fiction, such as the novel and the drama, in which the doings of characters interact, we can avoid the entanglement of art with morality. For first, there is the simple point that even to understand a work involving human interaction we cannot put aside whatever we understand of morality. How else could the novels of Jane Austen even be understood?

Moreover, whatever understanding of morality that we bring to a work may affect the quality of our understanding. This is simply a particular instance of the general truth that our preconceptions can affect our characterizations of people and events. (Consider, here, the widespread assumption that all Scots are near with money.) If, and this is a matter for moral philosophers to decide, it is possible to have erroneous moral views, then they can cause us to misunderstand works in which moral situations occur. Thus we might imagine those who have philosophized themselves into the belief that morality always progresses, so that moralities of past ages are always in some ways less satisfactory than our own. Such people may mischaracterize the situation in, say, Edith Wharton's *The age of innocence* through believing that the morality of old New York society *must* have been less liberating than a newer, and so more advanced morality, that puts personal happiness before duty. A second case would be one in which one's moral inadequacies prevent one from characterizing and appreciating a work aright. A case here might be someone overdosed on Baden-Powell who simply cannot see the xenophobia implicit in the Biggles works of Captain W. E. Johns. More complex perhaps is the case of someone taken in by Othello's presuicide self-justification. Any critic, determined to impose his own views of Christian redemptive tragedy on that play, is simply bound to get it wrong. And if one can get morality right, then one might claim to see the moral inadequacies lurking in even the greatest of works, because one is free enough of *those* inadequacies. An example here, upon which I pass no judgement, might be the way in which Leavis, for all that he finds Swift a writer of magnificent force, can none the less observe that this is a negative force, one in which the channels of life, as Leavis puts it, are blocked and perverted.

These are ways in which one's moral understanding impinges upon one's understanding and characterization of works of art. What we have to explore is how relevant this is to the judgements of works of art as art. For some have claimed that although we can make moral judgements about what happens in works of art, that is not aesthetic judgement.

Certain aspects of this matter will not concern me. Thus someone might think (indeed has thought) that *The naked Maja* is a magnificent work of art and yet doubt on moral grounds that it ought to be displayed where it will cause offence. What is being judged morally here is not the painting but the decision as to whether or not to hang it.

Nor shall I directly discuss questions about pornography or obscenity, questions, that is, about what makes things obscene or pornographic and questions about whether things that are these things should be available and, if so, to whom. If what I shall say is right, the judgement that a painting is pornographic or obscene, as opposed to erotic, does not stop it being art but does count against it when its artistic value is being weighed. The question whether, it being pornographic or obscene, the work should be allowed out in public, is not one for aesthetics.

A final preliminary: if we are looking for a way of understanding the importance of art, the relevance of truth and morality to art is a promising area to investigate. Not only are truth and morality central to our lives, so any art involved with them inherits some of this centrality, but in addition we persistently find the claim that art is in some important and special way a path to truth and understanding. The opposite, too, has been believed. Plato thought that the power of art to get people to believe false things to the detriment of themselves and society was so great that story-telling poets and representational painters were to be expelled from his ideal republic.

Report and reflection statements

There are two classes of problems about truth and morality, the division between which can be displayed by adopting Beardsley's distinction between report statements and reflection statements, that is, between the statements that create or occur *in* the world of a work of art and statements made *by* a work of art. The former includes assertions uttered by characters but not obviously endorsed or rejected by the work itself, as when Hamlet says "Denmark's a prison". It also contains statements that establish the world of the work, as when we are told that Superman is allergic to Kryptonite. Such statements may be fictional ("Titania fell out with Oberon"), factual ("Corfu is crowded in summer"), or a mix of both, as when we are told that Perdita (who does not exist) was abandoned on the sea coast (which it may not have had) of Bohemia (which most certainly exists, being the first country beaten by England at soccer on a continental tour). The reflection statements include any statements made or implied by the work itself, as when it is claimed that the works of Beckett express the thought that life is on the whole meaningless.

Although my interest is in reflection statements, completeness requires a little to be said about the report statements and the possible bearing of their truth-value on assessments of art.

Report statements

About these there are various matters more or less worth mentioning.

The truth-value of fictional statements

Suppose I read, "Mr Pickwick was fat". There being no such person, is what I say true or false? This is a problem for two sorts of people. One is the sort that believes that the meaning of a word is what is stands for. They have some explaining to do, for since "Mr Pickwick" stands for nothing, "Mr Pickwick is fat" has to be meaningless, which is absurd. The other is those who think that a statement must be either true or false with no third alternative. They have to explain, as Russell tried to do with the Theory of Definite Descriptions, what the status is of "Mr Pickwick is fat", since it seems to be neither clearly true nor clearly false. These are not questions for aesthetics but for the theory of meaning.

A reminder

To be sure there are questions, touched on earlier, which are more puzzling, about how we are able to engage imaginatively with fictions and respond to them with the appropriate emotions when we know that the objects of fictions do not exist. Here I refer the reader to that earlier discussion.

Report statements and appreciation

More interesting is whether the ways in which report statements can go wrong or go right bear on appreciation of a work of art.

An artist can simply get the facts wrong. Ignorance can lead to a painting of a salmon heading up stream at the wrong time of year. The Bond novels, celebrated for their factual detail, are often misinformed. In *On Her Majesty's secret service* someone is killed by being thrown onto a bobsleigh track and skinned by friction on the way down. It couldn't happen.

If there is something wrong with getting it wrong it is simply because its being wrong can interfere with one's entering imaginatively into a work. Whether such interference actually occurs is always relative to a state of knowledge. Someone ignorant of salmon fishing or friction may simply not notice, and so not be affected by, such errors. Even where something is factually wrong, as in the anatomical articulation of a depicted figure, that will be condoned if anatomical accuracy is subverted for expressive effect, as in Parmigiano's *Madonna of the long neck*.

191

Plausibility

Talking about novels or pictorial representations, even fictional ones, we happily use "plausible", "implausible", "true to life", "unrealistic", "improbable" and the like. There are difficulties in making the test here whether the representation matches reality.

If the representation is fictional, for example a novelistic representation of Mr Pickwick or a pictorial representation of Snoopy, there is nothing with which to compare the represented object. Further, as we saw earlier, if our interest is in the pictured object, then we should be interested in it and not in the question whether it does or does not have a counterpart in reality. That is what leads some to be suspicious of the relevance of considerations of truth to the appreciation of art.

The best discussion I know of what is going on when we use these terms is offered by Patrick Day (1962). His central claim is that when we talk about things as probable or improbable, we do so against a background of beliefs about what is likely or unlikely in the behaviour of human beings and natural objects. These beliefs are ultimately related to beliefs about the regularities to be found in human behaviour and the behaviour of natural things. When we refer to an action in a novel as implausible, it is because it does not accord with our background assumptions about these natural or psychological regularities.

A consequence is that our judgements of plausibility are revisable as our assumptions about such regularities change. The plausibility of events in H. G. Wells' *The time machine* may well be at the mercy of changes in our understanding of the laws of physics.

The way background assumptions operate can affect decisions on how a work is best structured. A sudden windfall seldom occurs at the very moment when it is most needed. So if it happens in a novel at the very moment when it is needed that will seem implausible. The coincidences in Thomas Hardy's novels are sometimes criticized on these grounds. Yet, since windfalls do occur, an answer is to start with one (as does John Fowles's novel *The collector*). Then, with whatever degree of plausibility the novelist can muster, the consequences of that can be traced. Sometimes implausibilities are tolerated, as when Alice shrinks or grows according as to the cake she eats, because we grasp when a novel expects us to ignore the causal laws of the physical universe and react to it as fantasy.

It is striking that many novels simply flout the presently known laws of physics. Alice falls down a rabbit hole and has time on the way down to read the labels on various jars. A time warp takes us to the planet of the apes long into the future, or takes the Star Ship Enterprise through light years. The same tolerance is not extended to violations of assumed psychological regularities. When, in a novel, natural laws are suspended, as when the protagonist of the *Satanic verses* falls safely to earth from an aeroplane, we still expect its characters to behave in ways deemed plausible by our beliefs about psychological regularities.

Kendal Walton has asked the interesting and related question, why, when reading a fiction, do we seem able to suspend our belief that people do not turn into insects, but not our belief that genocide is wrong? One suggestion I make is that it is a mistake to think that everything in a fiction has a fictional status. Kafka's Gregor Samsa is a fiction, a fact that not merely suspends but eliminates any antecedent beliefs about him. Genocide is not a fiction (although someone who believes it is right may be) and carries its properties into its temporary fictional resting place. In this sense a work of fiction can indeed be an imaginary garden with real toads in it. And the reason that there is an asymmetry is just that fiction may have two components, one of which need not be fictional. Compare here someone who embodies President Clinton in a fiction (this being the obverse of the case in which fiction embodied itself in Richard Nixon). Some real properties of Clinton must accompany him into his new home or it won't be Clinton who takes up residence there. (I think the same goes for Gregor Samsa, in so far as he is represented as a man.) This gives the same check to what we can imagine as true as incorporating the real phenomenon of genocide in one's work.

These plausibilities and implausibilities can affect our appreciation in various ways, but in the end they all come down to whether or not they interfere with our ability to enter imaginatively into the world of the work. If the excuse I am given for a late essay is simply implausible, I find it difficult to believe it. If what happens in a novel is simply implausible, I find it difficult to imagine it. And since, as we have seen, imagination is so important, so plausibility is important.

Reflection statements

But it is reflection statements that most interest me, for people do seem to develop likings and aversions to works of art in accordance with judgements about the beliefs and attitudes that are there articulated. Yet some say these considerations are irrelevant to aesthetic judgements. I can think of at least seven reasons why this might be said.

Firstly, those who did make truth a test of value, Plekhanov, Stalin and even Plato, for example, are in bad odour because of what they did or would have liked to have done, to art and artists.

Secondly, there is a set of reasons for eliminating considerations of truth that seem based on assumptions about the nature of art. Thus a reason, present in discussions by Isenberg and Beardsley, is that in order to determine whether an assertion is true or false something other has to be investigated than the fact that an assertion has been made. So, if a work contains the assertion, say, that the poor of Ireland in the eighteenth century were treated in abominable ways, then, in order to ascertain the truth of this, one has to leave the work and do some checking. As we have seen, some think that a proper interest in a work of art confines itself to what can be read from the work itself. And since the truth-value of its statements cannot be read from the work itself, these statements are irrelevant.

Thirdly, we bother to check the truth only of utterances that we take to be seriously asserted. If I hear you tell someone that his mother swims after troopships and know that you are rehearsing a play, I tend not to bother with the truth of what you say. Beardsley, as we have seen, does not think that a work of art contains genuine assertions. So he will feel that the questions of truth cannot arise.

Fourthly, since truth is something that things other than works of art possess, truth cannot be the thing we are interested in when we are interested in art.

Two further reasons have to do with what is involved in saying that something is true or false.

Thus, fifthly, for there to be considerations of truth at all, it must be possible to identify an assertion that says something about something. This is not generally possible in art. In music unaccompanied by words, it is impossible to identify what is being said about what. Further, even though in a painting we may identify a subject, a hay wain, for example, it is not clear what is being said about it.

Further, sixthly, the determination of the truth of an assertion goes with the possibility of ways of verifying that truth. Many of the reflective thoughts of many works seem not to allow this. Even if Beckett's plays do embody the thought that life is on the whole bleak, it is not clear how I would test that claim.

Finally, seventhly, it is argued, since we know of works that embody a false view of the world and are good (Dante's *Divina commedia?*) and works that embody a true view and are bad (Harriet Beecher-Stowe's *Uncle Tom's cabin?*), truth seems not to be relevant to judgements of artistic value.

Some of these arguments are simply feeble. Thus, firstly, the claim that since things other than works of art possess truth, truth is not relevant to judgements about art, would severely attenuate aesthetic discourse. Elegance and grace characterize natural objects as much as they characterize art, so these, by this line of reasoning, will have to be ignored in our dealings with art. The truth is that once a thing has been marked off as art, then many of the things it shares with things that are not art, like wit, grace and the like, become art-relevant properties.

Secondly, the moral stench that attaches to the crazed operations of Stalin show that what was done in the name of truth was indefensible. That no more shows the irrelevance of a proper reference to the truth-value of art than Stalin's quaintly conservative and bourgeois commitment to pictorial realism shows that we should abandon representation as irrelevant to art.

Thirdly, it is debatable that music and painting have no assertion content. True, if we know nothing of the context of a work, we may not realize that it has such a content. Shostakovich's Fifth Symphony and Picasso's *Guernica* do not reveal their propositions to the ignorant ear or eye. But that only excludes an interest in their propositional content if, as we do not, we have a proof that we should ignore the context of a work. The truth is that people do see that Goya's war paintings contain the thought that certain actions are dreadful, and Shostakovich's music was taken to be expressing attitudes to the state of the Soviet Union. Why else would Stalin have wished to silence him?

Next, the fact that some works articulating a view to which we assent are bad and some works articulating views to which we do not assent are good, does not show the irrelevance of truth-value to judgements about art. Some works containing wit are bad. Perhaps the wit is out of place (as might be a red-nosed comedy routine at a Quaker funeral). But that does not make wit irrelevant to judgements of merit. So, too, some bad works may be true and some good works false. But the bad might have been worse if false rather than true and the good better if true rather than false.

What of the assumption that relevant comments about a work are those that are confirmable solely by inspecting the work itself. Since that inspection, although it might tell us that a work contains a reflection statement, cannot, of itself, tell us whether it is true, that truth-value cannot, we are told, be relevant. The problem is that the assumption is hardly self-evident. When in *The four quartets* Eliot uses the word "harruspicate," mere inspection of this item on the page will not tell us its meaning. Is meaning therefore irrelevant because I have to leave the work and look it up in a dictionary? That an excellent parody is a parody might not be clear from an uncontextualized inspection of it. Is the fact that something is a parody irrelevant to judgements of it as art? The assumption behind this objection to the relevance of truth to art is simply too emaciating.

The claim that art is essentially a kind of pretending, its propositions not seriously asserted and so not to be assessed for truth or falsity fares no better. Firstly, many works of art are not like this. Goya was not pretending to the condemnations of war articulated in many of his paintings, no more than Dickens was pretending, in *Bleak House* to a condemnation of the law. Secondly, as we have seen, pretending is a real act and one that can be engaged in, as Nathan engaged in it after the murder of Uriah the Hittite, in order to make an assertion. If we can detect in imitations and pretendings the real hand of the imitators and pretenders, there seems no reason why we should not detect also, as we do with Dickens and Jane Austen, beliefs or attitudes articulated by those imitators and pretenders through their imitations and pretendings.

More interesting is the claim that questions of truth or falsity do not apply since the procedures of verification and falsification seem not to have a purchase on the reflective content of a work of art. For how are such work-embodied reflections as the reflection that life is on the whole bleak, to be tested. Aren't these expressions in the work of attitudes, which tell us about the response of an artist to a world, but not some truth about that world.

Here I invoke the suggestion, by J. L. Austin, that truth and falsity are only two of a whole set of appraisals that we have for measuring the fit between our beliefs, emotions, and attitudes to the world and the world to which they are attitudes. The words "true" and "false" belong to a group of appraisal words that includes also "prejudiced", "jaundiced", "biased", "slanted", "sane", "healthy, "intemperate", "balanced", "paranoid", "gloomy" and "optimistic". These words do not merely apply to propositions but to a wider class of items including beliefs, attitudes, points of view and perspectives. That these appraisal terms are sometimes difficult to apply and are often used, like "insane", merely to express unthinking hostility, does not establish that they cannot be used to signal various sorts of appraisals. Although a narrow sort of empirical verificationism does not work with the central reflective statements of works of art, this does not establish that usable analogues to the terms "proposition", "true", and "false" cannot be found that would operate on the reflective content of a work of art.

Inhabiting the work

Everything so far has been negative. No arguments have been found that absolutely rule out the possibility that a work of art might be true or false, or something analogous to it. But no positive argument has been given for that possibility.

Suppose, then, that it were no part of any artist's task to articulate his or her beliefs, feelings, attitudes and emotions to the subject matter of his or her art. That means that Goya confronted with the horrors of the War, Picasso confronted with Guernica, Ronald Searle confronted with the Japanese death camps, Sylvia Plath confronted with the nature of her life, Verdi confronted with contemporary events in Italy, had no business as artists in expressing attitudes to these situations. Not only is this laughably inaccurate as a picture of what artists have done, but it further entails that artists are cut off from comment on serious issues in a way that trivializes art.

Worse, an artist, such as Goya, can at best only create pictures of suffering as exercises in painterly design for the aesthetic edification and delight of his audience. That seems intolerable.

What I think worries some is that if comment on the important issues of life becomes part of art, there is no way of distinguishing art from other ways of expressing such comments. However, I have argued that we are not obliged to think that there is a difference in kind between expressions that are art and those that are not. Rather we might think, as Croce did, of a continuum of cases, running from expressions that we have little inclination to think of as art, through cases, like the sermons of Donne, up to those cases that because of the range and power with which they engage the imagination, we undoubtedly think of as great works of expressive art. Art may simply be, as Pope put it, "what oft was thought but ne'er so well expressed".

Any account of art has to be true to the experience of those who have dealings with it. For many, a response to art is affected by feelings of assent and dissent to the attitudes articulated in it. (That, it seems to me, is a central notion in a certain kind of "feminist" criticism.) For all that I admire Lawrence's novels, I am still uneasy about the attitude that they express. Again, I am utterly impressed by Picasso's artistic accomplishments, but, at times, the lavatorial attitude to the depiction of the female form affects my appreciation. I can think of cases in which an over-indulgence shown *in* a piece of music makes me pause in my approbation. In all these cases it does seem that appreciation is affected by some feeling that the attitudes or beliefs articulated in and through a work are defective. Contrariwise, when, as with Jane Austen, Henry Fielding, Rembrandt, and much of Mozart, I feel an assent to the attitude articulated in the work, that leads me to a more unqualified appreciation. Of course, the experience of an imaginative work of art can convert us to the view in it. That is merely to say that we come to share and approve of the attitude articulated in the work, and that enhances our approval.

I do not claim that if I do not share the world-view articulated in a work, then I must deny it all merit. I am suspicious of the attitudes expressed in Eliot's *The four quartets* and Dante's *Divina commedia*. That does not stop me thinking that these are great works. Similarly, I may share the attitude of a work without thinking that that work is unqualifiedly a good or great one. *Uncle Tom's cabin* may be a case in point. Truth or falsity, in a wider or narrower sense, are not the *only* things of relevance when we are assessing merit, but this does not stop them from being *among* the things that are relevant to that task. And I suspect that the works of art we think of as unqualifiedly great are not merely exemplary in their deployment of the techniques of art but are also works to the attitudes of which we give our assent. They are works, to use Ronald Hepburn's phrase, that we can inhabit. That makes our appraisals related immediately to our judgements as to whether there is or is not something right or wrong about the attitude, belief, or judgement articulated in a work of art relevant, though not conclusively relevant, to our appraisal.

A possible objection

Suppose our ability to respond to a work *is* affected by our judgement of the rightness or wrongness of any view it articulates. It could be said that such judgements are still not relevant to judgements of art as art. To use an analogy: someone's suffering from halitosis may prevent me getting near enough fully to appreciate the beauty of that person's teeth. But the judgement that someone has halitosis, although it affects my ability to make an aesthetic judgement, is not relevant to that aesthetic judgement. Similarly, my judgement that Leni Reifenstahl wrongly admired Hitler might put me off looking at the aesthetic merits of her work, but is not itself part of that aesthetic judgement.

In one sense this is true. If we think of an aesthetic delight as a delight in the looks or appearances of things, then judgements of the attitudes displayed in a work are not aesthetic judgements. That only brings us to the conclusion that they are irrelevant to art if one thinks that the only judgements relevant to art are aesthetic in this narrow sense. That looks simply bizarre. We are interested in far more than the looks and appearances of art. If the thing is art we are interested in the artistic qualities of a thing, the kind of choices that we see made in it and the kinds of qualities of mind and emotion displayed in those choices, as when we notice the discrimination that a composer shows in avoiding the temptation to mawkish descents into the minor for cheap effect. We are also interested in works as expressive – in giving us ways of articulating our attitudes and perceptions. And that is not a narrowly aesthetic matter.

Revelation

Quite apart from questions about whether works of art can, in some sense or other, be true and false, and quite apart from questions about whether, if they can, that truth or falsity bears on judgements about their artistic merit, there is another aspect to the question of art and truth. For people have sometimes spoken of art as revealing truths to us. What are we to make of this?

There seem to be two cases here. Firstly, a work of art might *change* in part or in whole one's way of seeing something. Possessed, say, of a knee jerk disapproval of radicals one might, through a work of literature, simply come to a different understanding. That is no more surprising or problematic than that acquaintance with the life of the trenches disinclined Wilfred Owen or Edward Thomas from continuing to feel and express a heroic attitude to modern warfare. Of course this leaves open the problem, which is not in the end a problem just for aesthetics, of the source of one's assumption that one is changed for the better. I know of too many cases of students who have been converted to the views of Ayn Rand through reading *Atlas shrugged* to be entirely happy with the thought that epiphanic artistic experiences are, so to speak, self-authenticating.

The more interesting case is the one in which a work occasions an experience, common in our dealings with art, which we articulate by saying that a work of art expresses what we already inchoately knew. In such cases we may exclaim "that's right!", as if the truth of the work were already in a sense known to us.

The phenomenon may occur in many contexts and not only in art. We may so express ourselves: after struggling with a proof in mathematics; after wondering how to say a line in a play; on finding a solution when struggling with a painting; on seeing the aptness of a description of someone or something; on suddenly coming to see one's life as answering to a certain characterization; on suddenly seeing through someone; on realizing, as Glenn Miller did, what combination of instruments gave him the sound he had long sought; on suddenly seeing the face in a puzzle picture; on struggling with a thought in a seminar and having someone articulate it perfectly: on simply reading something, as someone might feel "yes, that's it!" after reading Bogart's advice to Lauren Bacall on how to cope with the death of a lover.

Here are some particular cases. Firstly, we may feel that a work of art gives us a way of expressing what we already inchoately knew we were. That is why we exclaim, "that's right!". Only after Shakespeare had written Hamlet was it possible for Prufrock to express himself in the following lines (and only after Eliot had written them could it be possible for others to recognize themselves in them):

No! I am not Prince Hamlet, nor was meant to be;
Am an attendant lord, one that will do
To swell a progress, start a scene or two,
Advise the prince; no doubt, an easy tool,
Deferential, glad to be of use,
Politic, cautious, and meticulous,
Full of high sentence, but a bit obtuse;
At times, indeed, almost ridiculous –
Almost, at times, the Fool.

(The love song of J. Alfred Prufrock, Eliot, *Collected Poems 1909–62*. London: Faber, 1963)

Next, an imaginative narrative work of art may get us to see what we have done. So (in 2 Samuel 12) Nathan brought home to David what he had done in appropriating the wife of Uriah the Hittite and disposing of her husband by telling him a purely imaginative narrative about a man who misappropriated a lamb. The result was that:

David's anger was greatly kindled against the man; and he said to Nathan, As the Lord liveth the man that hath done this thing shall surely die . . .
And Nathan said to David, Thou art the man . . .

201

And David said unto Nathan, I have sinned against the Lord.

Finally an imaginative narrative may get us to *see* possibilities implicit in the morality to which we have subscribed. Such was the parable of the Good Samaritan, told to the lawyer who knew that he had to love his neighbour but could not see what range of persons to include in that category. He came to see, through an imaginative narrative, that neighbours are not just fellow members of one's tribe.

The experiences, both artistic and nonartistic, reported by "that's right!" seem to have an oddly double character. On the one hand we feel something has been *revealed* to us: yet, on the other, we also feel we already knew it. That can seem problematic. How could it be revealed if we already knew it? And how, if we already knew it, did we have to wait for it be revealed? How could one say, with a sense of recognition, "That is *exactly* what I was trying to say!" if one was not already, in some way, aware of what one wanted to say? How could a Lily Briscoe think, "Yes! that's the effect I was after!" if she did not already in some way know what effect was being sought? (And that carries with it the concomitant question how, if one knows already what one is after, one has so much trouble producing it and so much relief on doing so?)

The matter is an important one since these, so to speak, epiphanic experiences, have been thought central to art in at least two ways. Firstly, they occur in contexts in which the artist tries to solve an artistic problem, as when the artist is seeking the right word, the right combination of notes or the right compositional line. We saw how Lily Briscoe in *To the lighthouse* expresses herself when, of a sudden, light dawned and she resolved her compositional problem:

> She looked at her canvas; it was blurred. With a sudden intensity, as if she saw it clear for a second, she drew a line there, in the centre. It was done; it was finished. Yes, she thought, laying down the brush in extreme fatigue, I have had my vision.

Croce, indeed, we saw, made such experiences central to art.

Secondly, what innumerable people have valued in art is the way in which a work of art may bring to explicit and perfect articulation how, before its articulation, we already, but inchoately, felt the world and ourselves to be. So lovers appropriate Shakespeare's sonnets, finding in them something exactly apt for their own expressive purposes; and those who sense the losses of time might find this precisely articulated for them by, say, Hardy's *During wind and rain*. Similarly, after seeing a Turner painting, I might see a sunset and instead of that being a mere seeing, I might express myself by saying that the sunset is Turneresque. I may say "that's right!" not only when a work articulates the inner life of my emotions. It may also express the feeling that the work has given me a way of articulating what I know about the world. Ray Elliott (1966–7, p. 80) cites the lines from Pope, "So well bred spaniels civilly delight/In mumbling of the game they dare not bite", as getting us to see both how we feel both spaniels and the target of Pope's satire to be. Even (perhaps especially) in the case of music, as Helen Schlegel's experience reminds us, one can think that something correctly articulates both how it is with one and how one believes it is with the world. One can as well say "My emotions are all Mahler" as "That sunset is Turnesque". The inclination to say "that's right!", with its implications of finding a truth, arises as much in the case of music as it does in the case of the other arts. This sort of illumination is what Wollheim is seeking to clarify and understand, when he speaks of the way in which projecting our inner lives onto some objective correlate helps to restore to, or impose order onto, those internal lives (Wollheim 1993, pp. 5–6). What could be more important than this? And what, if not art, is to do it?

Puzzles

Although "epiphanic experiences" are familiar and of great importance, there are two things about the way these experiences are expressed that can seem puzzling. One is put thus by Wittgenstein: "One is tempted to use the following picture: what he really 'wanted to say', what he 'meant' was already *present somewhere* in his mind even before he gave it expression" (1953, para. 334). Later in the *Philosophical investigations*, Wittgenstein remarks: "James, in writing of this subject, is really trying to say: 'What a remarkable experience. The word is not there yet, and yet in a certain sense is there, – or something is there, which cannot grow into anything but this word"' (*ibid*. Part II, p. 219).

If I recognize something as what I *wanted* to say, I must already know that that is what I wanted to say. It must have been somewhere. Then we are tempted to think of it already being in some occult place, the mind, and of bringing what we recognize in the expression up against it in order to check that it *is* what is already there. This model makes it mysterious, both as to where this occult place is and – granted we do know already what we want to express – why we find it so hard to express it. This question is one for the more general philosophy of mind, of seeing what is wrong with the notion of the mind as an occult room.

Here I wish, rather, to deal with a problem for philosophical aesthetics, namely, granted people feel that these epiphanic experiences are so important in giving them ways of expressing the truth about themselves and the world, how do they know when they say "that's right!" that it *is* right? That this is a problem with epiphanic experiences in art is suggested by a quotation from T. S. Eliot's *Little Gidding*:

> Let me disclose the gifts reserved for age
> To set a crown upon your lifetime's effort.
> First, the cold friction of expiring sense
> Without enchantment, offering no promise
> But bitter tastelessness of shadow fruit
> As body and soul begin to fall asunder.
> Second, the conscious impotence of rage
> At human folly, and the laceration
> Of laughter at what ceases to amuse.
> And last, the rending pain of re-enactment
> Of all that you have done, and been; the shame
> Of motives late revealed, and the awareness
> Of things ill done and done to others' harm
> Which once you took for exercise of virtue.
> Then fools' approval stings, and honour stains.
> From wrong to wrong the exasperated spirit
> Proceeds, unless restored by that refining fire
> Where you must move in measure like a dancer.
>
> (*Little Gidding, The four quartets.* London: Faber, 1944)

Couldn't one think that one had been brought to see oneself or the world aright, and, indeed, live one's whole life in the spirit of that revelation and, at the last, come to realize that this was not right, just as the feeling that one had, of a sudden, come to an answer to a mathematical problem is, alas, compatible with not having got it right at all? And couldn't we think that we have found the solution to an artistic problem and others see that we have not? And couldn't we come to see that for ourselves at a later stage? By the same token, presumably, Helen Schlegel's thinking that Beethoven had told her what her life was is compatible with her finding out, as that life continued, that he hadn't. And can't I think that someone's sincerely felt, dollar-laden post-Ayn Rand epiphanies are simply barmy? As Wittgenstein asks "Can't we be mistaken in thinking we understand a question?". And "Don't I also sometimes imagine myself to understand a word . . . and then realize that I did not understand it?" (1953, para. 517, p. 53fn).

Here a real difficulty emerges. If Helen finds out that Beethoven had not revealed her life to her as it really is, it is presumably because, at some later time, she has a further epiphanic experience that revealed the falsity of what Beethoven had apparently revealed and the truth of something else. But, then, by parity of reasoning she could not trust that later epiphanic experience as genuinely revelatory. And then one might begin to wonder, if one cannot trust its revelations, what the value is of the claim that works of art have this revelatory power.

Could someone, be that person the artist or one of the audience, think "Yes! That's right! That's how I feel!" and be mistaken? Could an artist initially feel an inchoate restlessness, feel, subsequently, that a work expressed it clearly, as Lily Briscoe in one of my earlier examples claimed to feel, and be wrong? Could a person, reading *The love song of J. Alfred Prufrock*, think, "Yes! that's me: I'm past it" and be wrong? In one of the few coherent discussions of this matter (indeed, one of the few discussions of any sort) John Benson (1967) suggests that if an expression feels wrong, it *is* wrong and if it feels right, it *is* right. Is this so?

Two cases need to be distinguished here. Firstly, there is the case in which one inchoately feels past it, then feels, after reading a poem, that the poem expresses precisely that incohate feeling, and yet one is wrong in feeling, first inchoately and then articulately that one is past it. Here the poem truly articulates what one inarticulately feels about oneself, only one is wrong in feeling that about oneself. Secondly, there is the more interesting possibility that one might be wrong in asserting, with a sense of recognition, that a poem expresses articulately one's inner life. One says, with a sense either of recognition or revelation, "That's how it is with me", when that is *not* how it is.

The first of these cases is certainly possible, and it raises problems, to which we shortly return, about the epiphanic status of art. But the latter case is both intriguing in its own right, as well as worrying for those who think that works of art can clarify our lives in a reminding way.

In the latter case, one possibility seems to me to be relatively uninteresting. I might *carelessly* (but sincerely, in the sense of having no intention to mislead, lie or whatever) say, perhaps at a Bergman film, "Yes, that about sums up my world view", only to be persuaded that nothing of the sort is the case. Wittgenstein remarks: "it is the circumstances under which he had such an experience that justify him in saying in such a case that he understands" (Wittgenstein 1953, para. 155). And one of the circumstances seems to me to be how seriously the speaker took the matter. Did the speaker, so to speak, shoot from the hip, speak hastily, carelessly or whatever? And then I want to say that if a person speaks with due seriousness and consideration, *attentively*, let us say, then a gap cannot open between saying that a poem, for example, expresses what we incohately feel and what we in fact inchoately feel. That is the truth that Benson seems to me to have grasped.

But that still leaves it open that both the inchoate and expressed belief or feeling about oneself, about the world, about what one wanted to say, about what would or would not work artistically in a certain picture, could simply be mistaken. In that case, one could say "that's how it is (that's how the world is)" and be wrong, wrong not in describing one's feeling, inchoate or not, about how the world is, and asserting that the poem perfectly expresses this, but wrong in feeling that the world is so. Moreover, as the Eliot lines remind us, we *can* come to think that we erroneously believed ourselves to have had revelatory insights. What then becomes of the revelatory power of art?

Various possibilities exist here. One would be to invoke the notion, canvassed in Wittgenstein's *On certainty*, that certain beliefs, like the belief that there are objects, are not to be doubted, but rather constitute a context in which doubt becomes possible. (Doubt about objects makes sense only if there are objects.) Similarly, one might say that a work of art might bring something home to us with such force that doubt is not something we could seriously entertain. After reading Tolstoy's short story about the matter, I might be so struck with the horror of prostitution that I could not seriously ever again engage with any work that was in any way sympathetic to that institution. That, however, seems not to address the fact that some seemingly revelatory foundational experiences *do* come to be doubted, as might the foundational experiences mentioned in *On certainty* (Bernecker, 1995).

A second possibility is to claim that one can have a perfect title to say, on hearing the expression of a sentiment in a poem, "That's exactly right", meaning that one thinks both that the poem gets it right and, moreover, that it exactly expresses what one inchoately felt, even if one later comes to feel that it *doesn't* get it right. This seems to me to be of a piece with the claim that one can have a perfect title to say one is seeing a pig, even if that claim later turns out to be false.

The error here is to believe that revelation in art is of a piece with incorrigibility. That is erroneous for various reasons. Firstly, it supposes that there is in the end only one way to see things. That this is false, at least to the experience of art, is shown by the question "Which of Turner, Constable, Monet or Blake captured the way a sunset really looks?". There is a perfectly good sense in which these artists reveal to us ways of seeing sunsets, rather than *the* way a sunset looks (a conclusion, as I have said, which does not entail that there exists no sunset independent of those ways of seeing). It is further at odds with the fact that we may look back on the poems we loved in late adolescence and think of them as expressing a world view that is not so much false as inappropriate to our present condition.

Art aside, however, the claim that revelation is of a piece with incorrigibility seems to me not to do justice to the fact that our moral views, and more generally our views of life, are constantly brought to the bar of experience and can alter in consequence. We can never be sure when this is going to happen. One example of this is the case in which my belief as to how one should comport oneself in the face of the death of someone loved may simply not be sustainable when that actually happens to me.

Perhaps more importantly, a conviction that a sense of genuine revelation is of a piece with incorrigibility sits oddly with the fact that we engage with each other in moral and kindred inter-changes, interchanges that can effect a change in our views, an engagement that persuaded me earlier that there was something right about subjectivism. These debates are complex, and the agreements and disagreements that are reached are often patchily overlapping and sometimes fugitive, as they must be since we all bring to the interchanges our individual psychological histories.

This seems to me to happen in ethics and in our engagements with the moral expressions of art. I bring to the work my present moral and metaphysical posture and a work can affect it, and later works may affect it yet again. At each stage I may feel a revelation, but I must always be conscious that this revelation is at risk of what time and other insights may bring.

Avoiding oversimplification

So far I have spoken as if one brings one's moral views to the work and if one sees the work shares them, or if the work converts one to its view, one is moved to assent to it. But that is too simplistic.

Firstly we should guard against having too austere a view of what counts as our morality in our involvement with art. One overly austere model might work like this: we are committed, say, to opposition to genocide (although Western reaction to recent events in, say Timor, might indicate that the commitment is lip-service). We then encounter a work expressing an endorsement of genocide. This repels us enough to prevent our enjoying whatever the work might have to offer were it, so to speak, on our side. That counts as a defect in the work. Now one possibly minor point of moral psychology is that such an account leaves out cases like *'Till death do us part* (or *The bunkers* in its American incarnation). I became tired of hearing the righteous defending this as defeating evil with savage parody when it was obvious that a fair percentage of them (not to mention the public at large) were actually vicariously enjoying the saying of the unsayable. Indeed the very example of *The triumph of the will* brings before us the spectacle of the glamour of evil to which we may be attracted in the way in which Plato claimed we are attracted when we cannot take our eyes off a repellent corpse. It simply will not do to represent ourselves as simply switched off by the spectacle of that towards which we are at pains to voice our repugnance. We need a more sophisticated moral psychology.

More importantly, the account, cast as it is in terms of being switched off by works that clash with our morality, leaves out any consideration of the fact that some of the very greatest of art enacts its programme in the very areas where our morality is not secure, however vehemently we may protest it is. To be sure, if I, to use Professor Hepburn's excellent word, can "inhabit" the work, then I'll like it better, and if I can't, I'll be to some extent turned from it. But this needs to be supplemented by some notion of being morally challenged by a work. Though I have some moral certainties, I do not have enough to prevent my experience of art from being not a matter of attraction and repulsion, but (and here I think of Kafka and Beckett, not to forget Genet and Robert Mapplethorpe) an anxiety, the kind of anxiety felt by Huck Finn, trapped between a sense of duty to his racist society and his friendship with an escaped slave.

But there is another way in which an account of morality and its dealings with art may be too austere. It will be so if it concentrates on cases in which our attraction and repulsion to art is a matter of its according or not according with some moral principle to which we adhere. That certainly needs to be supplemented by a wider survey and etiology of the ways in which we can be put off art. I may, without this being strictly a moral matter, be put off, to take a few examples, by the pretentious (see *Lady Chatterley's lover*), the banal (see Betjeman's Laureate verses), the mawkish (see Keats's "Ode to Psyche"), the intellectually vague (see *Paradise lost* and parts of *The four quartets*) or the infantile lavatorial (see some of Picasso's later works and some of Swift's writings to Stella). Sometimes the failing might not be sufficient to prevent me from enjoying or even thinking highly of the work. What this suggests is that instead of taking on only the moral we should look more generally at the ways in which human qualities of a work of art may or may not make it possible for us to live with it.

Finally

Kafka writes in *Metamorphosis*: "As Gregor Samsa awoke one morning from uneasy dreams he found himself transformed in his bed into a gigantic insect." We can go along with a fictional world in which that sort of thing happens with no other sense of strain than the fictional world itself imposes on us, which, as Doctor Johnson found in the case of Lear, might be pretty considerable, but it will be a world that we can only imaginatively enter if it has a psychological truth, which is to say, if it accords with our assumptions about regularities shown in human behaviour.

Then we read:

> Thy husband is thy lord, thy life, thy keeper,
> Thy head, thy sovereign; one that cares for thee,
> And for thy maintenance commits his body
> To painful labour, both by sea and land;
> To watch the night in storms, the day in cold,
> While thou liest warm at home, secure and safe,
> And craves no other tribute at thy hands,
> But love, fair looks, and true obedience:
> Too little payment for so great a debt.
> Such duty as the subject owes the prince,
> Even such a woman oweth to her husband.

And now it seems harder to go along with those words, as witness the desperate attempts of recent directors to salvage an ironic intention notably ill-evidenced in the original passage. There is an asymmetry between our willingness to accept works of art in which unlikely if not impossible events occur and our unwillingness to ascribe to works of art that differ morally from our own. We find it harder to go along with the fictional world in which Kate's words are spoken. Here the claim that artists show themselves in works and my discussion of the relevance to art of truth and morality come together. For I am sure that the reason we might recoil, if we do, from those words of *The taming of the shrew* is not that we might find it hard to empathize with a fictional speaker saying those things in a repressive fictional world. Rather it is that we suspect, or better fear, that these sentiments were shared by a real person in a real world, namely the person who wrote the play. What upsets our assessments is not the morality of people and societies *in* works of art but the attitudes often displayed, wittingly or not, by the creators of those works in their very real acts of creation. For a work of art cannot be immoral, as opposed to containing instances of immorality, unless the morality it contains, if only by omission, is endorsed. The morality of a work of art can only be the morality displayed in the real act of articulating that work. That makes it as much part of the work as any of its other properties. But to say that is to say that moral considerations and with them considerations of the truth of those considerations must enter into our assessments of art.

Guide to reading

A good place to start, since it is clear and makes one valuable distinction is Beardsley's *Aesthetics* pp. 368–91. Note also his overview of Romanticism in his *Aesthetics from classical Greece to the present*. In Hanfling's *Philosophical aesthetics* there is another overview, "Truth and representation" by Rosalind Hursthouse. Those who like interesting historical figures will greatly enjoy Sir Philip Sidney's *Apology for* (sc. Defence of) *poetry*, where there is a lively debate (directed at Plato) about why poets are truth-tellers rather than liars. The long, but I think essential, J. P. Day article is "Artistic verisimilitude", *Dialogue*, 1(2&3) 1962, pp. 163–87, 278–304. D. Z. Phillips's *Through a darkening glass* (Oxford: Blackwell, 1982) is a series of discussions of examples of the way in which morality and art go together and displays a knowledge of and a sensitivity to literature that is rare in those who philosophize on that matter. Of a less explicitly philosophical intent, but exemplifying the way in which literature is bound up with morality, are the works of F. R. Leavis. His views are well discussed by J. Casey, *The language of criticism* (London: Methuen, 1966). I have referred to the way in which J. L. Austin widens the scope of what must be considered when truth is under examination. The best thing here is *How to do things with words* (Oxford: Oxford University Press, 1962). Two books, in relatively neglected ways have said interesting things about art truth and morality. One is Peter Jones, *Philosophy and the novel* (Oxford: Clarendon, 1975), where he introduces the useful notion of the availability of a work of art for use. This seems to me to throw light on the ways in which we appropriate a Shakespeare sonnet, say, for our own expressive purposes. The other is R. Beardsmore, *Art and morality* (London:Macmillan, 1971), which both surveys critically some popular views (aestheticism and moralism) and tries to show how a work of art might get us to see the wrongness of something like prostitution. On the matter of suspending belief in what one does not morally share see K. Walton & M. Tanner, "Morals in fiction and fictional morality", *Proceedings of the Aristotelian Society* supp. vol. **67**, 1994, pp. 27–66. We are now, I am told by neophiliacs, in the era of the New Humanism, the successor to poststructuralism. This movement has come round to seeing that ethics and literature do have something to do with each other. For more on this see David Parker's, *Ethics, theory and the novel* (Cambridge: Cambridge University Press, 1994) and Noël Carroll "Moderate Moralism", *British Journal of Aesthetics* **36**(3), 1996, pp. 223–37.

Various people have simply denied the relevance of truth. One is Arnold Isenberg in "The problem of belief" most accessibly available in Barrett's *Collected papers in aesthetics*, pp. 125–44 to which the admirable Ray Elliott's "Poetry and truth", *Analysis* **27**, 1966–7, pp. 77–85 was offered by way of a reply. Another is Douglas Morgan in "Must art tell the truth?", *Journal of Aesthetics and Art Criticism* **26**, 1967, pp. 17–21. J. Jobes has explored the revelatory aspect of art in his "A revelatory function of art", *British Journal of Aesthetics* **14**, 1974, pp. 124–33. Finally no list can afford to miss R. W. Hepburn's "Art, truth and the education of subjectivity", *Journal of Aesthetic Education* **24** (2), 1990, pp. 185–98.

Two groups have a special interest in truth in art: one is Marxists, the other is adherents to various religions. Both, however, can be subsumed under my discussion. Both claim to know how things are and to judge works on the ways in which they do or do not show a grasp of how things are: but that is compatible with my view that one's beliefs about how things are can condition one's opinions about a work of art. It is worth reading Sim on "Marxism and aesthetics" in the Hanfling volume. For total light relief I commend C. H. Rolph *The trial of Lady Chatterley* (London: Penguin 1960) with its rousing demonstration that humbug is not confined to (though it was amply spouted by) the unrighteous. Those who wish to look at a recent examination of pornography and obscenity (by a philosopher) can try B. Williams, *Obscenity and film censorship* (Cambridge: Cambridge University Press, 1981) an abridgement of the report of the Williams Committee on Obscenity and Film Censorship.

Chapter 10

The point of it all

To what extent has this work fulfilled the programme with which I began?

The avoidance of error

I said in the introduction that although the arts and nature offer us experiences of intense value, it is possible, when thinking about those experiences, to go wrong. If that error is confined to the interchanges of theorists, little harm is done. These errors are more pernicious when they affect those who teach the arts. In this work I have tried to show the errors of certain of these theories.

One is the belief that only a very narrow range of things is relevant to the appreciation of the arts. An extreme example of this is the view that an interest in works of art can only be an interest in their formal qualities. I have argued that we must continually resist attempts to restrict the knowledge that one needs to appreciate a work of art.

A second error is to take the model for proof in aesthetics as the model of citing things from which conclusions about merit and demerit *logically* follow. An aesthetic proof, rather, gets someone to *see* something, and although I can give you reasons for looking, I cannot give you reasons for seeing. I have argued, therefore, that the task of appreciation is to bring someone to respond with, "Yes, now I see it". What one wants to see is the value of a work as it emerges from and is dependent on the physical and semantic features of the work in question.

It is clear that the driving force behind many of the ills that I have attempted to diagnose has been a suspicion that appreciation of the arts is a subjective matter, where that means it records merely personal preference and as such is no material for the classroom. If it is to be studied academically we have to find something more objective to do, and what is more objective than counting vowels, measuring the wavelengths of tones, *ex post facto* musical analysis or talk of shapes and masses. That in turn leads to that *ignis fatuus* of twentieth century studies in appreciation, the search for a science of aesthetic judgement, where that means a way of deducing or inducing conclusions about the value of a work from statements about its "empirically observable" physical properties.

Faced with accusations of subjectivity one can try to show that aesthetic appreciation has a claim to be more than "just" subjective, whatever that means (and what it means is always worth asking of those who loosely bandy the word about). I tried to indicate that that is a viable strategy. But I also indicated that one might simply admit the charge that art involves our subjectivities and then show that appreciation can still be celebrated as a way of exploring the forms and limits of our communality as we discover the ways in which, in responding to art our subjectivities do and do not come together. At the very least this seems to me to offer a more interesting way of approaching the arts in the teaching situation.

One other remark while we are discussing theories of art: I overheard a colleague say recently that literature existed for him only as a stock of examples in terms of which to discuss theories of literature. That attitude goes a long way to explain the disaffection that many students feel with present-day methods of studying the arts. As a corrective I commend the attitude expressed by Philip Roth's "professor of desire" in the novel of that name, an attitude in the spirit of which I have tried to write this book. (Indeed I commend the whole of the soliloquy from which this extract is taken as a guide to what a teacher ought to feel.) The professor of desire says:

> You may even have grown a little weary of my insistence upon the connections between the novels you read ... even the most eccentric and offputting of novels, and what you know so far of life. You will discover (and not all will approve) that I do not hold with certain of my colleagues who tell us that literature, in its most valuable and intriguing moments, is "fundamentally non-referential" ... I am going to request nonetheless that you restrain yourselves from talking about "structure", "form", and "symbols" in my presence. It seems to me that many of you have been intimidated sufficiently ... and should be allowed to recover and restore to respectability those interests and enthusiasms that more than likely drew you to reading fiction to begin with and which you oughtn't to be ashamed of now. As an experiment you might even want ... to try living without any classroom terminology at all, to relinquish "plot" and "character" right along with those very exalted words with which not a few of you like to solemnize your observations, such as "epiphany", "persona", and, of course, "existential" as a modifier of everything existing under the sun. I suggest this in the hope that if you talk about *Madame Bovary* in more or less the same tongue you use with the grocer, or your lover, you may be placed in a more intimate, a more interesting, in what might be called a more *referential* relationship with Flaubert and his heroine ... Above all, I hope that by reading these books you will come to learn something of value about life in one of its most puzzling and maddening aspects.

> (*The professor of desire*, Philip Roth. London: Jonathan Cape, 1978)

Art

I said at the outset that our task is to understand the power of art. What progress has been made with that? *An* account of art has now begun to emerge. Someone has something inchoate to make clear. It might be something one wants to get clear about oneself, perhaps by writing a poem. It might be something one wants to articulate, in a painting perhaps, about the world as it seems to us. It might be an idea for a building or a story. One then sets about making something that will be finished only when one can say: "that's what I was after". When that is done one will have created something, all of whose elements will have been harnessed to produce the overall effect. Others who understand that object will grasp what is articulated in it and how its components have been arranged to express precisely that.

In all these cases an inner life is put into an object and thereby clarified. That object can be a natural object. I can project my mood onto nature and call it melancholy. In art, however, my control is greater. I create the object that embodies my vision and can ensure that precisely that vision will be articulated by it. One could be an artist in this sense, even if one did not know that this intention is something that people called "artists" have often self-consciously had. One *might* think, "I am in a certain internal state and I will become a painter or a novelist or a musician and make it clear". But one could, without knowing anything about all that, simply make something in order to clarify one's inner life. What is done by severely disabled people when they paint to articulate their visions meets Wollheim's condition even if they have no grasp of the uses of the term "art".

This is why I earlier argued that it is not easy to see where the line between deliberately made things that are art and those that are not is to be drawn. That in turn damages any attempt, like that made by Collingwood, to distinguish between art and craft, or any attempt to show that arts like architecture or the design of kitchen implements are not pure arts because they are bound up with the practical.

In architecture, for example, the intended practical end for the building (and, more generally, the intended end of a design object, a teapot, say) is part of what has to be forged into the aesthetic end product. A design problem bombards the designer with what Croce would call "unorganized material stimuli". These include, in architecture, such things as the location, the problems of the possibly cramped size of the site, its slopes, and its surrounding buildings, the wish to avoid hackneyed derivation, the needs of the users. The task of reconciling these elements presses on the mind of architect-artists and their task is to produce an object that leaves no lumps sticking out as unsolved problems. That one of the elements to be included in the organic whole is a practical demand does not show that the task of producing an object that meets all the demands is any the less artistic. That a chair has to be fit to sit on does not prevent a chair expressing its creator's conception of how furniture might be. We find furniture, clothes, chinaware, cutlery and buildings expressive of articulated conceptions.

Aesthetic matters, narrowly conceived, can, indeed, interfere with the practical. The new station at Euston may well have been a memorably uplifting visual spectacle, but when seats were excluded because the designers did not wish the purity of the design to become cluttered by human beings, the whole enterprise became bizarre.

Art's power

How does the kind of account I have given help us with the question, with which I began, of the power that art can have over us, a power that those who have felt it talk of as going as deep as our lives can go?

Firstly, we have come to a fuller characterization of the variety of the attractions of art. There is the interest in representation. This Aristotle rightly noted is something in which we take delight. Since delight is something that, in various degrees, uplifts us, that explains why we might seek out representations. It does not, though, explain why we can be so powerfully attracted to representations. Again there are the cases of the rapturous engagement with art in which all the capacities are fully engaged. The intensely pleasurable quality of such a state is again a reason why we might seek it. Then there are cases in which we find, perhaps after a struggle, a way of expressing, through creating or engaging with an object, something that has been hitherto inchoate in us. This is accompanied by a feeling of relief and illumination.

All these cases tell us that certain of our involvements with the arts lift and move us. But this is not as yet to have explained the power of art. What more is to be said?

I begin with a striking remark by Wittgenstein: "Anyone who listens to a child's crying and understands what is heard will know that it harbours dormant psychic forces, terrible forces different from anything commonly assumed. Profound rage, pain and lust for destruction" (Wittgenstein 1980, p. 2).

Here we are not merely told that a baby cries, but that there is a great power in that cry, a power linked to deep passions. That suggests that if we want to begin to explain the deep power of art we might try to link it with other cases in which we find an equal power and see if that leads to any illumination. Then I am reminded of a remark by Wollheim that "the expressiveness of a work of art derives from the human mind . . . the broad characteristics of art, including expressiveness, originate outside art" (Wollheim 1993, p. 5)

Croce, too, was at pains to stress that what we call art is a development of, and continuous with, the powers of the mind, although lacking a proper psychology he was unable to explain why that gave art such power. How would psychology help here?

Consider the case in which we call a landscape "melancholy". There is a way that landscape looks and there is a way that we feel, say lost and devastated. We possess a power to project that inner state onto the outer reality, and the look of the landscape invites us to do so. Why is this so important to us?

Croce correctly observed that merely to be at the mercy of the feelings blindly occasioned by the stimuli that fall on us is to be at the mercy of something that is not us. When we express these feelings, when we become clear about them, when we give them a form that articulates what we inchoately felt under their bombardment, we make them ours. If we do this by projecting our inner lives onto the world, we humanize nature and make ourselves at home in it.

We can now add this to Croce's account:

Of great significance however is another feature of projection that is rooted in the functions it serves. Over a widely varying range of conditions, from the benign to the pathological, the function of projection is to help the individual to achieve, or to restore, or to impose, internal order. (Wollheim *ibid.*, pp. 6–7)

Projection, with which expression is intimately connected, is an internal act in which we try to preserve what we value and is threatened or in which we try to come to terms with what we dread and that threatens us. Now we begin to see how the power of art, which we naturally think of as something to do with expression, is part and parcel of the power that expression, representation and projection have in the formation of our personalities. It is in particular related to those infant passions of which Wittgenstein spoke and a way of coming to terms with them.

Roads not taken

I am very conscious that there are things I have not done that I would wish to have done in a fuller introduction to aesthetics. One is to give a proper account of the vehemently interesting history of aesthetics, including, for example, an account of such extraordinarily important writers as Hegel and Nietzsche. The best I can do here is to say where the reader can go to remedy that lack. Another is to give a proper account of what modern philosophers in different traditions have done, especially Heidegger and Merleau-Ponty. Again I have tried to indicate where guides to them can be found.

If readers understand this book they will have made some beginning with the study of aesthetics. But I cannot leave this matter without indicating what seem to me fruitful lines of research for those who wish to do further work.

An obvious one is to fill out the account that I have just given of the way that the power of art is related to the central place of representational expression in any full account of the mind. When we have that, we begin to have something that will explain the power of art to us. It will, moreover, do so by demonstrating the truth of a claim we find in Kant and Croce and that has been rightly stressed by, among others, Scruton and Wollheim. We can have no proper account of art until we know how art fits into some fuller picture of the mind, into an account of its powers of imagination, thought and expression and of their origins and developments.

221

Another place where the reader may find an opportunity to become involved in unsolved problems is in discussions of the reasons why we are, as Wordsworth in the passage I quoted at the outset confessed himself to be, so powerfully affected by nature. That has become a central topic in philosophy, in part because of a realization that we harm our environment and from a wish to stop doing so. If we ask why we should change the mode of our present dealings with nature, one answer is that nature has an instrumental value. We need a flourishing environment if we are to flourish. But to some it seems that this instrumentalist approach is a facet of that anthropocentric selfishness that has got us into the present mess. So, too, if we say that we want nature preserved because we enjoy seeing it, that too, it will be said, takes too human a point of view.

One reaction to this is to argue that nature has values that are intrinsic to it, intrinsic in the sense that even had there never been and were there to be no humans, nature would still have these values. And with that goes the claim that the things that have these values, including even the mountains themselves, have rights against us. Whatever the coherence of that suggestion it seems to me to have the drawback of merely emphasizing the difference between us and our values and nature and *its* values, thus again separating us from nature. Moreover, it gives no guidance as to how conflicts between those values should be resolved.

We should ask ourselves why nature exerts over us the power and fascination that it does. That it does so at all is simply a reason for its preservation, even if we have no idea why it does. But if we knew why it does we might know, by knowing how our lives were bound up in it, why we need it.

One final area that I mention as needing further study is the relation between art and morality. We need a much fuller account of the ways in which what we bring to works of arts can affect our relations with them, an account that might lead us to see why sometimes we think that what we bring disqualifies us from sound judgement (as when the jealous man applauds in the wrong place in *Othello*) and why sometimes it seems a prerequisite for sound judgement (as only a person with moral sensibilities can appreciate just what is going on in the works of Genet). But we need, too, a far better account than we have yet of morality itself, of its roots

222

in the formative stages of our individualities, its forms, and its functions. Until we have that,we can say nothing of any real force about art and morality.

A final word: philosophical aesthetics owes to philosophy a duty to clarify our thinking about art and the aesthetic. But it owes to art a duty not to misrepresent it. Whether or not it does so will depend on whether what is says matches the experiences that people have of art before philosophy ever thinks about the matter. Those who read this book therefore should bring their own aesthetic experiences, of whatever kind, to what I have said and ask if that helps to make sense of them. If it even partially does then some progress will have been made. And do not forget, as my envoi will remind you, that your own aesthetic experiences, although they may seem to you outside the mainstream of what is talked about in academic books about aesthetics, may nonetheless have a value and importance.

Guide to reading

I have stressed the need to look at the history of aesthetics and mentioned, in particular, Beardsley's *Aesthetics from classical Greece to the present day*. I have tried, in various of the guides, to supplement that with reading on various figures I have not discussed in any detail. One or two more can be added. Thus you can make up for the paucity of my comments on Plato by reading C. Janaway, *Images of excellence: Plato's critique of the arts* (Oxford: Oxford University Press, 1995). Then Hegel's *Introductory lectures on aesthetics* (London: Penguin, 1993) is surprisingly readable, if one is prepared to make the effort. It is also worth reading F. Schiller, *[Letters] On the aesthetic education of man*, trans. E. Wilkinson & L. A. Willoughby, (Oxford: Oxford University Press, 1989).Those interested in Nietzsche's special contribution can be recommended Michael Tanner's brief but masterly *Nietzsche* (Oxford: Oxford University Press, 1994) and J. Young, *Nietzsche's philosophy of art* (Cambridge: Cambridge University Press, 1992). The various works of Paul Crowther are a useful introduction to a wide collection of concerns in contemporary European aesthetics.

On art and nature, begin with Allen Carlson "Environmental

aesthetics" in the *Cooper Companion to aesthetics*. Jane Howarth's "Nature's moods", *British Journal of Aesthetics*, April 1995, pp. 108–20 is a clear and stylish account of why nature may be important to us. We are fortunate in that a collection is now available: S. Kemal & I. Gaskell (eds), *Landscape, natural beauty and the arts* (Cambridge: Cambridge University Press, 1993). Professor Hepburn, who is in this collection, has also written "Contemporary aesthetics and the neglect of natural beauty" in *British analytical philosophy*, B. Williams & A. Montefiore (eds) (London: Routledge & Kegan Paul, 1966 pp. 285–310). My own tip is to explore the possibility that the rift (if any) between humans and nature will best be healed by adopting idealist models of knowledge that undermine any temptation to posit the opposites of dead and intrinsically meaningless nature and living and meaning-giving subjects. It is noticeable that able philosophers are beginning to nod towards more idealist ways of thought, notably J. McDowell, *Mind and world* (Cambridge, Massachusetts: Harvard University Press, 1994). If you can ignore the splashiness of Suzy Gablik's theorizing about culture, there is much of factual interest to be learned from her *The re-enchantment of art* (London: Thames and Hudson, 1991) about how artists, such as Andy Goldsworthy, are seeking different sorts of involvements with nature.

Envoi

The rape of the Holy Mother

to expose your ass on paper
terrifies some
and
it should:
the more you put down
the more you leave yourself
open
to those who label themselves
"critics."
they are offended by the out-
right antics of the
maddened.
they prefer their poesy to be
secretive
soft and
nearly
indecipherable.

their game has remained un-
molested for
centuries.
it has been the temple of
the snobs and the fakers.
to disrupt this sanctuary
is to them like
the Rape of the Holy Mother.

besides that, it would also
cost them
their wives
their automobiles
their girlfriends
their university
jobs.

The Academics have much to
fear
and they will not die
without
a dirty fight.
but we have long been ready

we have come from the alleys
and the bars and the
jails

we don't care how they
write the poem

but we insist that there are
other voices
other ways of creating
other ways of living the
life

and we intend to be
heard and heard and
heard

in this battle against the
centuries of the Inbred
Undead

let it be known that
we have arrived and
intend to
stay.

Charles Bukowski

References

Barthes, R. The death of the author. In *Image, music, text* (London: Fontana, 1977).

Beardsley, M. *Aesthetics* (NY: Harcourt, Brace & World, 1958).

Beardsley, M. *The possibility of criticism* (Detroit: Wayne State University Press, 1970).

Beardsley, M. & W. Wimsatt. The intentional fallacy. In *On literary intention*, D. Newton de Molina (ed.) (Edinburgh:Edinburgh University Press, 1976), pp. 1–13.

Bell, C. *Art* (London: Chatto, 1920).

Benson, J. Emotion and expression. *Philosophical Review* **76**, pp. 335–57, 1967.

Bernecker, S. The logical necessity of world pictures in Wittgenstein's *On Certainty*. In *Culture and value*, K. Johannessen & T. Nordenstam (eds) (The Austrian Ludwig Wittgenstein Society: Kirchberg am Wechsel, 1995), pp. 3–8.

Booth, W. *The rhetoric of fiction* (Chicago:The University of Chicago Press, 1961).

Cage, J. *Silence* (Cambridge, Massachusetts: The Massachusetts Institute of Technology Press, 1966).

REFERENCES

Cavell, S. The availability of Wittgenstein's later philosophy. In *Wittgenstein*, G. Pitcher (ed.) (London: Macmillan, 1968) pp.151–85.

Croce, B. *The aesthetic as the science of expression and of the linguistic in general* (trans. C. Lyas) (Cambridge: Cambridge University Press, 1992).

de Saussure, F. *Course in general linguistics* (trans. W. Baskin) (New York: McGraw-Hill, 1959).

Derrida, J. *Of grammatology* (Baltimore: The Johns Hopkins University Press, 1976).

Derrida, J. *Writing and difference* (trans. A. Bass) (London: Routledge & Kegan Paul, 1978).

Derrida, J. (1981a) *Margins of philosophy* (trans. A. Bass) (Chicago: The University of Chicago Press, 1981).

Derrida, J. (1981b) *Dissemination* (London: Athlone, 1981).

Derrida, J. *Memoires for Paul de Man* (NY: Columbia University Press, 1986).

Derrida, J. *Of spirit* (trans. G. Bennington & R. Bowlby) (Chicago: The University of Chicago Press, 1989).

Dickie, G. *Art and the aesthetic* (Ithaca: Cornell University Press, 1974).

Elliott, R. Poetry and truth. *Analysis* **27**, 1966–7, pp. 77–85.

Elliott, R. Imagination in the experience of art. In *Philosophy and the arts*, G. Vesey (ed.) (London: Macmillan, 1973).

Hepburn, R. W. Art truth and the education of subjectivity. *Journal of Aesthetic Education* **24**(2), 1990, pp. 185–98.

Hirsch, E. D. *Validity in interpretation* (New Haven: Yale University Press, 1967).

Hume, D. Of the standard of taste. In *Philosophy of art and aesthetics*, F. Tillman & S. Cahn (eds) (New York: Harper and Row, 1969).

Kant, I. *The critique of judgement* (trans. J. H. Bernard) (New York: Hafner, 1951).

Levinson, J. Defining art historically. *British Journal of Aesthetics* **19**, 1979, pp. 232–50.

Lévi-Strauss, C. *La pensee sauvage* (Paris: Plon, 1962).

Lyas, C. (ed.) *Philosophy and linguistics* (London: Macmillan, 1971)

Merleau-Ponty, M. *Signes* (Paris:Gallimard, 1960).

Nietzsche, F. *Thus spake Zarathustra* (London: Penguin, 1961).

Sartre, J. P. *Literary and philosophical essays* (trans. A. Michelson) (London: Rider, 1955).

Sharpe, R. A. What is the object of musical analysis? *The Music Review* **54**, 1993, pp. 63–72.

Staten H., *Wittgenstein and Derrida* (Oxford: Blackwell, 1985).

Tilghman, B. *Wittgenstein: ethics and aesthetics* (Basingstoke: Macmillan, 1991).

Tolstoy, L. *What is Art?* (London: Duckworth, 1994).

Trotsky, L. *Literature and revolution* (New York: Russell and Russell, 1957.

Wimsatt, W. Genesis: a fallacy revisited. In *On literary intention*, D. Newton de Molina (ed.) (Edinburgh: Edinburgh University Press, 1976), pp. 116–38.

Wittgenstein, L. *Philosophical investigations* (Oxford: Blackwell, 1953).

Wittgenstein, L. *The blue and brown books* (New York: Harper and Row, 1958).

Wittgenstein, L. *Culture and value* (Oxford: Blackwell, 1980).

Wollheim, R. *The mind and its depths* (Cambridge, Massachusetts: Harvard University Press, 1993).

Index